*To Salar Rawanduz*
*with hope for*
*the future*

# THE KURDS
## —— and the ——
## Future of Turkey

*Michael M Gunter*

### Michael M. Gunter

ST. MARTIN'S PRESS
NEW YORK

ISBN 0–312–17265–6

Library of Congress Cataloging-in-Publication Data

Gunter, Michael M.
    The Kurds and the future of Turkey / Michael M. Gunter.
        p.    cm.
    Includes bibliographical references (p.    ) and index.
    ISBN 0–312–17265–6
    1. Kurds—Turkey—Politics and government.    2. Turkey—Politics
and government—1980-    3. Turkey—Ethnic relations.    I. Title.
DR435.K87G85    1997
965.1'00491597—dc21                                          96-50177
                                                                CIP

*Dedicated to my wife
Judy*

# CONTENTS

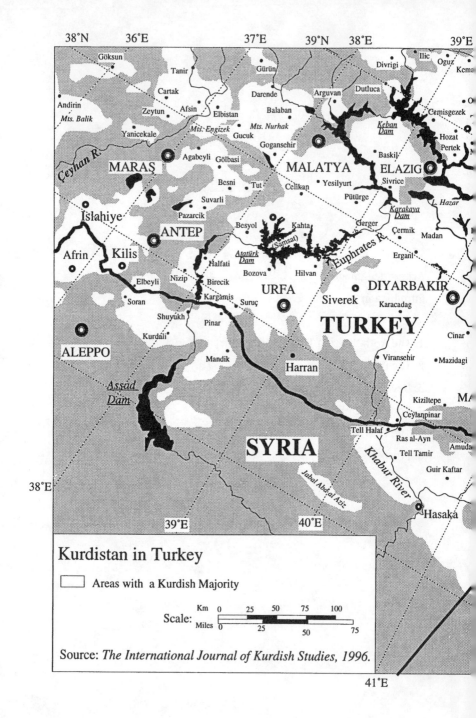

Kurdistan in Turkey

☐ Areas with a Kurdish Majority

Scale: Km 0 25 50 75 100
Miles 0 25 50 75

Source: *The International Journal of Kurdish Studies, 1996.*

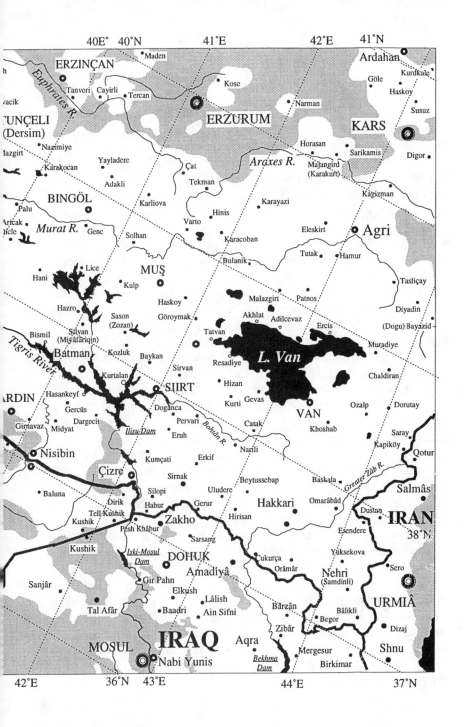

# ACKNOWLEDGMENTS

I would like to thank the Non-Instructional Faculty Assignment Committee at Tennessee Technological University, where I have taught since 1972, for giving me a semester of released time during which I was able to do a great deal of work on this book. Angelo Volpe, the president of Tennessee Tech, encouraged and supported me, for which I am most grateful. Paul Stephenson, the chairman of the political science department at Tennessee Tech throughout my career there, not only supported and encouraged me, but also provided technical help with computing problems. The library staff at Tennessee Tech helped me obtain a number of useful books and articles, as well as access items over Netscape on the Internet.

My year spent as a Senior Fulbright Lecturer in International Relations at the Middle East Technical University in Ankara, Turkey during the 1978-79 academic year first made me aware of the issues I have analyzed here. The Fulbright program was a tremendous educational experience for me. I hope it will always be supported, for it pays such rich dividends in international understanding and peace. I will never forget Turkey or the many wonderful people I met there, and will always wish the very best for them and their great country.

I want to thank the University Press of Kentucky, the Research Institute for the Study of Conflict and Terrorism, and the *International Journal of Kurdish Studies* for permitting me to use some material that appeared in earlier work I published for them. Thanks also go to Mehrdad Izady, the editor in chief of the *International Journal of Kurdish Studies,* for permitting me to use the map of Kurdistan in Turkey he constructed. Many others who helped me in the writing of this book are listed in the bibliography under interviews and correspondence. Others preferred to remain anonymous.

I will always owe a debt of gratitude to my late parents, Dr. Martin J. and Larissa Gunter. I miss them a great deal. Most of all, I want to acknowledge my wife, Judy, to whom this book is dedicated. She is very special.

I should also mention that I omitted the diacritical marks in foreign words to simplify the text; the meanings of the words have not been affected. I alone, of course, am responsible for any errors of fact or interpretation. Hopefully they are not too many, for it is my sincere wish that my book will help provide an objective analysis of the Kurdish problem in Turkey. Such an analysis might then help solve this problem to the benefit of Turkey and all its citizens of Turkish and Kurdish ancestry.

MICHAEL M. GUNTER
January 1997

# Introduction

Since August 1984, the Republic of Turkey has been suffering from an increasingly virulent guerrilla/terrorist insurgency led by the *Partiya Karkaren Kurdistan* (PKK), or Kurdistan Workers Party, headed by Abdullah (Apo) Ocalan. By the summer of 1996, more than 20,000 people had been killed and—by the admission of the Turkish government itself—another 2,000,000 internally displaced and more than 2,000 villages destroyed.[1] More and more the struggle was costing Turkey financially, diplomatically, domestically, and militarily. These costs, however, were just the tip of the iceberg, because it had become clear that Turkey's growing Kurdish population demanded long-term accommodations and solutions far beyond anything a military triumph over the PKK could offer.

In the summer of 1988[2] and the spring of 1990,[3] I published two of the first analyses in English of the Kurdish problem in Turkey. In them, I warned that the conflict potentially threatened the very existence of Turkey. My work was well-received,[4] and indeed proved prescient, because soon a number of additional studies appeared.[5]

Upon his return to the office of prime minister in November 1991, Suleyman Demirel described the Kurdish situation as "Turkey's top problem,"[6] while shortly before his death in April 1993, Turkish President Turgut Ozal warned his successor, Demirel, that it was "perhaps the most significant problem in the republic's history."[7]

More than eight years have passed since my *Middle East Journal* article appeared, and six since my book. During that time what was only a potential problem has, by the testimony of Turkey's own leaders, grown to challenge the very future of Turkey. Because of my continuing interest in the situation, it seems appropriate and even incumbent upon me to compile a new analysis based on the events and revelations that have occurred since my earlier work.

Many of my sources will be cited in the notes and bibliography. Certain individuals, however, have preferred to remain anonymous for various reasons. These people include certain U.S. and Turkish government officials, as well as Turkish and Kurdish scholars and activists. Some of these people I was able to meet during my trip through southeastern Turkey in August 1993, which was precisely the time that the U.S. State Department had temporarily banned travel to that area by its citizens because of the precarious situation.

In analyzing the failure of Turkey to solve its Kurdish problem I have been impressed by what I call the authoritarian tradition in the Republic of Turkey. This tradition not only has influenced the general attitudes of most government officials against a successful political solution, but has negatively affected human rights. Turkey has been prevented from taking the final steps toward becoming a genuine democracy, and there is a real possibility that the state will be split up, due to its failure to satisfy the legitimate demands of its citizens of Kurdish ethnic heritage, who constitute approximately 20 to 25 percent of the overall population.

With this background in place, I will then turn to a specific analysis of the PKK and its founder and longtime leader, Abdullah (Apo) Ocalan. Originally only one of several tiny Kurdish groups, Ocalan and the PKK have become increasingly identified with the Kurdish national movement itself both in Turkey and, recently, elsewhere.

Following the analysis of the PKK, I will trace the Kurdish struggle as it has developed in Turkey since the publication of my earlier work. My analysis largely coincides with events following the Gulf War against Saddam Hussein, an important turning point in the development of the Kurdish national movement not only in Turkey, but elsewhere such as in Iraq.

Next my attention will turn to foreign influences on the Kurdish problem and on how the Kurdish problem has come to be a major factor in Turkish foreign policy. Specifically, I will discuss the roles of Syria, Iraq, Iran, and Western Europe, as well as the triangular interaction among Turkey, the PKK, and the Iraqi Kurds. During October 1992, Turkey and the Iraqi Kurds were actually allies in a struggle against the PKK. In May 1994, the Iraqi Kurds themselves fell into their own civil war. Then, from August to December 1995, the PKK struck at the Kurdistan Democratic Party (KDP), one of the two main Iraqi Kurdish parties, in an attempt to prevent the implementation of a U.S.-Turkish brokered peace agreement between the Iraqi Kurds. In August 1996, renewed fighting among the Iraqi Kurds also involved Iran and Iraq, while threatening to embroil Turkey. All of these events heavily influenced the Kurdish problem in Turkey.

In my final chapter, which deals with the prospects for the future, I will argue that the preferred solution for the Kurdish problem is for Turkey to grant its citizens of Kurdish ethnic heritage their full cultural, social, and political rights as implied by democracy. In thus arguing, my thesis will have come full cycle, because this solution mandates that Turkey take the final large steps toward overcoming its authoritarian tradition and become a genuine democracy. If it does, most of Turkey's citizens of Kurdish ethnic heritage will become and remain loyal citizens of the Republic of Turkey.

# 1

# The Authoritarian Tradition in the Republic of Turkey

**B**eneath the veneer of modern democracy that most non-Western states such as Turkey today exhibit, there lies the continuing essence of diverse political, cultural, and historical heritages. Analyzing this very situation, Adda Bozeman concluded that "anyone attempting a comparative study of Western and Near Eastern approaches to law and organization . . . must face the fact that he is confronted here with totally different conceptions of the roles of law and government in society,"[1] and that these "locally and regionally prevalent theories . . . are likely to remain dominant in the future. . . . The world will continue to be multicultural under the surface of unifying technological and rhetorical arrangements."[2]

Thus, the modern Republic of Turkey,[3] which Mustafa Kemal (Ataturk)[4] proclaimed on October 29, 1923, from the ashes of the Ottoman Empire, can only be fully understood with reference to its political, cultural, and historical antecedents, as well as its own unique experiences. Once this legacy is examined, what may be called the authoritarian tradition in the Republic of Turkey becomes clear. This authoritarian tradition has proved an important factor in preventing the Republic of Turkey from solving its present Kurdish problem democratically.

## THE OTTOMAN LEGACY

The absolutism of the Ottoman Sultan and the related concept of "oriental despotism" are not pillars upon which a modern western democracy can be readily built. Feroz Ahmad has added that "the tradition of the strong, centralised state, identified with the nation, regarded as neutral and standing outside society, and representing no particularist interests"[5] has also helped to justify the military coups of 1960, 1971, and 1980 against what was perceived to be narrow, selfish interests.

Mustafa Kemal's famous title of *Ghazi*—which was granted him by the Turkish parliament following his victory over the invading Greeks in 1922—is another obvious legacy from the past. The title originally referred to the crusading spirit of the Islamic warrior striking against the Christian West. "Destroyer of Christians" was the traditional meaning of the term, according to Lord Kinross, the famous biographer of Ataturk.[6]

The seemingly obstinate refusal in the modern Republic of Turkey to admit that its citizens of Kurdish ethnic heritage constitute a minority can be understood in light of the old Ottoman principle that Islam took precedence over nationality among Muslims and that only non-Muslims could hold some type of officially recognized minority status. Indeed, this very position was acknowledged by the Treaty of Lausanne (1923)—under which the West recognized the new Republic of Turkey—as only non-Muslims such as Greeks, Armenians, and Jews were granted minority status in Turkey. Years later, Necmettin Erbakan—who became modern Turkey's first Islamist prime minister in July 1996—in reference to the current Kurdish problem, maintained the following: "We have bonds of brotherhood. There is nothing more absurd than ethnic differentiation among Muslim brothers."[7]

One might also understand Ankara's present refusal to grant Kurdish ethnic rights or some type of autonomy against the background of the gradual disintegration of the Ottoman Empire before the onslaughts of various nationalisms during the nineteenth and early twentieth centuries. Indeed, the modern Republic of Turkey itself was established only after a long and terrible struggle against the invading Greeks, who were pursuing their *Megali* Idea of a greater Greece after World War I with British encouragement, and a lesser but still serious war against the Armenians, pursuing their goal of a greater Armenia also with tacit allied backing. Finally, the Kurds themselves, during the Sheikh Said rebellion of 1925,[8] were seen as trying to destroy the new secular Republic by reinstating the Caliph and creating a Kurdish state in the southeast of Turkey.

However, one should also note that the Ottoman millet system (which guaranteed religious minorities virtual autonomy in cultural, religious, and educational affairs), the Tanzimat period of reform (1839-1876), the Constitution of 1876, and the Young Turk revolution and restoration of the Constitution in 1908 have all nourished republican instincts. In other words, as well as an authoritarian tradition, there was also a heritage upon which the Turks could call for support when they began to construct what might well be seen as the first modern democracy in the non-Western world.

## The Kemalist Legacy

During the desperate struggle to establish a Turkish national state in 1921, Mustafa Kemal became a virtual dictator by popular consensus. He took personal command of the army and was invested with all the powers of the nationalist parliament. The so-called Independence Tribunals dealt most severely with his opponents.

Following the victory in what came to be called the "Turkish War of Independence," the *Ghazi* handpicked the members of the new parliament—in which, according to the constitution written in 1924, all power resided—and also created what later became known as the Republican People's Party (RPP). An opposition Progressive Republican Party in 1924 proved short-lived.[9]

The Kurdish uprising in 1925 under Sheikh Said led to the reinstatement of two Independence Tribunals, one for the provinces in the Kurdish areas and the other for the remainder of the country. The Law on the Maintenance of Order passed in March 1925 gave the government the power to ban any organization or publication. It remained in force until 1929. Under this law some 7,500 people were arrested and 660 executed. The "Izmir Conspiracy," a plot to assassinate Mustafa Kemal, was uncovered in June 1926. It led to the arrest of a number of his opponents, several of whom were hanged. The Republic of Turkey had become an authoritarian, one-party regime. Indeed, following another brief experiment with a legal opposition (the Free Republican Party in 1930[10]) Mustafa Kemal's RPP officially declared Turkey a one-party state.

When Mustafa Kemal first began to form the Turkish nation-state, it was not clear what constituted a Turk.[11] Indeed, in appealing for Islamic unity against the Christian invaders, Ismet (Inonu)—Ataturk's famous lieutenant and eventual successor—initially spoke of the new state as being a "homeland for Kurds and Turks."[12] Kurdish troops played an indispensable role in the over-all nationalist victory. The nationalist parliament in Ankara included some 75 Kurdish deputies. For a while Mustafa Kemal apparently toyed with the idea of meaningful Kurdish autonomy in the new state. The minutes of the Amasya interview and the proceedings of the Erzurum and Sivas Congresses in 1919, as well as two other occurrences in 1922 and 1923, make this clear.[13] Kurdish autonomy, however, proved to be the road not taken.

Following the nationalist victory, a series of steps were taken in an attempt to eliminate the Kurdish presence in the new Republic of Turkey through legal fiat and gradual assimilation. On March 3, 1924, for example, a decree banned all Kurdish schools, organizations, and publications, as well as religious fraternities and *medressehs,* which were the last source of education for most Kurds. Deportations of Kurds to the west began after the Sheikh Said rebellion was crushed in 1925. The purpose was to dilute the Kurdish population in order to facilitate its assimilation. The Kurdish areas were declared a military zone forbidden to foreigners until 1965. In 1928, the entire civil and military administration of the Kurdish provinces in the east was placed under an "Inspector-General of the East." Given the Kemalist insistence on a unitary framework for the Turkish government, this latter measure was ironic, since it in effect placed the Kurdish provinces under a special administration.

In 1928, *Khoyboun* (Independence), a transnational Kurdish party that had been founded a year earlier in Lebanon, launched a major uprising around Mount Ararat under General Ihsan Noury Pasha. It was finally crushed in the summer of 1930. New deportations followed. Law No. 2510 in June 1934 sought further to disperse the Kurdish population to areas where it would constitute no more than 5 percent of the total. It was even suggested that Kurdish children be sent to boarding schools where they would speak exclusively in Turkish. Only the lack of state resources and the sheer size of the growing Kurdish population defeated the intention. One final, great Kurdish uprising occurred in Dersim (now Tunceli) from 1936 to 1938, but it too was finally defeated.

During the 1930s the basic principles of Kemalism (the "six arrows") were laid down: republicanism, secularism, nationalism, populism, statism, and revolutionism. A personality cult began to grow around Ataturk that presented him as the father, savior, and teacher of the nation. An extreme form of Turkish nationalism with its associated historical myths developed that had no place for Kurdish ethnic awareness. The Turkish Historical Thesis claimed that all the world's civilizations had been founded by the Turks, while the so-called Sun-Language Theory held that all languages derived from one original tongue spoken in central Asia. Turkish, the closest extant descendant of this primeval language, was the source from which all other languages had developed. Isolated in their mountain fastnesses, the Kurds had simply forgotten their mother tongue. "Kurdish" supposedly contained fewer than some 800 words and thus was not a real language. Indeed, the very word "Kurd" was said to be nothing more than a corruption of the crunching sound (kirt, kart, or kurt) one made while walking through the snow-covered mountains in the southeast. The much-abused and criticized appellation "Mountain Turks" when referring to the Turkish Kurds served as a code term for these actions.

During the 1960s, Turkish President Cemal Gursel lauded a book written by Sherif Firat that claimed that the Kurds were Turkish in origin, and helped to popularize the phrase "spit in the face of he who calls you a Kurd" as a way to make the word "Kurd" an insult.[14] At the same time, Law No. 1587 furthered the process of changing Kurdish names, "which hurt public opinion and are not suitable for our national culture, moral values, traditions and customs," into

Turkish names. As recently as 1995, the Turkish government suddenly announced that the Kurdish new year's holiday *Newroz*—which it now termed *Nevruz*—was in fact a Turkish holiday commemorating the day that the Turks first left their ancestral Asian homeland, Ergenekon. A year later the Turkish media launched a campaign to "prove" that the traditional Kurdish colors (green, red, and yellow) were actually those of certain crack Ottoman regiments. This concern with color recalled the recent attempt to alter traffic lights in some southeastern towns of Turkey such as Batman by replacing the supposed Kurdish green with blue. As an assessment by the U.S. Central Intelligence Agency put it: "In the early years of the Turkish Republic, the government responded . . . by ruthlessly . . . attempting, albeit unsuccessfully, to eliminate all manifestations of Kurdish culture and nationalism."[15] Obviously, such clumsy attempts continue even now.

After Ataturk's death in November 1938, his personality cult, if anything, grew even greater. The RPP's party statutes were changed to make him "the eternal party chairman," while his successor, Ismet Inonu, was made "permanent party chairman." "National Leader," a term which had been used for Ataturk at times in the 1930s, now became the official title of Inonu. Almost sixty years after his death, Ataturk remains the revered father figure, his portrait or bust virtually omnipresent and his mausoleum in Ankara the sacred symbol of the Turkish Republic.

That this remains so has something to do with the flexibility of Kemalism as an ideology, and much to do with Ataturk as a leader. Despite his authoritarian legacy, Ataturk inspired the Turkish people with his vision of a modern, secular, independent, and ultimately democratic Turkey. The authoritarianism was a necessary means to achieve an ultimate goal. Inonu was to take an important step toward that goal when he allowed the Democrat Party (DP) of Celal Bayar and Adnan Menderes to form in 1946 and, to his eternal credit, to assume power democratically following its overwhelming electoral victory in 1950. In addition, unlike its sometime fascist model, Kemalist Turkey disdained militaristic bombast and irredentist aims. "Peace at home and peace abroad" within the territorial confines of the Republic of Turkey Ataturk had created in the 1920s remained the guiding principle of Turkish foreign policy.

Given its authoritarian legacy, however, the attainment of complete democracy remained an uphill struggle for the Republic of Turkey. The new DP government of Menderes in the 1950s acted as if its majority entitled it to absolute power and legitimacy.[16] Since the 1924 constitution contained no checks and balances such as bicameralism or a constitutional court, the tyranny of the majority increasingly ran rampant in Turkey as Menderes extended his authority over the state bureaucracy, press, universities, and judiciary.

In April 1960, the DP government banned all political activity outside the parliament for three months until its parliamentary committee to investigate the opposition reported. Student demonstrations and riots finally led, on May 27, 1960, to a coup by the military, which saw itself as the guardian of the state and the heritage of Ataturk.[17] Almost lost in the ensuing actions of the new military government was the decision to arrest some 485 Kurdish notables in June 1960 and detain them for several months. The 55 most influential Kurds were exiled to western Turkey for two years. All but one of them had been members of the DP. Menderes claimed that some of them had attempted to use their positions of power to achieve Kurdish independence.[18]

Ironically, the military government, in an attempt to prevent the unbridled concentration of majority power again in the future, produced a new, greatly liberalized constitution and a series of other laws that gave Turks much more democracy than they had had before. For example, the new constitution contained a full range of civil liberties, and trade unions were given the right to strike.

Proportional representation was introduced to lessen the chance of one party winning an overwhelming majority. A much wider spectrum of political activity from left to right was permitted, which resulted in the emergence of such genuinely leftist but legal groups as the Turkish Workers Party. In October 1970 this party passed a remarkable resolution concerning the Kurds that stated: "There is a Kurdish people in the East of Turkey. . . . The fascist authorities representing the ruling classes have subjected the Kurdish people to a policy of assimilation and intimidation which has often become a bloody repression."[19] This was the first time a legal political party in the Turkish parliament had ever recognized the existence of the Kurdish people.

A second parliamentary chamber called the Senate was created to help implement these new checks and balances. Legislation would now have to pass through both chambers. In addition, an independent Constitutional Court that could reject legislation it considered unconstitutional was introduced, while the remainder of the court system, universities, and mass media were given full autonomy.

The 1961 constitution, however, also provided a constitutional role for the military for the first time by establishing the *Milli Guvenlik Kurulu* (MGK), or National Security Council (NSC) of ten members to advise the government on internal and external security. Chaired by the president (or in his absence the prime minister), the NSC also consisted of the chief of the general staff, four military service chiefs, and the defense, foreign affairs, and interior ministers. Thus, although the military's chief of staff theoretically reported to the president, the NSC consisted of an even number of military and civilian members.

In the succeeding years the NSC gradually extended its power over governmental policy, at times replacing the cabinet as the ultimate center of power over issues of national security. After the "coup by memorandum" on March 12, 1971, for example, the NSC was given the power to give binding, unsolicited advice to the cabinet. Following the military coup of September 12, 1980, for a while all power was concentrated in the NSC chaired by the chief of staff, General Kenan Evren, who eventually became president from 1982 to 1989. Before handing power back to the civilians under a considerably more restricted constitution, the NSC banned a number of leading politicians from further political activity for ten years. Although its actions greatly reduced the rampant terrorism in Turkey, a major price was paid in terms of human rights. (See below.)

During the 1990s the NSC began to exercise virtually total authority over security matters dealing with the Kurdish problem. In April 1996, for example, the Turkish Defense Minister Oltan Sungurlu noted that while "Turkey is a democratic country . . . it is not correct to sharply criticize our Army."[20] He added that "Article 125 of the Constitution bars any legal recourse against the Council's decisions." Thus the NSC became both the symbol and reality of the continuing authoritarian tradition in the Republic of Turkey.

The new 1982 constitution drawn up by the military represented a reversal of the more liberal constitution of 1961. Article 118 institutionalized the military's predominant position in the country through the NSC. Other provisions strengthened the powers of the president while limiting civil liberties, the freedom of the press, and trade union rights. The national vote to ratify the new document was held under a decree banning all criticism of it or of the speeches made in favor of it by General Evren. Approval also carried with it the elevation of the NSC head General Evren to the presidency.

The present (1982) constitution contains a number of specific provisions that seek to limit even speaking or writing in Kurdish. Its preamble, for example, declares: "The determination that no protection shall be afforded to thoughts or opinions contrary to Turkish national interests, the principle of the existence of Turkey as an indivisible entity with its state and territory, Turkish historical and moral values, or the nationalism, principles, reforms and modernism of Ataturk." Two articles ban the spoken and written usage of the Kurdish language without specifically naming it. Article 26 provides that "no language prohibited by law shall be used in the expression and dissemination of thought. Any written or printed documents, phonograph records, magnetic or video tapes, and other means of expression used in contravention of this provision shall be seized." Article 28 states that "publication shall not be made in any language prohibited by law."

Law No. 2932 published on October 22, 1983, reinforced these constitutional provisions regarding the Kurdish language by declaring that "it is forbidden to express, diffuse or publish opinions in any language other than the main official language of states recognized by the Turkish state." This new law also proclaimed that "the mother tongue of Turkish citizens is Turkish. It is forbidden . . . to use as a mother tongue any language other than Turkish, and . . . to carry, at public gatherings and assemblies, placards, banners, signs, boards, posters and the like, written in a language other than Turkish." Those violating the law faced sentences of between six months and two years in prison.

Further constitutional provisions were added to ban any type of regional autonomy for ethnic groups such as the Kurds. Article 14 of the constitution, for example, prohibits "violating the indivisible integrity of the State . . . or creating discrimination on the basis of language, race, religion or sect, or of establishing by any other means a system of government based on these concepts and ideas."

Although restrictions on the usage of the Kurdish language were eased following the Gulf War in 1991, Article 8 of the Anti-Terrorism Law that entered into force in April 1991, made it possible to consider academics, intellectuals, and journalists speaking up for Kurdish rights to be engaging in terrorist acts: "Written and oral propaganda and assemblies, meetings and demonstrations aimed at damaging the indivisible unity of the Turkish Republic, with its territory and nation are prohibited, regardless of the methods, intentions and ideas behind such activities." Similarly, under Article 312 of the Turkish Penal Code, mere verbal or written support for Kurdish rights could lead one to be charged with "provoking hatred or animosity between groups of different race, religion, region or social class." Yasar Kemal, one of Turkey's most famous novelists, and Aliza Marcus, a Reuters correspondent and U.S. citizen, were indicted in 1995 for violating these provisions concerning what critics of the government came to term "thought crime." Although in both of these cases the accused were eventually vindicated, the mere threat implied by indictment is often enough to deter exercising what should be normal constitutional rights in a genuine democracy.

Despite these stifling restrictions, the constitution of the third Turkish Republic was approved by more than 90 percent of the voting electorate. (The only relatively high percentage of "no" votes came from the Kurdish areas in the southeast.) Within a year, however, disillusionment with the military's strong hand had grown and the military's handpicked party to form the new government was resoundingly defeated in the elections. The one party that wanted the military out of politics but was still permitted to participate in the elections, Turgut Ozal's *Anavatan Partisi* or Motherland Party, emerged with a tremendous victory, in part because of Ozal's cautious opposition to the military.

Although eventually tainted by charges of corruption and nepotism, Ozal may well be remembered—after only Ataturk himself—as the greatest and most important Turkish politician of the twentieth century. His electoral victory in 1983 was seen as at least a partial triumph for civilian government. From this he went on successfully to reject the military's candidate for chief of staff in 1987 (the "civilian coup"), and in 1989 he became Turkey's first civilian president since Bayar was removed by the military in 1960. In addition, Ozal dramatically and irrevocably restructured the heretofore autarkic Turkish economy toward an export-oriented free market integrated into the international economic system. Although the results have been mixed, Turkey's economic face has been altered forever.

It was during Ozal's tenure that the current Kurdish problem began, slowly escalated, and then exploded. Although Ozal at first responded with such harsh and unimaginative measures as the emergency rule in the southeast and village guards (see below), by the end of his life he had evolved to become the only important Turkish statesman politically and intellectually capable of conceiving imaginative, democratic solutions. Unfortunately, he suddenly died from a heart attack in April 1993. To date, his successors have proven incapable of regaining his level of accomplishment.

## HUMAN RIGHTS

The situation concerning human rights is one of the most obvious and important consequences of the authoritarian tradition in the Republic of Turkey. It particularly affects the Kurdish problem.

Critics of Turkey's human rights problems often fail to understand the need to override normal civil liberties in times of emergency such as the current Kurdish insurgency. Even Article I, Section 8 of the Constitution of the United States allows for the suspension of the writ of habeas corpus "when in Cases of Rebellion or Invasion the public Safety may require it." In 1995, however, General Ahmet Corekci, the vice chief of staff, went so far as to argue that democratic conditions and human rights protections prevented an effective military response against terrorism. He added that demands for Kurdish language and education rights were part of the "salami tactic. . . . The more slices we cut the more they will take."[21]

In partial explanation of such a position, one must again remember that Turkey has a cultural legacy that permits actions seen in the West, at least since the nineteenth century, as illegitimate. In addition, the fact that Turkey is a much more open society than most other non-Western states probably has enabled more unfavorable observations to be made of Turkey's behavior, when in reality the more closed non-Western states are much more guilty of human rights violations. Nevertheless, if Turkey truly aspires to become a genuine democracy—as I believe it does—and, in addition, to solve its Kurdish problem, it will have to make major new commitments toward human rights.

Critics of Turkey's human rights record have focused their attention on the following areas:[22] (1) torture and the suspicious deaths of prisoners held in detention; (2) disappearances and extrajudicial killings of opposition politicians, human rights activists, journalists, and Kurdish nationalists; (3) government infringements on the freedoms of speech, press, and association; (4) denial of due process to persons under the jurisdiction of State Security Courts and in the state of emergency region; (5) the murder of Kurdish civilians and the destruction of Kurdish villages in the southeast by the Turkish military; and (6) the suppression of Kurdish cultural expression.

In the spring of 1995, more than 100 journalists and other writers were being held in Turkish jails for supporting the Kurdish cause in their writings. These included such well known figures as Ismail Besikci, Fikret Baskaya, Haluk Gerger, Mehdi Zana, Eren Keskin, and Yilmaz Odabasi. They were joined by six former DEP members of the Turkish parliament, among them Leyla Zana. Some 2,500 other people had been convicted of similar charges and were awaiting the outcome of their appeals, while more than 5,600 others were in the process of being tried on similar charges.

Following the closure of the pro-Kurdish newspaper 2000 *Ikibine Dogru* (Towards 2000) early in 1992, a series of successors promptly met a similar fate: *Gundem* (Agenda) 1992-93, *Ozgur Gundem* (Free Agenda) 1993-94, *Ozgur Ulke* (Free Land) 1994-95, and *Yeni Politika* (New Policy) 1995. *Ozgur Politika* (Free Policy) was still publishing in 1996. Ludicrously, Turkish law allowed thinly disguised retreads to reappear, but only ephemerally. And during their brief lives, all were subject to regular confiscations, while their workers and buildings were targeted for fatal attacks. Musa Anter, the famous Kurdish writer and intellectual, was gunned down in September 1992, while a pair of explosions ripped through the Istanbul and Ankara offices of *Ozgur Ulke* in December 1994. DEP MP Mehmet Sincar was murdered in broad daylight while attending a political rally in the southeastern city of Batman on September 4, 1992. Suspicions abounded concerning the culpability of the state, but his killers have never been apprehended.

The U.S. State Department, Amnesty International, and Human Rights Watch have all issued damning reports of Turkish human rights violations, many of which directly concern the Kurdish problem. Although prone to be more lenient than the others because of geostrategic reasons, the annual U.S. State Department report devoted 36 pages to Turkey in 1995, more than any other country except China, which got 39. Only Iran, Iraq, North Korea, Burma, and Cuba were listed as bigger offenders.

In 1996, the State Department report[23] declared that although "the human rights situation improved in a number of areas . . . very serious problems remain." Specifically mentioned were "torture"; "extrajudicial" or "mystery killings" that occurred "mostly in the east and southeast of the country"; "evacuation and burning of villages"; and "limits on freedom of expression." The report added that "according to [Turkish] government statistics, during the first 9 months of 1995, 5,893 persons were under arrest charged with offenses under the Anti-Terror Law, and 2,861 had been convicted." The law in question, claimed the report, contained a "broad and ambiguous definition of terrorism." The report mentioned that the PKK also had "committed many human rights abuses."

Amnesty International accused the Turkish government of encouraging torture, disappearances, and extrajudicial killings.[24] Additional reports claimed that human rights workers and lawyers in Turkey were subject to arbitrary arrest and detention, and that they then became victims of torture.[25] Human Rights Watch made similar criticisms,[26] as did the Human Rights Association and Human Rights Foundation in Turkey itself.

In its annual report for 1994, the Turkish Human Rights Foundation declared that "human rights and freedoms, including the primary right to life, were continuously abused during the year."[27] Extrajudicial executions, murders, and torture were specifically mentioned. "The most vital issue for the country in 1994 continued to be the Kurdish problem. . . . Dissenters were heavily penalized. Journalists and writers were arrested and sentenced. . . . The Kurdish problem caused great damage to the Turkish economy too. . . . During the year, more than 1000 villages and hamlets were evacuated." Algan Hacaloglu, the state minister responsible for human rights in Turkey, cautiously criticized the government for burning villages in the southeast to preempt the villagers from supporting the PKK.[28]

Even the Turkish parliamentary commission established to investigate unsolved political killings reported that the state bore guilt: "Due to [the] absence of strong state controls over these people [certain state officials], they set up criminal organizations and are engaged in arms smuggling, killing, drug smuggling, etc."[29] As a result of its "anti-state elements," many members of the commission refused to sign the report.[30] Obviously frustrated, State Minister Ayvaz Gokdemir clumsily called three female European MPs (Catherine Lalumiere of France, Claudia Roth of Germany, and Pauline Green of Britain) "European sluts of dubious intent" after they added their insights into the Turkish human rights situation.[31]

## State Security Courts

Toned-down, modern-day versions of the earlier Independence Tribunals, Turkey's eight State Security Courts (DGMs) have jurisdiction over civilian cases involving the Anti-Terrorism Act of 1991 that contains the notorious Article 8, which covers drug smuggling, membership in illegal organizations, and the propagation of ideas banned by law as damaging the indivisible unity of the state. Each court consists of panels of five members: two civilian judges, one military judge, and two prosecutors. In all, there are a total of 18 such State Security Court panels. These courts may detain people twice as long before arraignment as other courts, as well as hold closed hearings. Their verdicts may be appealed only to a specialized department of the High Court of Appeals dealing with crimes against state security.

In his rulings and comments, Nusret Demiral, the chief prosecutor of the Ankara State Security Court, has become both the symbol and reality of the problem these courts present to democratic freedoms. Demiral's reply to a journalist's inquiry was illustrative of his thought processes:

> If he tries to spread the views of an outlawed organization for the destruction of the state . . . he will not be considered to have been convicted because of expression of his thought, because the crime he has committed is the crime of spreading propaganda. . . . The freedom of expression also has legal limits. This limit has been stipulated in constitutional article 14. This article prescribes that none of the rights and freedoms set forth in the Constitution can be used to upset the indivisible integrity of the state.[32]

## DEP

The predicament of the Democracy Party (DEP) members of parliament provides a specific example of the human rights problems associated with the State Security Courts. In November 1992, Demiral announced that he would seek the death penalty against eighteen members of DEP's predecessor in parliament, HEP,[33] for subversive statements they had made in their recent congress. The accused had chanted slogans praising the PKK, described a section of Turkey as "Kurdistan," and referred to the Turkish army in southeastern Turkey as "illegal, occupation forces."[34] "These people hold opinions which violate the indivisibility of the state and nation,"[35] Demiral declared.

Early in March 1994, the Turkish parliament finally voted to lift the immunity of six DEP members: Hatip Dicle, the party's new chair; Ahmet Turk, the party's former chair; Leyla Zana; Sirri Sakik; Orhan Dogan; and Selim Sadak. All were to be tried under Article 125 of the Turkish Penal Code: "Any person . . . who carries out any action intended to destroy the unity of the Turkish state or to separate any part of the territory from the control of the Turkish state shall be punished by death." Turkish popular opinion had become infuriated by DEP chair Hatip Dicle's statement that the five Turkish NCO cadets killed at the Tuzla train station in Istanbul by a PKK bombing a month earlier were normal casualties of war. Embattled Turkish Prime Minister Tansu Ciller also took credit for "driving the PKK out of parliament."

On June 16, 1994, DEP was formally banned by the Constitutional Court, and on December 8, 1994, five of the above-mentioned DEP MPs were sentenced to 15-year prison terms, while the sixth was sentenced to a 7-and-a-half-year term. Although the decisions were roundly denounced in the West as an unjustified attempt to stifle freedom of expression, Demiral appealed them on the grounds that some of the accused still deserved the death penalty.

On October 26, 1995, the High Court (*Yargitay*) upheld the 15-year sentences of Zana, Dicle, Sadak, and Dogan, while reducing the remaining two sentences to time served. The Court argued that the aims of the first four DEP MPs were one and the same as those of the PKK. Among the charges considered proven were that Zana had received political training in a PKK camp in Lebanon and that Dicle's remarks about the bombing that killed the NCO cadets constituted an offense. Such activities demonstrated that they were members of the PKK. The other two DEP members whose terms were reduced were deemed guilty of oral and written statements that spread hatred, enmity, and separatism that made it clear they wanted to divide the state between the Turks and Kurds on the basis of race.

In the minds of many, the legitimacy of Demiral's fervor in prosecuting the DEP case could be questioned by his failure to seriously pursue leads implicating rightists in the car-bombing murder of the famous leftist journalist Ugur Mumcu on January 24, 1993. Similarly, Demiral's response to the notorious arson attack by Sunni fundamentalists—which killed 37 leftist Alevis in Sivas on July 2, 1993—was to threaten to prosecute the actual target of that attack, the author Aziz Nesin, who had supposedly infuriated the mob by translating some passages of Salman Rushdie's *The Satanic Verses.* Early in November 1995, the parliament of the European Union (EU) awarded the Sakharov Award for freedom of thought to the imprisoned Leyla Zana.

## Yasar Kemal

The recent situation concerning Yasar Kemal, probably Turkey's greatest living writer and perennial candidate for the Nobel Prize in Literature, provides one of the most egregious examples of how Turkey's authoritarian heritage has negatively affected an intelligent response to the Kurdish problem and human rights abuses. Of Kurdish ethnic heritage, Kemal's most famous work, *Memet,*

*My Hawk,* is the story of a Robin Hood-like bandit in the Taurus Mountains, and it won him international fame in the 1950s. Since then he has written more than 35 other books, which have been translated into some 30 different languages, and he has been awarded an honorary degree by the University of Humane Sciences in Strasbourg, the Legion d'Honneur from the French government, and a Hellman/Hammett grant for writers suffering from political persecution, among many other honors.

Kemal ran afoul of the Turkish authorities for an article entitled "Campaign of Lies" he published in the January 10, 1995, issue of the well-known German magazine *Der Spiegel.* Given the international reputation of the author and the powerful eloquence of his prose, it seems particularly appropriate to cite from his article at some length.[36]

> From the day of its inauguration, 29 October 1923, up to the present day, the Turkish Republic has been developing into a system of unbearable constraints and cruelty. It has tried to hide this from the eyes of humanity with oriental duplicity and disingenuousness. . . . While the Turkish people, paralysed by decades of oppression, acquiesced, resistance stirred within the Kurdish people, albeit in a hesitant, cautious form. It was, after all, the Kurdish people who were being oppressed most brutally under this rule of force. They were suffering hunger, were crushed by poverty and were subjected to ethnic massacres. Their language had been legally banned, their identity as Kurds had been denied, instead they were officially known as "Mountain Turks," and every 10 to 15 years they were driven to all four corners of Anatolia. . . . As far as I know, there were only very few Kurds in Turkey who wanted to have an independent state. And did they not have a right to demand this? In accordance with all human rights declarations, every people has the right to determine its own fate. Now Turkey is the scene of the vilest war imaginable. Holding the flag in one hand and the Koran in the other, the leader of our government emphatically denied that our State's armed forces had set any villages or forests alight. And the helicopters? They had been brought in from Armenia and Afghanistan by the PKK. And they were the ones who were setting the towns and villages aflame. . . . When the Turkish Republic was established, it should have given the Kurds the basic rights which it afforded the Turkish people. On the threshold of the 21st century, no people and no ethnic group should be denied human rights. . . . The Turkish Republic should not go into the 21st century with the curse of this war still hanging over its head. . . . We in Turkey should always be aware that the road to true democracy must lie in a peaceful solution to the Kurdish question. . . . That the leadership has tried to kill the language and culture of the Kurds is a

crime against humanity, even if this pressure has recently been relaxed. . . . The honour of a country and its humanitarian record will be on trial.

Controversial, but accurate words! In response, the State Security Court in Istanbul first considered trying Kemal under Article 125 of the penal code, which theoretically carries the death penalty. Although Kemal argued that he had always supported the unity of the Turkish state and a peaceful solution to the Kurdish problem, the state persisted, finally bringing him to trial under Article 8 of the Anti-Terrorism Law. Inanely, the Turkish president Suleyman Demirel declared with an air of resignation:

> Yasar Kemal is a very famous author. I like him very much. . . . He uses Turkish. But he is coming from a Kurdish family—that's all right. But what he did in his article, that's unfortunate. I don't think the whole thing is bad. People in Turkey were divided—many said he shouldn't have done it. He did it. The prosecutor cannot do anything else.[37]

Probably influenced by all the negative publicity Turkey was receiving and a desire to win approval to join the European Customs Union later that month, the court gave Kemal a suspended sentence early in December 1995. Although it could have been worse, the entire affair clearly demonstrated the glaring inconsistencies in the human rights record of the Republic of Turkey.

## Aliza Marcus

In 1995, Aliza Marcus, a 33-year-old American reporter writing for the Reuters News Agency in Turkey, became one of the first foreigners to be charged and tried under Turkey's stringent security laws for an article she wrote entitled "Kurdish Villages the Target of the Army." It was published in the November 27, 1994, issue of the pro-Kurdish newspaper *Ozgur Ulke*, which has since been closed down by the state. In her article, Marcus wrote that "forcibly evacuating and even torching Kurdish villages in southeastern Turkey is now a central part of the military's 10-year battle against Kurdish rebels."[38] She cited as sources "villagers and human rights activists." For her efforts she was charged under Article 312/2 of the Turkish Penal Code with "provoking enmity and hatred by displaying racism or regionalism," and she was tried in the Fifth State Security Court.

The Marcus case once again illustrated the continuing limits on the freedom of the press in Turkey, in particular regarding the Kurdish problem. Although finally acquitted at the end of 1995, the entire matter added yet another dimension to the human rights problem associated with the Kurdish question in Turkey, involving as it did a U.S. citizen.

## Atakurt

On April 17, 1995, Ahmet Altan, a prominent leftist journalist, published a bitingly iconoclastic satire on Turkey's official history in *Milliyet* entitled *Atakurt*. The ironic reference, of course, was to the last name of the country's famous founder, Ataturk [Father of the Turks]. In his editorial, Altan imagined what it would be like if Ataturk had been Kurdish instead of Turkish and had, therefore, founded a Republic of Kurdey instead of Turkey after the War of Independence in the early 1920s.[39]

> If we were called Kurds, because all the citizens of the Republic of Kurdey were "Kurds," if on the walls of Taksim, Kadikoy, Kizilay [prominent locations in Istanbul and Ankara], there were signs which read "Happy is he who can call himself a Kurd." If in Kurdey (Kurdiye) it were declared that the Turks do not exist, that the so-called Turks were simply Kurds, that those who considered themselves Turks were really "Sea Kurds" (*Deniz Kurdi*). If we had to learn in school that the Kurds have 7000 years of history behind them, that Anatolia belonged to them alone, that in fact the Mongols, Huns and Etruscans should be considered their ancestors. . . . If it were forbidden to bear the [Turkish] names of Teoman, Cengiz, Attila or Osman, if it were compulsory to take the [Kurdish] first names of Berfin, Biruj, Tiruj or Nevruz. If the creation of a Turkish television station were prohibited, and if all the television programs were in Kurdish. If we were compelled to write our novels, stories and poems in Kurdish, if we could listen only to Kurdish songs and if we had to publish our newspapers in Kurdish. If, in school, the lessons were only given in Kurdish and if it were strictly forbidden to give them in Turkish. If for claiming that "we are Turks, we have a language and a history," we could be arbitrarily thrown into jail. . . . Would we take it? . . . Today we ask the Kurds to accept things that we ourselves would probably have refused as "Turks." This pretentiousness has brought us to the point of explosion and has led the country first to terrorism and then to civil war. . . . To be a democrat means above all to listen to the Kurds' demands, demands which would have been our own if we had lived in the Republic of Kurdey.

The Turkish establishment, however, was not amused, and Altan was quickly fired from his job at *Milliyet*. A few days later the State Security Court in Istanbul charged him under Article 312/2 of the penal code with "provoking enmity and hatred by displaying racism or regionalism." In October 1995 he was sentenced to two years in prison, but it was reduced to a 20-month suspended sentence provided he did not commit a similar crime. For defending Altan in his column in *Yeni Yuzyil,* Ali Bayramoglu also faced charges under Article 312/2.

## Improvements

In the spring of 1991, President Turgut Ozal legalized the usage of Kurdish in everyday conversation and folkloric music recordings by rescinding Law no. 2932, which had been enacted by the military in October 1983. Usage of Kurdish in the media and education, however, remained prohibited.

In November 1992, a piece of legislation known by its Turkish acronym CMUK was enacted in a supposed attempt to bring "Turkish law into conformity with international standards in the vital areas of detention periods, arrest procedures and interrogation practices."[40] According to one careful study of CMUK's effects, "the law is a very positive beginning," but does "not apply equally to the State Security Courts, to so-called 'terrorist' crimes, or to the state of emergency area of the Southeast."[41]

The most recent (1996) Human Rights Report issued by the U.S. State Department agreed that "under the CMUK, detainees are entitled to immediate access to an attorney and may meet and confer with the attorney at any time," but that this did not apply to those detained by the State Security Courts. In general, the State Department Report found that "the human rights situation improved in a number of areas, but very serious problems remain."

In March 1995, Turkey was unfairly criticized in much of the Western media for its large military incursion into northern Iraq against PKK guerrillas raiding into southeastern Turkey from their safehouses there. This criticism of Turkey failed to distinguish between legitimate self-defense actions in hot pursuit of PKK guerrillas on the one hand and human rights abuses against civilian Kurds on the other. Indeed, the supposed Iraqi Kurdish "victims" of this Turkish incursion in fact largely supported it, since the PKK was challenging their authority in northern Iraq. Similarly, in November 1992, the Iraqi Kurds had actually joined the Turks in attacking the PKK in northern Iraq. Then in August 1995, the PKK launched attacks against Massoud Barzani's Kurdistan Democratic Party (KDP), one of the two main Iraqi Kurdish parties.

During 1995, Turkey came under considerable pressure to correct its most egregious human rights abuses in order to win approval from the European parliament to join the European Customs Union. The Turkish parliament's approval of amendments to fifteen articles of the Constitution as well as the Preamble in July 1995 played an important part in this action. These amendments included lowering the voting age to 18, increasing the seats in parliament by 100, removing bans on political activity by unions and other organizations, and granting civil servants the right to form trade unions. It was the first time that the Constitution had ever been amended by a civilian government.

Three months later the Turkish parliament amended Article 8 of the Anti-Terrorism Law, supposedly to remove the ambiguity in it that had allowed practically anybody to be imprisoned for advocating a political solution to the Kurdish problem. In addition, the amendment required that conscious intent to commit separatism be proven before a conviction could be reached by eliminating the phrase "regardless of the means, purpose or intention." Maximum penalties were reduced from five to three years, a change that made suspended sentences or their commutation to mere fines more likely. Finally, the newly amended Article 8 was made retroactive to allow 123 people in prison under its provisions to be freed.

On the negative side, however, the expression of Kurdish nationalist views continued to be a crime under the new version of Article 8. In addition, parliament inserted a new clause in the law making radio and television stations liable to closure for 15-day periods for broadcasts deemed separatist. What is more, other provisions in the penal code continued to make it possible to indict, detain, and harass those who spoke out on the Kurdish problem. As a result, critics of Turkey denounced the constitutional amendments and change in Article 8 as merely cosmetic. The European parliament, however, was satisfied, and in December 1995 it admitted Turkey into the Customs Union, a coveted reward long sought by Turkish governments aspiring to eventual membership in the EU itself.

## CONTINUING LEGACY

By Western standards, people in Turkey are not encouraged to think for themselves, let alone be different from others.[42] Pressures to conform come from parents who find it only natural they should dictate to their children what careers they should choose and whom they should marry. Those who think, dress, or eat differently are in a small minority. A whole range of taboos exist, starting with the Kurdish problem.

What is more, the authorities frequently abuse citizens' rights, while few try to improve matters. When these few do, they often are accused of separatism or worse. Civil society is embryonic at best. Only a small portion of the population belongs to any kind of formal civilian organization. What social groups exist are usually of migrants from the same province, followed by trade unions and professional associations. The majority of the population does what it is told and reads what is provided. Despite the supposed constitutional and legal reforms in 1995, few seemed to care.

The deteriorating economic situation most people face probably bears a large blame for this state of lethargy. The fact that an elite few are becoming ever richer, often through dubious means, does not help matters. Saying the "correct" thing remains a good strategy in a country which has seen three military coups since 1960. In the educational system too, the rewards are for those who learn to repeat the correct things and accept the information given them without question.

When members of the government-sponsored public service trade unions marched through Ankara in October 1995, the police did not intervene. When independent public service trade unions had tried to stage similar marches in the Istanbul district of Kadikoy on May Day in 1995, however, the police resorted to wanton violence and arrests. When members of the Alevi community were sprayed with bullets in a coffeehouse in the Istanbul district of Gaziosmanpasha in March 1995, the police shot and killed more than 20 Alevis who were protesting what had happened. Prime Minister Ciller ludicrously blamed the Greeks.

Members of Alpaslan Turkes' right-wing Nationalist Action Party apparently provided the backbone for the special team forces that with official connivance attacked civilians of Kurdish ethnic heritage in Tunceli in 1994. Non-violent Kurdish nationalist politicians and intellectuals, however, are quickly portrayed as dangerous separatists and treated as criminals by a state supported by large sections of the population. Indeed, the Kurdish problem has provided Turkey's rightists with such a free hand that it is difficult not to believe that the rightists have been and still are deliberately fanning the flames. Whether this final interpretation is simply another example of the ever-present conspiracy theories that the state and its supporters use to explain the Kurdish problem and how it is instigated from abroad, however, remains to be seen. What is clear is that Turkey's authoritarian tradition continues to lay a heavy legacy upon attempts to move toward a complete and genuine democracy that would integrate those citizens of Kurdish ethnic heritage completely and willingly into the Turkish body politic.

# 2

# The PKK

## ORIGINS

The *Partiya Karkaren Kurdistan* (PKK), or Kurdistan Workers Party, grew out of two separate but related sources: (1) the Kurdish nationalist movement, and (2) the leftist, Marxist movement that had formed in the 1960s.[1] The former had seemingly been crushed in Dersim in 1938 but began to revive again in the 1960s due, in part, to the relative freedoms enjoyed under the 1961 Constitution, the influence of Mulla Mustafa Barzani's exploits to the south in northern Iraq, and a sense of economic deprivation. The leftist movement also grew from the liberties granted by the 1961 Constitution, growing frustration with an economic situation rife with un- and under-employment and limited possibilities for entry into the over-crowded universities, and, possibly, the influence of the leftist student movement in the West. Compared to what the Kemalists offered, long-suppressed Kurds discovered a more sympathetic hearing from this new left.

Both the Kurdish nationalist and the leftist movements spawned a bewildering plethora of organizations, groups, and parties, many of which proved short-lived or went through a series of combinations, alliances, splits (often violent), and name changes. Due to the shadowy, illegal nature many groups had, it is impossible to detail all of them accurately. Nevertheless, the basic outlines seem clear.

During the 1960s, two leftist organizations that proved crucial to later developments were formed: the *Turkiye Isci Partisi* (TIP), or Turkish Workers Party (TWP), a legal socialist party permitted by the new, liberal constitution; and *Dev Genc* (Revolutionary Youth). The TWP won 15 seats in parliament during the 1965 election, and, as mentioned in chapter one, passed a pro-Kurdish resolution in 1970. This latter action led to its closure following the military intervention of 1971. *Dev Genc,* on the other hand, was a radical, militant student-based organization that gave birth to a host of other, even more violent, leftist organizations and parties in the 1970s. The groundswell of organizations was facilitated, inadvertently perhaps, by the Bulent Ecevit government's general amnesty in 1974 that freed many imprisoned terrorists, radicals, and leftists who had been sentenced after the military coup in 1971.

Because of internal disputes and splits, the original *Dev Genc* movement that had been established in 1969 led in 1976 to the establishment of *Dev Yol* (Revolutionary Way) and in 1978 to *Dev Sol* (Revolutionary Left). (A faction of *Dev Sol* still exists as a violent terrorist organization in Turkey but now calls itself the Revolutionary Peoples Liberation Party-Front [DHKP-C].) One might also say that three other tendencies grew out of Dev Genc: (1) Mahir Cayan's *Turkiye Halk Kurtulus Partisi ve Cephesi* (THKP-C); (2) Ibrahim Kaypakkaya's Turkish Communist Party–Marxist Leninist (TKP/ML) and its armed flank the *Turkiye Isci Koylu Kurtulus Ordusu* (TIKKO), or Turkish Workers Peasants Liberation Army; and (3) Deniz Gezmis's *Turkiye Halk Kurtulus Ordusu* (THKO), or Turkish People's Liberation Army. Each tendency spawned a host of mutually hostile successors following the deaths of their original leaders in the early 1970s.

Cahir's strategy of armed propaganda proved important in the early days of the PKK. He argued that the "Turkish oligarchy," in cooperation with western imperialism, had created an "artificial balance" with better living standards and fear of the state that enabled it to pacify the people and keep them under control. Revolution in Turkey could only be achieved if this "artificial balance" could be shown to be weaker than thought. The way to accomplish this was through "armed propaganda," violent attacks against certain unpopular state targets that would attract public attention and show the state as incapable of protecting its own. The people then would gain the courage to side with the revolution. To announce its creation in 1978, the PKK carried out just such an action when it tried unsuccessfully to assassinate Mehmet Celal Bucak, a local landlord and Justice Party MP for Siverek.

During the fervor of the 1960s and 1970s, a dizzying series of leftist Kurdish groups were formed, including: the *Devrimci Dogu Kultur Ocaklari* (DDKO), or Revolutionary Eastern Culture Clubs, in 1969; *Devrimci Democratik Kultur Dernekleri* (DDKD), or Revolutionary Democratic Culture Associations, in 1975; *Ozgurluk Yolu* (Road of Freedom, the Turkish name of its monthly journal), or (Turkish) Kurdistan Socialist Party, associated with Kemal Burkay and Mehdi Zana in 1975; KAWA (named after a legendary Kurdish folk hero associated with the Kurdish new year's holiday *Newroz*) in 1976; *Rizgari* (Liberation) in 1977; and *Kurdistan Ulusal Kurtulusculari* (KUK), or Kurdistan National Liberationists, in 1978. As with their leftist cousins, these Kurdish organizations suffered from bitter divisions and violent clashes among themselves. Although they all had their brief moments in the limelight, with the partial exception of Burkay's Kurdistan Socialist Party, which still exists in exile, all were eventually wiped out following the military intervention of 1980, if not earlier.

It was within this milieu that Abdullah (Apo) Ocalan—a Turkish Kurd from the Hilvan-Siverek region in the province of Urfa and a former student in the political science faculty of Ankara University—first formed the Ankara Higher Education Association (AYOD) at a *Dev Genc* meeting in the home of Riza Altun in the Tuzlucayir district of Ankara in 1974. Of the seven to eleven persons said to have been present at this first meeting, Cemil (Cuma) Bayik and Ali Haydar (Fuat) Kaytan, in addition to Ocalan himself, were later announced as being members of the PKK's Central Committee of 30 and its Leadership Council of 6 following the PKK's fifth congress in January 1995.[2]

Ocalan told this first meeting that since the necessary conditions then existed for a Kurdish nationalist movement in Turkey, the group should break its relations with the other leftist movements that refused to recognize Kurdish national rights. Further meetings were held, and the fledgling group decided to call itself the *Ulusal Kurtulus Ordusu* (UKO) or National Liberation Army. Given Ocalan's preeminence, however, the group soon began to be called "Apocular," or followers of Apo.

In 1975, the group departed from Ankara and began its operations in the Kurdish areas from where they had originally come. This entailed recruitment and indoctrination activities that by the late 1970s had spilled over into violence against leftist groups termed "social chauvinists" and other Kurdish groups, such as the KUK, which were called "primitive nationalists" or "nationalist reformists." (Almost 20 years later such violence continued when the PKK suddenly attacked Barzani's KDP in northern Iraq in August 1995. See below.)

According to Martin van Bruinessen, an astute observer of Kurdish affairs, the Apocular were "the only [Kurdish] organization whose members were drawn almost exclusively from the lowest social classes—the uprooted, half-educated village and small-town youth who knew what it felt like to be oppressed and who wanted action, not ideological sophistication."[3] One should also note that Ocalan himself was the only contemporary Kurdish national leader who did not come from the traditional elite classes. Bruinessen further noted that the Apo's group "represents the most marginal sections of Kurdish society, the ones who feel excluded from the country's social and economic development, [and the] victims of the rural transformation with frustrated expectations." Although much of the violence seemed to be mindless, petty feuds, "there was also a definite aspect of class struggle to these conflicts. . . . Much of the . . . violence was directed against the haves in the name of the have-nots." Ocalan offered his supporters "a simple and appropriate theory, and lots of opportunities for action, heroism and martyrdom."

By the end of 1978, Ocalan felt that the necessary conditions for creating a formal party had arrived. On November 27, the founding members met at the house of a "patriotic" landlord called "Seyfettin" in the village of Fis in the Lice township of the province of Diyarbakir and formally established the PKK. Only seven people were named to the party's first Central Committee: Abdullah Ocalan (General Secretary), Kesire Yildirim (at that time Ocalan's wife), Sahin Donmez (who later became a "repentant" or informer for the government), Cemil Bayik (long considered to be the number two person in the PKK), Mehmet Karasungur, Mahsun Dogan, and Mehmet Hayri Durmus. (Dogan and Durmus died in the Diyarbakir prison in 1982.)

## Escape to Syria

Sensing the military coup that finally did occur in September 1980, Ocalan fled to Syria in May 1979.[4] He chose Syria because he was aware of the Palestinian organizations based in that country and how they already had helped certain radical leftist groups from Turkey to locate there and in Lebanon. Lacking allies on the Turkish left, however, he initially had to settle for the help of a Turkish Kurd, Mehmet Sait, who had relatives living in Syria.

Thus, Ocalan first arrived in Syria with Sait and stayed for a few days with his relatives. From there he went on to Damascus where he was able to contact certain Palestinians. Although they were initially suspicious of him—after all, the Kurds from Iraq that they knew had relations with Israel and the Shah of Iran—Ocalan finally gained their support to bring in his men and train them. By the summer of 1979, Kemal Pir[5] and Halil Atac, two top PKK leaders, had joined him. Cemil Bayik also visited and upon returning to Turkey arranged for the first 50 recruits to be sent over.

Under the code name "Ali,"[6] Ocalan soon established contacts with almost all the various regional movements in Syria and Lebanon as well as representatives from the Eastern bloc including the Soviets, Bulgarians, and Cubans. He also developed his first contacts with Jalal Talabani, the leader of one of the two main Kurdish groups in Iraq, the Patriotic Union of Kurdistan (PUK). Talabani proved helpful in arranging for financial aid from Turkish Kurdish laborers living throughout the Middle East. In addition, support arrived from Kurds living in Germany and Sweden as well as Armenians in the Bekaa valley. The training opportunities provided by Nayef Hawatmeh's Popular Democratic Front for the Liberation of Palestine (PDFLP) also proved very useful. According to Ahmet Ersever, a former Turkish intelligence officer with keen insights into these early days, the PKK fighters were distributed in groups of five or ten to Hawatmeh's camps, where contacts with the Soviet Union and Bulgaria were particularly important.[7]

During 1980, the first PKK fighters infiltrated back into Turkey over the Syrian border under the leadership of Mehmet Karasungur. Although some of them actually reached Siverek and even Batman, most of them were killed by the Turkish troops. At the same time, Cemil Assad, the brother of the Syrian leader Hafez Assad and responsible for his country's relations with the Kurdish world, established contact with Ocalan. Rifad, another well-placed Assad brother, also entered the picture. Indeed, according to Cemil Bayik, "Rifad had great sympathy for the organization [PKK] from the very beginning. . . . He placed great value on us."[8] As a result, the Syrians allowed the PKK to expand its influence among the Syrian Kurds and create recruitment offices, safehouses, and several training camps within the country. The Mazlum (Mahsun) Korkmaz camp in the Bekaa valley of Lebanon on the Syrian border—originally called the "Helve camp," but renamed for a famous PKK leader killed in 1986 by the Turks—was the most famous. Occupied and controlled by the PKK from 1981 on, it was finally closed down as a sop to the Turks in 1992. But, of course, by then the PKK had plenty of other sources upon which to fall back.

## ABDULLAH (APO) OCALAN

From its inception, the PKK has been so closely associated with the views and actions of its *Serok* (leader) Abdullah "Apo" Ocalan that a brief biography would seem appropriate at this juncture.[9] His nickname "Apo" is a shortened form of the very common first name in the Middle East "Abdullah" (literally "slave of Allah") and also means "uncle." His surname "Ocalan" means "revenger," which one might see as appropriate.

The first born in a family of poor farmers in the village of Omerli in Turkey's (Sanli) Urfa province, Apo Ocalan apparently had six brothers and sisters.[10] One of them, Osman (Ferhat) Ocalan, was a leading member of the PKK for many years, reportedly active in Iran and, in the 1990s, northern Iraq; he may still be a member of its Central Committee. However, he reportedly has been in at least temporary eclipse since his forces were deemed to have performed poorly when attacked by the Iraqi Kurds and then the Turks in northern Iraq in October 1992. After that, he was for some time the PKK commander at the Zaleh camp in northeastern Iraqi Kurdistan, where his forces were supposedly being interned by those of Talabani's PUK. Commenting about Osman, Apo declared that "in some ways he is a sacrificial lamb for his big brother," but that there was "nothing much" to their ties as brothers. Another brother, Mehmet Ocalan, said to be a member of the PKK, was caught near Izmir, Turkey in September 1995, trying to illegally flee by boat to Greece.

Ocalan's mother, Uveys Ocalan, was a powerful woman. In September 1992, shortly before her death, she attended a meeting of the pro-Kurdish HEP party in Ankara, where much deference was shown her. Ocalan's father, on the other hand, has been described as a "man without authority." Indeed, Ocalan himself later declared that his father was "such a weak person that his reaction to injustices was to go up to the roof of the house and scream and swear."[11] A clash with his father led Ocalan to conclude that Kurdish families are "deeply feudal" and that it was necessary to revolt against such oppressive bonds to be free. A great-grandfather, Husune Oce, however, was famous for his armed resistance to the Turks. Even after finally being forced to accept Turkish authority, he was said to have instilled a desire for revenge into his offspring.

Although he became a Marxist as an adult, Ocalan was known in elementary school for his knowledge of the Koran, which he had supposedly learned by heart. (Interestingly, another even more famous secular Kurd, Mulla Mustafa Barzani, was also said to have memorized long verses from the Islamic holy book.) In his early days as a student in Ankara, Ocalan attended prayers five times a day and frequently attended conferences held at the Maltepe mosque, as well as seminars of the Association to Fight Communism.

Ocalan grew up in a village where Armenian formerly had been spoken. Some Armenians apparently still lived there. For five years he walked to elementary school past the nearby village of Cibin that contained a mosque that formerly had been an Armenian church. The Armenian massacres troubled him: "I feel a repugnance when I see that this church has been transformed into a mosque. . . . In fact, my father was a friend of Armenians, despite the fact that he was a Muslim and was attached to his prayers."[12] Ocalan also claims that as a young boy he could not speak Turkish, only learning to do so gradually in elementary school. As an adult, however, Turkish became his working language; it is ironic, given his life mission: "I think and plan completely in Turkish. Kurdish comes second."

For a time during the 1960s, Ocalan worked in the cotton fields of Adana and other temporary jobs to earn money for his family and further schooling. When he first visited Ankara in 1966 to take the university entrance examinations, he thought of himself as a Turk. Upon seeing the equestrian statue of Ataturk in the district of Ulus, for example, he was deeply moved and excited. He was also a dedicated fan of the Istanbul Galatasaray football club and one of its leading players at that time, Metin. He finally managed to obtain a place in a business school where he finished in the eighteenth position and then took a white-collar job in the civil service in Diyarbakir for a year.

Ocalan participated in his first mass demonstration in 1969, the funeral ceremony in Ankara held for former appeals court chief justice Imran Oktem. After failing to gain admission to the Turkish War Academy, Ocalan entered the political science faculty of Ankara University, where he particularly enjoyed classes in economic history. He also spent seven months in prison in 1970 for participating in an illegal student demonstration, an experience that apparently proved a turning point. He became a leftist; scientific socialism and dialectic materialism replaced religion.

The first book he read in this field was called *The Alphabet of Socialism.* He also seems to have been influenced by the ideas of Leo Huberman, a rather obscure American, Marxist journalist still active in the 1960s, and was "truly touched" by Lenin's treatise on national self-determination. According to Cemil Bayik and Kemal Pir, two of the original founders of the PKK, Ocalan "was incredibly literate compared to us. . . . He just read on and on." Ocalan also enjoyed the Kurdish ethnic-origin author Yasar Kemal, mentioned above, and filmmaker Yilmaz Guney because they tried to see into the "Kurdish reality."

Many years later, Ocalan specifically testified that he had been affected by the careers of Deniz Gezmis and Mahir Cayan, the two radical leftist leaders of the early 1970s discussed above: "The ideas for which they waged a struggle influenced me personally and were enough to push me to the left and later in a socialist direction."[13] He also recalled how he had heard Cayan, at a meeting held at Istanbul Technical University, denounce Kemalism as "chauvinistic and nationalistic, and that the Kurdish problem must be resolved by getting rid of the Kemalist influence." According to Ocalan, this "influenced us deeply." When Cayan was killed by Turkish security forces during the famous shootout at the village of Kizildere on March 30, 1972, Ocalan was deeply moved: "The execution of Deniz and the ruthless massacre of Mahir . . . caused us to take action. . . . We hoisted this resistance flag over the blood of Mahir and his friends . . . [who] were martyred in Kizildere."

Ocalan went on to declare that after he had led the AYOD organization of Ankara students, "we realized that a joint organization would not be very beneficial" and that "an organization based specifically on the Kurdistan issue and one that aims at solving the Kurdish national problem would also lead the way for a Turkish revolution." Since this was also the view of such Turkish leftists as Kemal Pir and others, "together with them, we started to work as a group." Despite all that had happened since, Ocalan still claimed in 1996 that "our struggle is an integral part of the struggle of the Turkish people, enhances their struggle, and acts as its guarantee." In so arguing, Ocalan was maintaining loyalty to and still advocating the alternative leftist road that Turkey had failed to follow in the early 1970s.

During the latter part of the 1970s, Ocalan married Kesire Yildirim. Earlier she had been the fiancee of another militant named Ismet Dogru. At the time, some accused Kesire of associating with Ocalan simply to further her career, and indeed she was one of the people both present at the AYOD meeting in Ankara in 1974 and an original member of the PKK's first Central Committee in 1978.

In 1987, they were divorced. Following a brief house arrest in Lebanon, Kesire managed to escape to Sweden where she became a member of an alternative movement called the PKK-*Vejin* (Resurrection). Ocalan accused her of being a Turkish agent, said she was "as cold as a snake,"[14] and claimed that being married to her "was like being with a corpse."[15] He did credit her, however, with making him sensitive to feminist demands. In another interview, the PKK leader claimed that he found "it shameful to go and find a girl," but admitted that "unfortunately, in the shelters, we could not control our urges and engaged in sexual relations."[16] He also asserted he was not interested in having any children, given the many he had seen without any future.

In some more-recent interviews Ocalan has seemingly tested his interlocutors' judgment by claiming, on the one hand, that "I could not even kill a fly,"[17] but, on the other, that "we will fight to the last man. Much blood will be shed."[18] To yet another interviewer, Ocalan possibly manifested a messianic complex by claiming that a Christian priest had told him quite frankly that he was "a Kurdish Jesus."[19] "That might be. . . . Often I compare my deeds with those of the prophets. . . . When I see you [the Christian priest Ocalan was talking to], I start thinking about Jesus and say to myself, 'what . . . good friends we could have been.' And I am sure that there is a very close resemblance between us."[20]

More to the point, perhaps, in this same interview concerning Ocalan's supposed likeness to Jesus, the PKK leader offered the following insights into the PKK: "I often liken my colleagues to Jesus' disciples, and tell them that they should emulate them. Forty is the average age of my colleagues. They have no homes and families, own nothing for themselves, and believe they are living to serve mankind."[21] One should also recall that as a Muslim, Ocalan would look upon Jesus as a great prophet, not the son of God.

Ocalan evinced a philosophically mystical aspect to his character when he told the famous Turkish journalist Mehmet Ali Birand: "I am increasingly moving away from the feeling of death. That is so. . . . The more I deal with huge and frightening things, I move away from the feeling of death, from the danger of death, as well. That is also strange, but true."[22]

Ocalan has been described in recent appearances as being stout, speaking Turkish in a husky voice, and having dark, glinting eyes and bushy eyebrows. Although he has almost certainly not left his Syrian-Lebanese safehouse since he first arrived there in 1979, various sources have from time to time placed him in northern Iraq, southeastern Turkey, the Lachin area of Armenia, Moscow, or even the Melkonian Institute in Greek Cyprus. When he gives interviews from his apartment in Damascus, he does so on the condition that they be datelined the "Bekaa valley" so as not to embarrass Syria. In May 1996,

Ocalan survived yet another assassination attempt when a bomb blast at his flat in Damascus occurred while he was away.

In 1991, *Serxwebun* (Independence), the PKK's sophisticated magazine produced in Germany, published Ocalan's book, *Kurdistan'da Halk Savasi Ve Gerilla* (Popular War and the Guerrilla in Kurdistan). It constituted a valuable insight into his strategy for successfully waging a guerrilla war. A year later, Ocalan published *12th September Fascism and the PKK Rebellion.* Its publisher, Unsal Ozturk, the owner of the Yurt publishing house in Turkey, was sentenced to one year in prison and fined TL 100 million (approximately $5,000). In 1994, Agri-Verlag in Cologne, Germany, published yet another book by Ocalan, *Kurdish Reality Since the 19th Century and the PKK Movement.*

When Selim (Tilki [Fox]) Curukkaya—a former PKK leader in Europe, said to have made a great deal of money through drug dealing, and sentenced to death by the party for "treason"—fled to Germany and published a book in 1994 entitled *Verses of Apo,* its Kurdish readers were attacked by PKK militants. In his book, Curukkaya called Ocalan a "murderer" and "dictator" and referred to him as being "the biggest betrayer of the already betrayed Kurdish revolution."[23] He also called for the establishment of a new Kurdish party. At approximately the same time, the PKK reported that "Dr. Baran" (Muslum Durgun), its longtime commander in the Dersim area of Turkey, had committed suicide. Others believed, however, that he was executed on orders of Ocalan for "passivism"—that is, failing to launch attacks on Turkish targets. These incidents recalled the earlier case of Huseyin Yildirim, a Kurdish lawyer who for several years served as a spokesman for the PKK in Europe. Yildirim broke with Ocalan in the late 1980s over the party's policy of killing civilians who collaborated with the state; he helped to establish the *Vejin* movement mentioned above. At the time there was a great deal of polemics and even violence exchanged over the issue. A number of other PKK members apparently have been executed over the years for various transgressions they supposedly committed against the party.

## ORGANIZATION

Although the PKK is ultimately a single entity, it consists of a number of different divisions or related organizations, themselves subdivided, which operate at various levels of command. Superficially, at least, this organization resembles the traditional model of a communist party: an ultimate leader ("General Secretary" until the fifth party congress in January 1995, since then "Chairman" or "President"); the equivalent of a politburo (termed "leadership council" by the fifth congress); a central committee (CC or Central Executive Committee);

and various bureaus operating under the CC. In addition, there is a much larger popular front organization, the ERNK, which supposedly limits itself to political work, and a professional guerrilla army, the ARGK. One might also mention Tev-Sal, the Kurdistan Intelligence Network Ocalan set up in Damascus in 1989 to collect intelligence on Turkish military targets and Islamic activities in southeastern Anatolia. Other sub-organs of the PKK include the Patriotic Youth Union (YXWK), Patriotic Women Union (YJWK), Patriotic Workers Union (YKWK), Patriotic Religious Men's Union (YDWK), and Patriotic Artists Union (YRWK). In addition, Kurd-A, a PKK-affiliated news agency, has operated out of Germany for several years, while MED-TV began operations from Britain and Belgium in the spring of 1995.

Over the years, five party congresses are said to have been held (1981, 1982, 1986, 1990, and 1995), as well as three national conferences (1988, 1990, and 1994). There are military commands set up on a provincial level in Turkey and certain areas in northern Iraq, while in Europe there are, in effect, national offices of the ERNK in such countries as Germany, France, Sweden, Belgium (which at the present time houses the ERNK's European headquarters), the Netherlands, Austria, Denmark, Britain, Greece, and Switzerland. Even in the United States there is a small but active American Kurdish Information Network (AKIN) in Washington, D.C. that is, in effect, connected to the ERNK. The PKK also produces some 30 different publications in various countries. Finally, one should mention the Kurdistan Parliament-in-Exile that first met in the Netherlands in April 1995 and has since convened in Austria, Russia, Denmark, Italy, and Norway.

Although the PKK in part grew out of the leftist unrest and violence prevalent in Turkey during the 1960s and 1970s and is still termed a "Marxist-Leninist Communist Party and terrorist organization" by the Turkish government, it clearly is first a Kurdish nationalist movement. Indeed, it was this very Kurdishness that caused the original Apocular to break from its leftist associates in the mid-1970s. This, of course, is not to deny that even in its most recent (1995) congress, the PKK reiterated its commitment "to socialism . . . despite the contrary developments in the world,"[24] and, in Ocalan, maintains an all-powerful, ruthless leader who himself has declared he is "without pity,"[25] and thus suggests a miniature Stalin or Mao. What is more, the PKK guidelines remind one of the Leninist principle of democratic centralism: "It is always necessary for the order to be carried out from the top unit to the bottom unit without discussion. As for the report, every member should be reporting on the situation and waiting for the commands that come from the Center."[26] Various observers still comment about the continuing dedication to Marxist ideology within the PKK's leadership as distinguished from its foot soldiers and mere supporters.[27] Even after the fall of communism in the Soviet Union, Ocalan still maintained that he believed "that socialism is an august ideology which should be upheld. . . . I respectfully remember socialism's distinguished militants and I maintain the view that that ideology should not be allowed to be defamed or blamed. That also applies to Cuba, Stalin, and Lenin."[28]

This Marxism, however, has always been secondary to the Kurdish nationalist essence. As Ocalan himself recently said: "When the PKK was founded I was not a true Marxist. . . . The Kurdish cause was the thing I was most interested in. . . . That is the PKK's ideology, not Islamism and not Communism."[29] This tendency has become increasingly evident over the years and was officially ratified by the changes instituted during the party's fifth congress in January 1995. (See below.)

## Central Committee

At its very inception in November 1978, the PKK named its first Central Committee (CC) of seven persons. (See above.) Although there has normally been a smaller leadership group that corresponds to a politburo, usually it is the CC that officially has acted as the highest organ of the PKK, subordinate, of course, to the General Secretary (since 1995, Chairman) Ocalan.

The party's fifth congress in January 1995 named 30 members to the most recent Central Executive Committee or CC.[30] A listing of those names available would be useful: Abdullah (Apo) Ocalan, Cemil Bayik (Cuma), Duran Kalkan (Abbas), Murat Karayilan (Cemal), Mustafa Karasu (Huseyin Ali), Halil Atac (Abu Bakir), Ali Haydar Kaytan (Fuat), Semdin Sakik (Buyuk or Parmaksiz [Fingerless] Zeki), Sabri Ok, Ahmet Uman (Baver), Hidir Sarikaya (Ekrem), Dursun Ali Kucuk, Mehmet Esiyok (Berxwedan), Mehmet Can Yuce, Mahmut Gun (Cemal), an unidentified Syrian national using the alias of "Khabat" (Struggle), an unidentified northern Iraqi Kurd known as "Halil," one of the officials in charge of northern camps known as "Ali," a member responsible for the province of Garzan (corresponding roughly to the Turkish province of Bitlis) known as "Kemal," a member responsible for the northern Iraqi region of Khwakurk near the Turkish and Iranian borders known as "Ferhan," the Amed (Diyarbakir) province coordinator known as "Yilmaz," and two other members known as "Sozdar" and Hane." The names or even aliases of the seven remaining members were not available, although the following were announced as alternate members of the CC: Muzaffer Ayata, Nedim Seven (Behzat), Nedim Ates (Kerem), Nizamettin Tas (Botan), and Sakine Altinmakas (Fatma).

The following seven members of the CC were also named to the party's Leadership Council (Politburo). As such, they may be assumed to be the leading members of the PKK, possibly in the very order that their names are listed:

Abdullah (Apo) Ocalan, Cemil Bayik (Cuma [Friday]), Duran Kalkan (Abbas), Murat Karayilan (Cemal), Halil Atac (Abu Bakir), Mustafa Karasu (Huseyin Ali), and Ali Haydar Kaytan (Fuat). Although all have been longtime associates of Ocalan, only Bayik was with him at the first meeting of the AYOD in 1974 and was a member of the first CC in 1978. Born in the southeastern Turkish province of Elazig in 1955, the eldest of four, Bayik proved an excellent student and won a state scholarship to attend a teacher training college in Malayta. Bayik then went on to study in Ankara University where he met Kemal Pir, who later introduced him to Ocalan.

For many years Bayik was the head of the ARGK, the party's professional army. At the fifth party congress in 1995, however, he was relieved of this position. Nevertheless, Bayik and Kalkan were the only two members of the Leadership Council who were listed as being members of two of the five additional bureaus working presumably under the CC and Leadership Council. In addition, the back injury Bayik suffered in 1992 might have played a role in his moving into a new position of authority. Thus, it would appear that Bayik remains the number two person in the PKK, and with the exception of Ocalan's personal aide, a Syrian Kurd called "Hamit," the only person who sees Ocalan on a daily basis.

Beside Atac and Karayilan, Suleyman Kaydi (Celal) was assigned to the military bureau responsible for the operations of the ARGK. This was the bureau Bayik had headed for many years. The front bureau for directing the activities of the ERNK, the party's political front described in detail below, consisted of Karasu from the leadership bureau, Faysal Ates (Ferhan), and a third member identified only by his alias "Zuhat." Possibly Ates was the same "Ferhan" listed as the alias for one of the CC members, listed above, but this is simply speculation. Karasu had been imprisoned for many years following the military coup in 1980 and after his release had worked for three years in the party's European organization. He had now been called to the "center" by Ocalan to gain "experience in the [battle] region."

The somewhat confusingly named political bureau was to be directed by Bayik. His two associates were listed as Numan Ucar (Mahir) and Ali Sapan, a longtime, important PKK operative in Europe. The organization-education bureau was placed under the responsibility of Bayik and Kalkan (two of the seven members of the Leadership Council) and a third member using the alias "Sirzat." Previously, Kalkan had served as the General Secretary of the *Hazen Rizgariya Kurdistan* (HRK), or Kurdistan Freedom Brigades, a forerunner of the ERNK and ARGK that had been established in 1984 and abolished in 1986 when the ARGK had been created. Although Kalkan was considered by some to be the second in command to Ocalan in 1988, Kalkan reportedly broke with him in that year over violence against Kurdish villages, which he believed hurt the party's recruitment efforts. After being imprisoned in West Germany in 1989, he had been tried and punished by the party itself. He recently was rehabilitated after he recanted and pledged to work more loyally.

The ideological bureau consisted of Kalkan and Kaytan, another member of the seven-man leadership council. He too had been returned to active party work in Lebanon's Bekaa valley after his release from prison in Germany. Dursun Ali Kucuk, a member of the CC, was the third member of this bureau. It is possible that the members of these five bureaus not specifically listed above as members of the CC were some of the seven members of the CC whose names were not available.

Kani Yilmaz (whose real name is Faysal Dumlayici)—possibly the third highest ranking member of the PKK and in charge of all its European activities before his imprisonment in Britain as "a threat to national security" in October 1994—was also possibly one of these *in petto* members of the CC, as was Akif Hasan, another important PKK leader in Europe. To maintain their cover as merely members of the political front organization, the ERNK, the PKK would be reticent to announce that they belonged to its CC. Riza Altun, a longtime confidant of Ocalan who spent a hard nine years in the Diyarbakir prison, is now in charge of the technical aspect of party communications and may also be a member of the CC. As recently as 1993, it was reported that there was also a member of the CC in charge of activities in the United States named "Dilan," who was possibly a woman. Furthermore, the ARGK's approximately seven regional commanders, some of whose code names already were listed above as being CC members, are all supposedly members of the CC. Again, for reasons of security it is likely that in certain cases the party does not want to reveal their names. Finally, in addition to the bureaus and their members listed above, a central disciplinary board was also announced: Mahmut Dora (Serhat), Selahattin Gun (Dogan), Engin Karaaslan (Haydar), Salih Kubat (Sinan), and Osman Tekin (Sari Sadun).

The CC is clearly too large, makeshift, and geographically dispersed to meet regularly and make decisions as a collective body. On the other hand, the "party leadership," a term used for Ocalan himself, probably does confer closely with the other members of the leadership council, since its membership is small and geographically concentrated in the Syrian-Lebanese safehouse.

## ERNK

In March 1985, the PKK established the *Eniye Rizgariye Nevata Kurdistan* (ERNK), or Kurdistan National Liberation Front, as a popular front and propaganda division. Mahsun or Mazlum (Agit) Korkmaz, described at the time as

"Ocalan's right-hand man," was named as its first commander. After his death in action the following year, the main PKK training camp in the Bekaa valley was renamed in his honor.

Although it usually masks itself in the West as solely a peaceful popular front, the ERNK has also been involved in armed actions from its inception. Indeed, armed attacks have even been carried out in its name. Only as the ARGK developed as a professional guerrilla army in the late 1980s did the ERNK begin to play down these armed aspects, but it has never disavowed them.

Today the ERNK plays the key role in public relations and propaganda activities. In Turkey, it is mainly in charge of urban activities such as producing local recruits for the PKK and ARGK, organizing PKK activities such as mass riots, collecting money and information, liaison, carrying out Islamic activities and propaganda for the PKK, maintaining the logistical supply lines to ARGK guerrillas in the mountains, and organizing the rural settlements. In Europe, the ERNK liases with the PKK leadership abroad, carries on propaganda activities and stages demonstrations to attract attention to the PKK cause, finds new recruits for the ARGK, and camouflages ARGK militants.

Anyone can support the PKK by being a sympathizer with or member of the ERNK. Indeed, at the end of 1989, the PKK even secured the services of Melle Abdullah, a prominent 89-year-old Islamic theologian, to help establish the *Yurtsever Dinadamlari Birligi,* or Patriotic Men of Religion, a unit connected to the ERNK, and probably the same organ as the Patriotic Religious Men's Union mentioned above. Despite its Marxist philosophy, when appropriate, PKK propaganda releases would now begin with *"Bismillahirrahmanirrahim"* (in the name of Allah), and end with "Amen." Verses from the Koran on the legitimacy of struggle were cited: "Whoever attacks you, attack him with as much force as he has attacked you." Muslim clerics were also enlisted in campaigns to increase the fertility rate among Kurds. In recent years the Turkish government has shown concern about the long-term implications of the Kurds having a higher birthrate than the Turks. The PKK, however, is determined to encourage this growth.

In 1993, the PKK established the Kurdistan Islamic Movement (KIM) in Europe, apparently to replace the earlier Kurdistan Religious Union. Although the KIM lacked an official leader since the death of Melle Abdullah, Abdurrahman Durre acted as its organizer and spokesman. He was a member of the Kurdish Institute in Berlin, which was affiliated with the ERNK. Previously he had worked for the Turkish Religious Affairs Directorate for 13 years, but he had been removed because of his pro-Kurdish views. In its first communique, the KIM declared: "Like all Muslim peoples, the Kurdish people also have the right to be independent and free [and] to fight . . . Kemalism."[31] The KIM had six mosques in Germany, one in Austria, and one in France.

Unlike the 500 mosques in Europe owned by the Turkish Islamic Refah Party, the KIM mosques had an ethnic character. Its Sheikh Said mosque in Hamburg was similar to a social establishment as it also contained a butcher shop, grocery, and even a barber shop.

In July 1994, Ocalan sent a taped message to a meeting held in Berlin to discuss "the Kurdistan problem and the Islamic solution" in which he declared that "the Kemalist ideology is a *Dadjdajl* [Arabic term meaning "deception"] regime," thus implying that the present Turkish government was a betrayal of Islam.[32] The PKK leader then declared: "Today our struggle resembles the first days of Islam. At the end of our fight, we could achieve a situation similar to that of the Prophet Muhammad and his four caliphs." Warming to his theme, he even claimed that "the Kurdish problem is an Islamic issue, and we are the closest movement to Islam" and then speculated that "a solution to the Kurdish problem might mean Kurdistan could become the cradle of international Islam."

Although ERNK members still can fight, they do not wear uniforms. During the day they may work as waiters, students, shopkeepers, and peasants. A member of the ERNK is not necessarily a formal member of the PKK, while by definition a member of the ARGK is. In short, the ERNK is the PKK's militia and may have as many as 50,000 formal members and an additional 315,000 sympathizers, depending on how they are counted. The ARGK, on the other hand, has maybe around only 10,000 members.[33] If their cover is blown, members of the ERNK can easily join the ARGK in the mountains. The common misconception that the ERNK is solely a peaceful popular front thus "imposes a serious threat for western countries."[34] ERNK members supposedly operating in Europe as peaceful members of a popular front, may actually be professional guerrillas on loan from the ARGK.

## ARGK

The *Artes-i Rizgariye Geli Kurdistan* (ARGK), or Kurdistan Peoples Liberation Army, was reportedly established by the PKK's third congress in October 1986 to be the party's professional guerrilla army. Although in practice there is an easy interchange between members of the ARGK and ERNK, the former are always supposed to be party members, wear military uniforms, and operate under stricter codes of discipline, while the latter need not even belong to the party, just be sympathizers. As Ismet G. Imset, probably the single most knowledgeable observer of the PKK, has put it: "In simplest terms, the ARGK is composed of the 'mountain units' of the PKK while the ERNK is composed of 'urban-rural units' living in settlements."[35] This difference is a result of the decision that professional guerrilla activities should be formally separated from the actions of urban groups.

Although most accounts list the strength of the ARGK at approximately 10,000, Ocalan himself claimed that there were 15,000 members in October 1993, a figure that would double by the following year.[36] Indeed, in August 1994, Kani Yilmaz, a very high-ranking member of the PKK, claimed that it then had 30,000 "professional fighters" and that this would increase by 20,000 in the next six months.[37] Despite these claims, there were indications that the ARGK was having trouble expanding to such numbers and was even having to turn down some volunteers for the time being. Ocalan admitted as much when he declared in June 1994 that "We cannot continue to be satisfied with the present level. The number . . . has to be increased to 50,000, otherwise we cannot achieve a strategic result."[38] In September 1996, Ocalan claimed that there were more than 35,000 "fighters" both in "the mountains of Kurdistan and in key areas on the borders with Russia, Armenia, Iran, Iraq, and Syria."[39] He did not make clear, however, whether this figure included only ARGK fighters or also ERNK militia.

During large-scale Turkish military operations in Tunceli province in the fall of 1994, it was reported that there were some 2,000 to 3,000 PKK guerrillas opposing the Turkish army.[40] The Turks claimed there were 1,600 guerrillas, including 300 female fighters, in the Zaleh camp in northern Iraq when they bombed it at the end of January 1994.[41] The following spring the Turks estimated that there were some 2,400 to 2,800 PKK guerrillas in northern Iraq when they invaded in an attempt to eliminate them.[42]

By the early 1990s, the ARGK maintained a regional command system in Turkey's southeast as well as in northern Iraq and (theoretically at least) the Kurdish area in Iran. As mentioned above, each regional commander was also supposedly a member of the PKK's CC. The organization used a sophisticated wireless system and code book to maintain communications. It would be useful to list these regions by their Kurdish names and the data available concerning them.[43]

Botan (the name of a powerful Kurdish emirate in the first half of the nineteenth century) covered the area of furthest southeastern Anatolia along the borders of Iraq and Iran and roughly corresponded to the Turkish provinces of Hakkari, Siirt, and Sirnak. At times the ARGK distinguished between northern Botan, or the Zagros region whose commander during the spring of 1993 was "Cemal" (Murat Karayilan), and Shin (southern) Botan, or Cukurca, whose commander was identified as "Derya-Shin." In 1990, Nizamettin (Botan) Tas had been the commander of the entire Botan region. In November 1993, Ocalan declared that the Botan area had become a "red" area or liberated zone. In such an area guerrillas could stage attacks or defend themselves with units of up to 1,000 fighters for as long as a week, and the people had fully accepted PKK authority.

Garzan corresponded roughly to the Turkish provinces of Batman and Bitlis. Its commander was "Abu Bakir" (Halil Atac). According to Ocalan, this province could be turned into a red zone. "Dr. Baran" (Muslun Durgun) still commanded in the province of Dersim (Tunceli). Following his death in 1994, "Parmaksiz Zeki" (Semdin Sakik), a.k.a. "Semo," eventually became the new commander. Earlier, Sakik had commanded in Amed, which roughly corresponded to the Turkish provinces of Diyarbakir, Mus, and Bingol. In this role, Sakik was considered a hardliner; he eventually forced Ocalan to terminate the cease-fire he had declared in March 1993 by capturing and then killing some 33 unarmed Turkish soldiers near Bingol at the end of May 1993 (see below). He was called "Parmaksiz" (Fingerless) because he earlier had blown off a thumb while firing a rocket. Apparently, Sakik also might have suffered from kidney problems at the time he left his Amed command. His brother Sirri Sakik was one of the six DEP members ejected from the Turkish parliament and arrested in March 1994. In the past, Sirri had mentioned how his brother was "a Kurdish general." According to Ocalan, red zones were possible in Dersim and Amed, but caution had to be used in the latter area, especially given past experiences. After Sakik left Amed early in 1994, he was replaced by a commander known as "Munzur." A year later, however, "Yilmaz" was reported to be the new "provincial coordinator." By April 1996 this post was occupied by the high-ranking CC member "Cemal" (Murat Karayilan).

A person known as "Ali" was the commander of Serhat, which roughly corresponded to the Turkish provinces of Agi, Erzurum, Kars, and Van. Ocalan felt that this area also could become a red area. The Mardin commander was "Kara Omer." Ocalan felt that Mardin was a "mixed" zone, which meant that the guerrilla campaign was not yet developed and operations were still in the form of small units. Thus although the PKK could attack, it could not control zones or sustain long conflicts with the Turkish forces. In such areas secrecy was essential and only very rapid and safe raids should be carried out. In such areas, therefore, ERNK activities were more important. Faysal Kut, supposedly a former ARGK commander in Mardin, had been executed by the party after being accused of stealing one billion Turkish Lira from it. A "Dr. Kemal" had also commanded in Mardin at one time, but apparently was killed in action early in 1993. Another official with the same name "Kemal" was elected to the CC in 1995 and since then has been listed as being "responsible" for Garzan.

"Region 44," or Zelve, in northern Iraq (usually known by the Kurds as "Bahdinan") was still commanded in early 1993 by Ocalan's younger brother "Ferhat" (Osman). Shortly after most of his fighters were forced into a mild type of internment under the authority of the Iraqi Kurdish leader Jalal Talabani in November 1992, he was replaced by "Mahir," who possibly was Numan Celik or Numan Ucar. "Ali" and "Ferhan" were two members of the CC in 1995 also listed as responsible respectively for "northern Iraqi camps" and "the northern Iraqi region of Khwakurk," which lies east of the Bahdinan region. This area too was considered as a red or liberated zone.

Other "provinces" or regions according to the ARGK command structure included: Orta (Middle), covering such towns as Karliova, Varto, Hinis, Bulanik, Malazgirt, and Tulak, and supposedly a red area; the Southwest, covering Kahramanmaras, Gaziantep, Sanliurfa (Ocalan's home area), and Adiyaman; GAP (the Turkish acronym for the Southeast Anatolia Project to harness the waters of the Euphrates and Tigris rivers), covering Hilvan, Siverek, Viransehir, and Cinar, and supposedly a "mixed" zone; and the so-called Eastern Province, or Iranian Kurdistan.

In addition to red and mixed zones, Ocalan identified what he termed "white" zones. These were areas where the Turkish forces had total control. The PKK was thus advised to enter in full secrecy only for hit-and-run attacks conducted from the outside. The militia (ERNK) should be developed in these areas.

During the summer of 1994, Ocalan toyed with the idea of reorganizing his provincial command structure into a larger, more simplified one of three "field" commands for the north, center, and south to improve coordination, but the plan failed to be carried out. This attempt to create a new command structure followed the tremendous escalation of the military struggle after May 1993 that for a while threatened to wrestle actual control of large areas from the state, but by 1994 had clearly failed to do so. In response to the increased Turkish pressure, there were indications by the spring of 1996 that the PKK's central military command headquarters had been moved to northern Iraq, and Ali Haydar Kaytan appointed to head it.

The fifth congress of the PKK[44] in January 1995 concluded that "the main reasons for not establishing an adequate army and not evaluating popular uprisings," stemmed from "the notion of coming to power quickly by means of individuals" and "that all sorts of fanatical, hypocritical, and aghaish [tribal chieftain-type] approaches were widespread in the past." The congress "decided to establish a national army comprised of semi-regular units apart from the already-established guerrilla units." In addition, the party would establish a general staff headquarters to assume command of the ARGK. As of the summer of 1996, however, the ARGK still seemed to be established according to the provincial command structure outlined above and had been implementing a partial cease-fire since December of the previous year.

One of the most striking characteristics of the ARGK is its very young female fighters. Jake Border, a combat photographer and journalist, visited an ARGK camp in northern Iraq in 1992.[45] There he met Soz Dar, a 12-year-old female guerrilla originally from the Turkish border town of Cizre. Although officially a guerrilla must be at least 16, she was proof that this requirement is not always strictly enforced. "Boys and girls are treated as equals by the Party. Female guerrillas form an integral part of all attack groups." Another young female guerrilla said: "There is no other type of life better than the life of a revolutionary."

Michael Ignatieff also visited a much larger ARGK camp in northern Iraq commanded by Ocalan's younger brother, Osman.[46] Upon first arriving, he realized "that there are women everywhere; single files of them, in combat gear, carrying rifles, running up the goat tracks towards the heights." He was told that he had happened upon a women's conference. "The astonishing thing is how young they all are: most in their teens, the oldest in their late 20s, unsmiling, earnest, youthful faces, some with rimless glasses, their hair pushed up beneath berets or tied in ponytails; all in the shapeless baggy uniforms worn by the men."

One of the female guerrillas Ignatieff met was "Milan"—at 25, older than most of the others, and surprisingly, originally from Australia, which explained "the Australian lilt in her accent." Only as a teenager had she discovered her Kurdish roots. Quickly, she had then managed to contact the PKK and join it in the Bekaa, where she was trained. When asked why so many women joined the organization, she replied: "Feminism is at the centre of our party. We want to change the condition of women in Kurdistan." "Milan" claimed that Ocalan "has encouraged the women to think for themselves, to speak up and make their voices heard." Both Border and Ignatieff also reported that ARGK members of both sexes claimed that they had no time for marriage, which would have to come later. By Ocalan's own testimony cited above, however, PKK political correctness is not always implemented here. Nevertheless, there can be no doubt that women have been given opportunities in the PKK that they never would have had elsewhere. As a recent PKK publication claimed:

> The Kurdish liberation movement is the only movement in the Middle East which has taken practical steps to achieve an equal status for women in social life. Women today can assume leadership positions within the liberation movement. . . . Today, Kurdish men cannot hit women at will, nor rule over them like kings. These developments have also led to women going to join the guerrillas in order to fight for their freedom and equality.[47]

Border found the ARGK guerrillas he visited in northern Iraq "a disciplined and polite group."[48] The largest camp he saw held 180 to 200 guerrillas who were mostly Turkish Kurds, but with a few who came from Iraq and Syria. Of the three camps he visited, two were set up for Turkish speakers and one for those who used Kurdish. Living conditions were "austere, but not grim." The tents had plastic sheeting to keep them dry and woodburning stoves for heat. The regular fighters "existed on a basic diet of rice, bread and tea," while the senior commanders had more. There was no other distinction between the fighters. All the guerrillas attended compulsory four-hour political lessons each morning, the most important of which dealt with Kurdish history and culture. Care was taken not to challenge the religious beliefs of the average fighters.

Border reported that "the basic fighting unit of the PKK is the *manga,* a squad of about 15. Three of these units made a *takim* and three of these constituted a *buluk.*" During his visit, he saw "a prolific variety of hardware" including 7.62 x 39mm Kalashnikovs from the Soviet Union, Yugoslavia, Romania, Hungary, East Germany, China, and Iraq. Also common were 7.62 x 54R PKM and 7.62 x 39mm RPK and RPD machine guns. The American M16s, favored by the guerrillas for their lightness, are not as common as H & K G3s of Turkish, West German, and Iranian origins. The commander possessed an M-203 and a Beretta PM12 submachine gun. He told Border, however, that "the best weapons for guerrillas is the AK. You can drop it in the mud, get it dirty or full of dust, and it will still fire."

Yet another observer reported "the region awash with weaponry of all types."[49] An ARGK guerrilla, for example, can buy a RPG-7 launcher for $6 in Iranian Kurdistan. Jake Border agreed that "most gun are cheap," reporting that AKs are priced from as little as $50 up to $150 depending on their condition. Thirty rounds of AK ammunition only costs $1, while Soviet RGD-5 hand grenades sell for just 50¢ each.[50] The former chief of staff of the Turkish armed forces, General Dogan Gures, explained that the collapse of the Soviet Union had led to "very cheap arms markets," and added that "the power vacuum" in northern Iraq following the Gulf War also had encouraged the proliferation of weapons.[51] As a result of Operation Steel, their large-scale military incursion into northern Iraq in the spring of 1995, the Turks reportedly discovered that the PKK had acquired Stinger missiles from Afghanistan. In addition, the Turks found 2 recoilless rifles with 101 rockets, 21 handguns, 933 infantry rifles, 32 machine guns, 5 antiaircraft machine guns known as Dochkas (DShks), 31 mortars, 118 rocket launchers, 8 grenade launchers, 6 antitank guided missiles, 3,492 magazines, 290 antitank mines, 7,500 mortar shells, 3,500 RPG-7/11 missiles, 75,000 rounds of ammunition for Dochka machine guns, and 3,853 hand grenades, among other types of weapons.[52]

Although the ARGK will never be able to match the firepower of the Turkish military, it often does possess superior knowledge of the terrain. And despite the Turkish usage of village guards and "repentant" guerrillas, the ARGK usually enjoys better intelligence because of its ethnic relationship to the people in the area, as well as the people's hatred of the harsh Turkish military tactics and their fear of possible PKK retaliation. Furthermore, the mountains upon which the ARGK camps are located are thousands of feet high and honeycombed with innumerable caves, which make excellent hiding places. These tactical advantages have enabled the ARGK to pursue successfully such guerrilla techniques as ambushes against government security and troop transit patrols; raids on police stations and isolated gendarmerie outposts; sabotage against government economic targets such as factories, communications and transportation facilities, and pipelines and radar installations; assassination of key government supporters; and mine laying. In short, the ARGK would seem able to maintain its guerrilla struggle for many years into the future.

## Parliament-in-Exile

To equate the sum of the PKK's activities solely with the continuing guerrilla struggle waged by the ARGK would constitute the gravest of mistakes. From the PKK's very inception political activities have also played an important role, as readily illustrated by the establishment of the ERNK in 1985.

During its self-proclaimed cease-fire that lasted from March to May 1993, the PKK attempted to initiate a Kurdistan National Congress (KUM) that had been elected near the end of the previous year. The KUM hopefully would include most of the other illegal, but more moderate, Kurdish parties and movements of Turkey, and later, the Iraqi Kurdistan Front in northern Iraq, which had established its own parliament in Irbil following elections in May 1992. Kemal Burkay, the leader of the Kurdistan Socialist Party of Turkey and long an opponent of the PKK, was mentioned as a possible head of the KUM. Ocalan envisioned such a structure evolving into something analogous to the African National Congress (ANC) or Indian Congress Party. But his hopes for the KUM were disappointed. The PKK's fifth congress in January 1995 revived the idea of what was to become the *Parlamana Kurdistane Li Derveyi Welat* (PKDW), or Kurdistan Parliament-in-Exile, which held its first plenary session in The Hague, The Netherlands, April 12-16, 1995. According to its founding bylaws, the parliament consisted of 65 members elected from the exiled Kurdish (DEP) parliamentarians, mayors, Kurdish personalities, Assyrians, women, and representatives from national institutions, youth organizations, and trade associations.[53] It represented "the will of people both inside and outside of Kurdistan" and would "constitute the first step of the new Kurdistan National Congress." Indeed, as Ocalan himself declared, the new body was "the first necessary step"[54] toward creating federative districts for the entire Kurdish population living in Turkey, Iraq, Iran, and Syria.

In practice, the 65 deputies included the 6 former DEP members of the Turkish parliament who had escaped abroad, 12 members of the ERNK, and various Kurds and a few others living abroad who were favorably disposed toward the PKK, such as the distinguished Kurdish scholar Ismet Cheriff Vanly. As the oldest member, Vanly served as the body's temporary chair until Yasar Kaya, the first chair of DEP and former owner of the pro-Kurdish newspaper in Turkey *Ozgur Gundem,* was elected the permanent speaker.

The parliament's first session also elected a 15-person executive council chaired by Zubeyir Aydar, a former DEP member of the Turkish parliament. Another DEP member, Remzi Kartal, was elected secretary, while Ali Sapan, as noted above a leader of the ERNK in Europe and probably a member of the PKK's CC, was chosen council spokesman. The 12 other members of the council were: Ali Akbaba, Aydin Gul, Ali Yigit, Helin Ates, Necdet Buldan, Petros Karatay, Cafer Kocgirilli, Masallah Ozturk, Rustem Bruyi, Abdurrahman Durre, Ismet Cheriff Vanly, and Felemez Basboga. All were sympathetic to the PKK.

The seven committees and their chairs were: judiciary (Vanly), international affairs (Akbaba), education, culture and the arts (Ozturk), ethnic and religious communities (Karatay), public relations and information (Gul), finance (Yigit), and women and the youth (Ates). The partial list of those who sent messages of support and solidarity included Ocalan himself and the ARGK of the following "provinces": Amed, Bahdinan, Botan, Dersim, Garzan, and Guneybati. The ARGK from Erzurum was also cited.

Following these procedural matters, the executive council then announced a 35-point program. A listing of some of these more important points will give an idea of the range of functions the parliament envisioned for itself: establishing "a national parliament of a free Kurdistan"; "entering into voluntary agreements with the neighboring peoples"; strengthening "the national liberation struggle to end the foreign occupation of Kurdistan"; undertaking "programs to safeguard the political, cultural and social rights of the Kurds"; implementing "the rules of war that relate to the Geneva Conventions of 1949 and those of 1977 to bring about a mutual cease-fire"; taking "the question of Kurdistan to the United Nations, to the Organizations of the Security and Cooperation in Europe, to the European Council, to the European Parliament, [and] to the agenda of the International institutions to secure an observer status for the Kurds"; pressuring the "international community to initiate military, economic and political embargoes on the Turkish state"; working to establish "the union of all of the political parties, organizations, institutions and influential personalities to ensure the national cohesion" and ending "the fratricidal war that is going on between the Kurdish parties in the south"[55]; preparing draft resolutions concerning a "constitution, citizenship laws, conscription laws, civil laws, tax laws, penal laws, and environmental protection"; ending the "oppression visiting the women"; improving the "Kurdish language"; laying the "foundations for a national library" and undertaking "projects to honor the Kurdish writer Ahmede Xani . . . who was the first Kurd to think of the Kurds and Kurdistan in terms of a nation-state towards the end of the 17th century"; establishing "schools, including the universities"; dissuading the "Kurdish youth not to serve in the enemy armies; it will urge them to do that in the Kurdish national army"; and building "friendships with the other peoples" and "the democratic public in Turkey."

Headquartered since April 1996 in Brussels, Belgium, further plenary sessions of the peripatetic parliament have been held in Vienna in the summer of 1995, Moscow in October 1995, Copenhagen in March 1996, Rome in July 1996, and Norway in November 1996. There was even talk of holding a future meeting in northern Iraq in an attempt to broaden the parliament's support. When not in session, the members of the now 69-member body fan out over Europe.

Although it meets monthly, the executive council has been criticized for not being active enough. From its inception, moreover, the parliament has been handicapped by its image of being an organ of the PKK. As a result, the major states such as the United States, Britain, France, and Germany have refused to recognize it. In addition, moderate Kurds from Turkey such as Kemal Burkay refused to join it. Turkey, of course, has put great pressure on foreign states not to cooperate with the parliament, putting The Netherlands for a time on its "red list" of states from which it would not purchase weapons. In September 1996, as part of a European-wide crackdown on the PKK, the Belgian police searched the parliament's premises and seized some of its equipment.

## STRATEGY AND TACTICS

In 1977, Ocalan and his associates met in the Bagcilar district of Diyarbakir and produced a stridently nationalist, separatist, and Marxist program entitled *Kurdistan Devriminim Yolu,* or Path of the Kurdish Revolution. Although greatly altered by developments in the 1990s, this program still provides a valuable insight into the PKK's founding strategy and tactics.[56]

Kurdistan has been divided into four separate sections by what were in effect colonial exploiters: Turkey, Iraq, Iran, and Syria. These exploiting states encouraged the continuation of feudal relations of production throughout Kurdistan. Turkish Kurdistan will lead a national democratic revolution whose minimum objective is an independent, non-aligned Kurdish state, and whose maximum goal is a state based on Marxist-Leninist principles. In alliance, the proletariat would provide the political leadership of the revolution, while the peasantry would constitute the main force. The Turkish revolutionary movement, other patriotic forces in Kurdistan, socialist countries, workers movements in capitalist countries, and international liberation movements would provide additional help. Broadly based propaganda activities including "armed propaganda" would help win supporters. Opponents included fascists (the *Ulkucus,* or Idealists, of Alpaslan Turkes' Nationalist Action Party [NAP]), social-chauvinists (the Turkish left who believed that the Kurdish cause would be satisfied by the left's victory), agents and other state supporters in Kurdish territory, and feudal landlords. For the time being, however, the Turkish security forces were not listed as being a main target, probably so that the Apocular would have an easier time establishing itself by not directly antagonizing the state.

The resulting violence was simply a small part of the much larger violence Turkey was suffering from in the late 1970s that finally called forth the military intervention of September 12, 1980. According to its own tallies, the new military government of General (later President) Kenan Evren apprehended and placed on trial almost 20,000 suspects.[57] Only 3,177 were accused of "separatist activities," with PKK suspects numbering 1,790 of them. The formal indictment claimed that the PKK was a "clandestine separatist organisation . . . aspiring to establish a Marxist-Leninist state in Eastern and Southeastern Anatolia after an armed struggle."[58] Many of the accused were given lengthy prison terms; such PKK leaders as Mehmet Hayri Durmus, Kemal Pir, and Mazlum Dogan died in prison.

Safely ensconced in his Syrian-Lebanese safehouse from 1979 on, however, Ocalan was able to develop his strategy and tactics of guerrilla warfare.[59] In his guerrilla handbook he argued: "Kurdistan is a country full of false friends. . . . Those in the middle are bogus revolutionaries." He asserted that "one of the main reasons for so many losses in the past is that our people did not behave like guerrillas. They missed the heat of houses, they missed the food and a cup of tea. I know tens of people killed only because they stopped at a village for some tea." Analyzing the situation in 1994, the PKK leader declared that "there are targets that will be hit by our guerrillas either by infiltration or through assassination."[60] He explained that "secrecy is the weapon of the guerrilla to the end, unlike in the story of Don Quixote. We will chop them up and eat them bit by bit. The militia will be in action."

Murat Karayilan, a leading lieutenant, elaborated: "While the enemy attacks a particular area of ours, we launch attacks on all fronts. Besides, we do not insist on holding areas under massive attack. We are employing guerrilla tactics."[61] Explaining the strategy and tactics of the ARGK in a recent battle on Mount Cudi near Cizre and the Turkish border with Iraq, Karayilan added: "When the enemy masses 30,000 troops, we disperse our forces. We strike at the enemy's weakest point. This is a guerrilla tactic. . . . Our aim is not to defend Cudi at all cost, but to defeat the Turkish Army."

Since the formal establishment of the PKK on November 27, 1978, and its subsequent move to the Syrian-Lebanese safehouse, the evolution—and at times dramatic changes—in its strategy and tactics may be usefully analyzed in terms of the five congresses and three conferences it has held over the years. Not only will such an analysis allow insight into the PKK's strategy and tactics in its own words, but also provide useful dates for these developments.

At its first congress held at the Lebanese-Syrian border July 15-26, 1981, the PKK laid out for itself a long-term, Vietcong-style, guerrilla-war strategy that would rely heavily on its supporters and sympathizers throughout the countryside by depending on what became its militia or the ERNK in 1985. The party also criticized itself for its pre-1980 Turkish-coup strategy and tactics of clashing with the Turkish left and such Kurdish opponents as the KUK. Plans were made to establish an alliance with Iraqi Kurdish movements such as Barzani's KDP. (See below.)

A year later, the PKK held its second congress again on Syrian territory. Ocalan declared that the Kurdish revolution would begin with weak forces against a strong enemy as a long-term national war of liberation. Three stages of this struggle were identified: (1) strategic defense, (2) strategic balance or balance of forces, and (3) strategic attack period. The first phase of strategic defense was expected to last until 1995. It was a period in which the forces of the PKK would be relatively weak, while those of the enemy would be relatively strong. Thus, this period would involve armed propaganda, attacks against state collaborators, and the preparation of an armed movement that would return to the homeland. This occurred with the creation of the *Hazen Rizgariya Kurdistan* (HRK), or Kurdistan Freedom Brigades, and its two well-coordinated attacks on Eruh and Semdinli, villages in southeastern Turkey separated by more than 200 miles of rugged, mountainous terrain, on August 15, 1984.

The second period of a strategic balance was projected for 1995-2000. This phase consisted of the creation of liberated zones in which the PKK could hide and prepare for action; an alliance with the radical, armed Turkish left; the ability to prevent the state from launching serious blows to the party; and the establishment of armed forces adequate for carrying out a large-scale guerrilla war. The third and final stage of strategic attack would see the abandonment of "active defense" in favor of a full-scale offensive that would amount to a popular uprising throughout the southeast after 2000.

By 1993, the PKK had clearly achieved the goals of the first period. Following the breakdown of its unilaterally declared cease-fire of March 20, 1993, the party quickly—and in hindsight, precipitously—entered the second and even third periods of strategic balance and then attack. For a while during the remainder of 1993, the PKK appeared to be gaining control of the situation, but eventually the Turkish armed forces responded so strongly as to reduce the situation back to that contemplated in the first period of strategic defense. (See below.)

At its third congress, held October 25-30, 1986, in Syria, the PKK was able to bask in the light of what it saw as a "year of great advances." "Public relations," on the other hand, were identified as its most important problem. Accordingly, the HRK was abolished, steps were initiated to strengthen the ERNK that had been created the previous year, and the ARGK was established. Such actions would hopefully create mass support. The PKK's third congress also decided to step up its attacks against the *Korucu,* or village guards system of Kurdish villagers loyal to the government, which had been created on April 4, 1985, to help ward off PKK attacks. The PKK viewed the village guards as a new version of the old Turkish policy of *Kurdu Kurde kirdirmak,* or using the Kurds to kill the Kurds. Soon Turkish newspapers were filled with stories of PKK massacres of Kurdish civilians who were, of course, the village guards and their families.

On April 15, 1988, some 300 PKK delegates and representatives of such other Kurdish parties as the KUK, KAWA, *Rizgari,* PUK, KDP, the Iraqi Communist Party (ICP), and an Iranian Kurdish party called *Komala* gathered in Lazkiye, Syria for two weeks to hold the PKK's first party conference.[62] Most of the decisions reached concerned methods to consolidate and thus strengthen the party. Although Kurdish independence was still mentioned, one of the conference's decisions also hinted at a possible compromise by mentioning "a strong alliance" between the Kurdish and Turkish people that would create "a revolutionary-democratic popular administration." Among other goals, this "administration" would terminate "all agreements signed with NATO and the United States." The conference also looked forward to "a national assembly" or "Kurdistan National Congress . . . to solve the [Kurdish] national problem and determine laws and principles." Finally, the conference had to deal with the defection of the party's then European representative Huseyin Yildirim over tactics that included the killing of Kurdish civilians who supported the government. Ocalan, however, was able to maintain his personal ascendancy.

The party held its second conference on May 3-13, 1990, in the Bekaa valley.[63] It identified the Botan region as constituting the "central headquarters to develop the war. . . . The war will expand from there." "To exploit . . . structures within the enemy," the conference decided "to exist within a legal socialist party [the HEP] with our mass forces, . . . establish friendship with religious movements," and work with green and women's movements. The party also would seek "to attack" not only military, but also "economic and financial institutions" of the state.

The party held its fourth congress in Syria on December 25-31, 1990. It was at this time that the idea of a federation, instead of independence, was first broached as a possible solution to the Kurdish problem in Turkey. In the succeeding years, Ocalan and his associates elaborated upon this concept in much greater detail. (See below.) The fourth congress also decided to abandon village raids that led to civilian deaths and massacres. Instead, the party decided to offer the village guards (and their families) who had been the victims of this earlier policy an unconditional general amnesty if they would quit the program by the end of 1991. At the same time, the congress also decided to step up the degree of armed violence, but concentrate it mainly against military targets, including the feared *ozel tim,* or special forces. The *ozel tim* were a highly trained, ideologically motivated force capable of using counter-guerrilla tactics and apparently drawn from among Turkey's ultra-nationalist, right-wing groups. (See below.) Finally, the PKK adopted a "visa system" that demanded that foreign visitors to the southeast of Turkey receive permission in advance from ERNK offices in Europe.

By the end of 1991, the PKK was making its first offers of a cease-fire, to which, however, the Turkish government made no official response. Then in March 1993, Ocalan made a dramatic cease-fire declaration, which was in effect until the end of May. For the first time since the military struggle had begun in 1984, a peaceful end seemed in sight. Speaking from one of his bases in Barr Ilyas in Lebanon's Bekaa valley, Ocalan declared that he did not want "to split the country." Rather, a federation would make "for healthy unity. . . . It is important that the status of the Kurds in Turkey becomes a constitutional article."[64] In Europe, Akif Hasan, a high-ranking member of the PKK, elaborated: "The first condition is that the Turkish government must recognize our national identity—the Kurdish reality."[65] He maintained that "we do not equate independence with national borders. On the contrary, what we want is a federation that unites people." As analyzed in detail below, however, the cease-fire of the spring of 1993 broke down, and the renewed struggle saw the violence rise to heights earlier unimagined.

Reflecting this intensification of the struggle, the PKK's third conference, held March 5-15, 1994, decided "to stage all-out revolutionary war in response to the enemy's all-out war of destruction."[66] Employing formulations first defined at its second congress twelve years earlier, the conference claimed that "the struggle which the PKK carries out has left the stage of strategic defense and entered that of strategic balance." Thus, "it is inevitable that we escalate our struggle. . . . All economic, political, military, social and cultural organizations, institutions, formations—and those who serve in them—have become targets. The entire country has become the battlefield."

Specific targets included "all radio and TV channels, newspapers and magazines which are the tools of special warfare [and] . . . financial organizations and institutions which finance the dirty war." Also "included are tourist facilities, mines, oil pipelines, power stations, factories, the arms industry, transportation and communications systems, and economic organizations." Not to be ignored were "the entire army . . . all the special units, special teams, counterguerrilla units and village guards . . . all the internal security units, the police force, the National Intelligence Organization (MIT) and civilian defense units."

To further these aims, the conference decided to allow the members of the ERNK—normally confined to support services, propaganda, and logistics—to join the attack. This decision implied carrying the violence to the cities, as the ERNK was primarily located in urban areas. Finally, the conference called for centralizing the military structure of the party under a general staff, enlarging the ARGK to 50,000 members, and setting up state assemblies and governments as well as a separate judiciary in the Kurdish areas.

At the same time, Ocalan renewed his call for a peaceful solution that would not destroy Turkey's territorial integrity. In a message sent to the "International Conference on North West Kurdistan (South East Turkey)," which met in Brussels, Belgium, on March 12-13, 1994, the PKK leader declared:

> I would like to emphasise that we are not insistent on the division of Turkey, and that such propaganda does not reflect our approach to the question. I want to state that I am ready to sit down with the Turkish government to discuss the issues if talks are based on dialogue within a democratic framework, where we can express the legitimate demands of our people. We have never been opposed to tangible proposals for a solution. We are ready to discuss any alternatives, including federation.[67]

In a public letter to the Western leaders, international organizations, and other notables near the end of 1994, Ocalan continued this emphasis on a peaceful approach and asked them to do more to further such a purpose: "On various occasions, we have informed the public that a solution could be found by debating various alternatives, including a federation, without undermining the present borders. . . . We believe that the influential states and/or international organizations could play an important role in its [the current violence] solution."[68] A few days later, the PKK leader announced that his organization would abide by the Geneva Conventions on the law of war and human rights: "The PKK definitely pledges to comply with the provisions of the Geneva Convention."[69] He also reiterated that "we do not intend to have the country divided and fragmented," and claimed, "our movement is aimed at strengthening Turkey, democracy, and the people. . . . There are many ways to resolve the problem within the framework of Turkey's unity."

The fifth congress of the PKK was held corresponding to these diplomatic moves toward improving the party's image. In an apparent attempt to prevent the congress from being somehow sabotaged, conflicting reports at first were released regarding its dates and location. One release claimed that the congress met in late November 1994 in northern Iraq on the fifteenth anniversary of the PKK's formal establishment.[70] Later, however, it became clear that it was actually held January 8-27, 1995, probably in the same Syrian-Lebanese safehouse in which earlier conventions had been staged. Possibly the earlier date referred to some type of preliminary meeting.

A total of 317 delegates participated, 231 of them having speaking and voting rights and 86 of them having only the right to speak.[71] Female delegates numbered 63. "All the provinces of our country were represented, as were all the regions of activity abroad." Although the congress claimed that "the immediate future" would "be a period of intense warfare," it "emphasize[d]" that the party was still "open to dialogue." Continuing the de-emphasis on the strident Marxism that marked its earlier days, the congress declared that "former party regulations . . . which were accepted at the party's founding congress . . . were replaced by new regulations." Symbolically, the hammer and sickle were dropped from the party's flag.

The congress denounced "the Soviet socialists' depoliticized and dogmatic ruling tactics" that "have added to the downfall of humanity" and called "Soviet [Real-existing] socialism . . . a kind of deviation" and a "rough and wild phase of socialism." On the other hand, "the PKK's approach to socialism is scientific and creative," and "goes beyond the practices of other socialist organizations in the world." The PKK's scientific socialism "deals with all questions facing humanity, including morality, science, culture, the question of women, democracy, protecting the environment, and so on."

The congress claimed that "the total war of the Turkish Republic has failed and instead led to an escalation of the war, which has caused severe conditions of economic and political bankruptcy." Somewhat disingenuously, given its failure to establish and maintain "liberated zones" during the preceding year, the congress maintained that "our national liberation struggle has entered the period of victory and for the first time in the history of Kurdistan the Kurdish struggle prevails. . . . Guerrilla warfare had been established on a firm footing everywhere in Kurdistan. . . . Popular uprisings everywhere in Kurdistan have spread fear in the colonialist enemy." The PKK gathering even went so far as to argue that "the ongoing struggle in South [Iraqi] Kurdistan has emerged as a result of the direct impact of the struggle in North-West [Turkish] Kurdistan," and credited "the unprecedented leadership of our party."

The congress also engaged in some self-criticism, blaming "the reason for a lack of success in the past" on "any deviation of attitude to right or left" which "will cause heavy casualties. The notion of coming to power quickly by means of individuals spread throughout the party's organs like an illness." Ambition "caused opportunistic individuals from the middle-class to dominate the party's organs" and led to "attitudes [that] had eroded the vanguard of the party and prevented the growth of the party." The congress claimed that "these were the main reasons for not establishing an adequate army and not evaluating popular uprisings." On the other hand, the congress "also identified some unjust punishments in past struggles" and restored "the victims with full honours." These actions had led the present congress to be "a great congress of judgment and justice" and enabled it to start "its main project, increasing membership of the party in the upcoming year."

Moving on, the congress decided "to establish preparatory committees with the aim of forming people's institutions. This will include assemblies and administrations of the people at the local, regional, and provincial level." Additional "important tasks are to promptly organize the Kurdistan National Assembly and proclaim a revolutionary government." The PKK would "form relations between the ERNK and other Kurdish forces with the aim of achieving power." The fifth congress also claimed that it was "the first congress in which women have made such a great contribution" and announced "a plan to convene a Women's Congress."

Calling "the Turkish people the closest and most strategic ally of the Kurdish people," the congress regretted that the Turkish people were "without leadership and disorganized." It called "on the Turkish people . . . to see the reality and not to support the genocidal war, not to be deceived by the propaganda and lies of the fascist, colonialist, ruling classes [and] . . . to struggle and fight alongside the Kurdish people in solidarity against the fascist regime." To implement these calls, the congress "decided to make a maximum effort to develop the democratic and revolutionary movement of Turkey through a variety of approaches and to support the democratic and revolutionary popular forces of Turkey more than before." In addition, the congress resolved "to further develop relations with environmental, liberal, human and civil rights groups worldwide," as well as "to participate in international forums and to work to develop revolutionary international socialist alliances."

On December 15, 1995, the PKK announced another cease-fire: "This cease-fire is designed to contribute to the realization of elections in Turkey [which were held on December 24], the settlement of the Kurdish question which is the source of all the problems, the development of a political approach, [and] an end to the ongoing war."[72] The party warned that "if the Turkish government does not respond to our call, the current crisis in Turkey will get deeper." Ominously, the PKK declared that "we know very well how this dirty war is being supported underhandedly, especially by Germany, France, Great Britain, and the United States with huge amounts of weaponry and financial support," and warned that "we shall observe the positions of each state, each institution, and each organization and draw our policies accordingly."

In his *Newroz* (March 21) new year's message three months later, Ocalan specifically threatened the United States and Germany: "This is not your war and do not move against the PKK. We do not want to fight against you as well!"[73] But, "if like the enemy you come towards us for a fight, you too will sustain great losses. The people you have stripped of their dignity and national identity will explode in your midst, too."

For the Turks, he threatened "suicide brigades" to attack the cities. "If you are going to ignore our peace initiatives, and carry on your dirty war against our people, then prepare yourselves for the war to heat up. . . . The suicide brigades can strike . . . the city centers, in factories, and employment places, wherever the regime gets its support." Indeed, a few weeks later Ocalan decided to train some 100 young female sympathizers how to disguise large quantities of explosives as a pregnant stomach and then detonate themselves at selected sites. The reluctance of the male police to search such women would aid in their attacks.

On June 30, 1996, the first such deadly suicide attack occurred in Tunceli during a ceremony involved in the raising of the Turkish flag. A 24-year-old woman named Zeynab Kinali Zilan, with grenades tied to her body, blew herself up, killing 9 soldiers and wounding 30. On September 25, 1996, three police and one civilian were killed by a female suicide bomber in front of the special forces bureau in Adana, while yet another suicide attack occurred in front of the police headquarters in Sivas on October 29, 1996, Turkey's Republic Day. Moreover, in December 1996, as a possible harbinger for the future, the PKK announced an agreement for joint actions with *Dev Sol* (now called the Revolutionary Peoples Liberation Party-Front or DHKP-C), a notorious Turkish left-wing, terrorist organization long active in urban areas.

Ocalan closed his *Newroz* 1996 message, however, on a more conciliatory note, repeating his call for democracy: "We do not want to divide Turkey. We want democracy in Turkey. We want fraternal relations amongst the people." Once again Ocalan seemed prepared to use the seemingly contradictory tactic of pursuing a cease-fire and peace by escalating the violence. Moreover, despite the suicide bombings and new agreement with *Dev Sol,* it seemed unlikely that he would want the PKK to begin earning a reputation as a mindless perpetrator of terrorism and indiscriminate suicide bombings. An earlier agreement between the PKK and *Dev Sol* for cooperation made in 1989 had come to nothing.

## FINANCES

The evidence concerning PKK finances is contradictory in regard to both the role of drug dealing and the total amount received from all sources. According to Ismet G. Imset, PKK financing is based on: (1) voluntary donations, (2) taxation, (3) protection money, (4) small and medium business investments, (5) robberies, and (6) narcotics.[74] *Turkish Probe,* another highly respected source, reported that the PKK enjoyed "vast financial resources" that were "obtained by extortion and 'enforced contributions,' as well as drug trafficking and clandestine business organizations operating under the cover of legitimate ventures in Turkey and Europe."[75] The American weekly magazine Time declared that "much of the money is raised through so-called contributions—in some cases plain extortion—from the estimated 1.5 million [Turks and] Kurds working in Europe and from Kurd-owned businesses that are forced to pay a 'revolutionary tax.' Millions of dollars more come from the drug trade."[76] In France, another report detailed how the PKK allegedly collected FF 6 million (about $1.2 million) per year in the early 1990s through what it called "voluntary gifts" or a "revolutionary tax," but which others termed "extortion of funds" or a "racket."[77]

According to Imset, "the most profitable PKK financial operation to date has been this organization's increasing involvement in the international traffic of drugs which, according to one official, has provided the organization with an annual income of not less than DM 500 million (about $333.3 million).[78] Two years later Imset wrote that according to Interpol the PKK "was earning some $400 million annually from drug trafficking and by extorting money from Kurdish and Turkish businessmen in Europe."[79]

Ocalan has vehemently denied such accusations, claiming that "it is the counter-guerrilla forces [of Turkey itself] who are mixed up in the heavy amount of drug-trafficking in the area. Our party strictly prohibits not only the sale but also the consumption of drugs."[80] In another recent interview, the PKK leader charged that "the Turkish government fabricated this lie in order to cover up its own genocidal crime against our people," and he suggested that the drug charges were Turkish disinformation to discredit his organization in a manner similar to the earlier false charges that the PKK was responsible for the assassination of Swedish Prime Minister Olof Palme in 1986.[81] Cemil Bayik, the number two man in the PKK, explained that while claims of Kurdish involvement in the drug trade may be true, this did not mean the PKK was involved:

"There are Kurds who do this and, even here, they are trying to involve our organization in the trade. . . . But we refuse to accept their offers."[82]

Recent revelations concerning so-called "uniformed gangs" in the southeastern Turkish city of Yuksekova and elsewhere partially support PKK protestations here.[83] Two Republican Peoples Party (CHP) reports in 1996 indicated that various members of the Turkish police and special team members apparently had been working together with such criminal groups as the Soylemez brothers gang in drug trafficking since at least 1993. Five such "uniformed gangs" had been uncovered by the fall of 1996. The notorious car accident in Susurluk, Turkey on November 3, 1996—in which in the same vehicle a well-known, right-wing terrorist and convicted drug dealer supposedly a fugitive from justice, was killed along with a high-ranking police official, while a village guard chieftain who sat as a DYP MP was seriously injured—seemed to give credence to allegations of a state infiltrated at the highest levels by organized crime. Given the nationwide shortage, by 8,000, of judges and prosecutors, and the fact that only 0.009 percent of the national budget is allocated to the justice system, such situations are not surprising.

One also should notice how some reports of PKK drug dealing do indeed name specific Kurds, but fail to make the actual connection with the PKK. *Hurriyet,* for example, a leading Turkish newspaper, recently headlined an article "US: PKK Involved in Drug Trafficking," which seemed to implicate the PKK in some major way by citing Ambassador Robert Gelbard, the Assistant Secretary of State for International Narcotics and Law Enforcement Affairs. In the actual article, however, all Gelbard really said was: "We are concerned about the dramatic flow of drug trafficking through Turkey and other nations in the region, some of which has been associated with some individuals who are members of the PKK."[84]

On the other hand, a year earlier Gelbard did indeed declare that his government believed the PKK was "involved in the transit of drugs . . . as a fundraising mechanism."[85] Phil Wilcox, the U.S. State Department counter-terrorism coordinator, added that the PKK had been involved "in narcotics trafficking in Western Europe and elsewhere."[86] Hans-Ulrich Klaus, the German Social Democratic Party assembly group chairman, asserted that "there is strong evidence that the PKK is running the drug traffic in Germany."[87] Frank J. Gaffney, Jr., the director of the Center for Security Policy in Washington, D.C., agreed: "The PKK relies heavily on illicit international drug traffic to finance its operations."[88]

Tangible evidence of PKK drug dealing supposedly surfaced when the Turkish freighter *Kismetim* was scuttled by its own crew on December 15, 1992, to avoid capture by American and Turkish agents trying to board it on the high seas.[89] Reportedly the ship was carrying 3.8 tons of morphine base. Agents had actually watched it being loaded, but wanted to wait until it had reached Turkish waters before making an arrest. A month later the *Lucky S* was seized off the Turkish port of Bodrum with 2.7 tons of morphine base. Even the report of these two incidents, however, made it clear that Turkish criminals were also involved, and that it was admittedly "a far murkier area of investigation" to conclude that the PKK "is funding part of its insurgency from the heroin trade." Nevertheless, the report did conclude that "German and other European narcotics agents have come to share the belief that either by demanding 'transit fees' from drug smugglers in eastern Turkey or through direct involvement some PKK supporters have at least become closely associated with the drug trade."

Divided as they are by artificial international borders, Kurds have long been involved in smuggling activities. Michael Ignatieff, for example, wrote how one young PKK fighter he met during his visit to a PKK camp in northern Iraq near the Iranian border whispered to him how "the smugglers and the guerrillas work together. Meaning? I can only assume the smugglers hand them a cut of their profits, in money or in kind, and the guerrillas provide protection."[90]

As mentioned above, Selim (Tilki) Curukkaya, a high-ranking PKK official in Europe until he fell out with the party in 1993, was said to have pocketed large sums of money from drug deals. The chief prosecutor in the German city of Frankfurt recently declared that 80 percent of the drugs seized in Europe were PKK-linked and that the money obtained in this way was being used to purchase arms.[91] During its incursion into northern Iraq in the spring of 1995, the Turkish military found and seized a 4.5 ton cache of drugs hidden away in a cave by the fleeing PKK guerrillas.[92]

A recent report[93] concluded that there was an "incredible" amount of heroin being made in Turkey and that "the bulk of the trafficking is controlled by several families in eastern Turkey, many of them ethnic Kurds" who had business alliances in Iran and Afghanistan and family connections in Germany, the Netherlands, and elsewhere in Europe. Government corruption protected the big drug bosses in Turkey, while in western Europe fear that "if we point the finger at the PKK, we will have these guys bombing and shooting in the streets."

Similarly difficult to pinpoint are the total finances of the PKK. While figures of DM 500 million ($333.3 million) and $400 million a year were mentioned above, other sources have listed lesser amounts. A recent analysis of the PKK by a Turkish scholar stated that the total annual budget from drug dealing and extortion both in Turkey and abroad only added up to $86 million.[94] During a briefing in the summer of 1993, the Turkish military released seemingly contradictory figures, claiming first that the PKK's revenues in 1992 were TL 135 billion—only some $6.75 million—and then that the money it collected in 1992 totaled TL 280 billion ($14 million).[95] No explanation for the different fig-

ures was offered. Certainly, however, the nearly triple-digit inflation rate in
Turkey makes it difficult to calculate precisely what a figure given in Turkish
lira would be worth in U.S. dollars. In January 1997, Ocalan himself declared
that although he had "not calculated it," the PKK's annual budget "must be
more than $100 million."[96] Given the magnitude of the PKK's activities, the
higher figures would seem more accurate.

The PKK, for example, proved to have the finances to start up its own television channel in May 1995. Broadcasting from London but with its principal
production studios located in Brussels, MED-TV was reaching an estimated
audience of some 50 million in 34 different countries, including Turkey, by the
summer of 1996. In September 1996, a simultaneous crackdown against the PKK
across Belgium, Britain, and Germany reputedly yielded further evidence concerning the organization's financial sources. Operation Sputnik in Belgium
raided the premises of MED-TV and the Kurdistan parliament-in-exile, supposedly obtaining evidence of mafia-type operations very active in the suspicious
transfers of money originating from drugs and arms trafficking, kidnaping,
and rackets operating within the Kurdish population.[97] Five people were arrested
for money laundering, while other arrests seemed likely for illicit work, residence, and the carrying of arms. Yasar Kaya, the president of the Kurdistan parliament, indignantly denied the charges, blaming them on Turkish provocation.[98]

# 3

# Developments since the Gulf War

The Gulf War in 1991 proved a major watershed in the development of the Kurdish problem in Turkey.[1] Following Saddam's defeat, a de facto, autonomous area in northern Iraq was created for the Iraqi Kurds, under the protection of the allied Operation Provide Comfort (OPC) housed in Turkey. Not only was this Iraqi Kurdish proto-state a powerful inspiration to Turkey's Kurds, but increasingly, as the Iraqi Kurds fell into fratricidal conflict, the resulting vacuum of authority in northern Iraq created a valuable new safehouse for the PKK. For his part, Turkish president Turgut Ozal initiated modest but potentially far-reaching reforms in his country's longstanding policy towards the Kurds. Ozal moved on this issue not only because of the immediacy created by the Gulf War, but also on account of a host of background factors involving the Kurds. One of these was the growth of the Kurdish population within Turkey.

Kurdish assimilation into the over-all Turkish population and deportation of Kurds to the Turkish areas in the west had given the false impression that the Kurdish problem in Turkey was being solved.[2] As a result, a few of the harsher restrictions against the Kurdish language and culture were relaxed in the 1950s and early 1960s, only to be reinstated when the government realized what was really occurring.[3] The poor socioeconomic condition in which Turkish Kurdistan remained had helped lead to a Kurdish population explosion, while the demographic curve of the Turks themselves, reflecting their relative socio-economic prosperity, lagged behind. By 1990, some 13.7 million Kurds were living in Turkey, a figure that constituted 24.1 per cent of the total Turkish population.[4] What is more, "if present demographic trends hold, as they are likely to, in about two generations' time the Kurds will also replace the Turks as the largest ethnic group in Turkey herself, re-establishing an Indo-European language (Kurdish) as the principal language in that land."

Already, "Kurdish demographic growth in many Turkish cities on the peripheries of Kurdistan and beyond . . . is changing their ethnic composition."[5] Erzincan, Elazig, Malatya, Antep, and Maras—Turkish cities on the western fringes of Turkish Kurdistan—either have now or soon will have a Kurdish majority. These cities are the first stops Kurdish migrant workers make as they move west. Long considered the unofficial capital and largest city in Turkish Kurdistan, Diyarbakir may soon lose its position.

Equally startling was a declaration by the late Turkish president Turgut Ozal that "60 percent of the Kurds live west of Ankara."[6] Kurdish-speaking people can be seen everywhere, from the construction fields in Istanbul to the ports or fishing markets in Izmir, from the marketplaces or open bazaars in Ankara to the vast cotton fields of Adana. As many as three million Kurds may now live in Istanbul, making that storied metropolis the home of more Kurds than any other city in the world. More than a million Kurds live in both Ankara and Izmir, the second and third largest cities in Turkey.

The result has been an increase in interaction between ethnic Turks and Kurds as never before. Already parts of Turkey outside the original trouble zone are experiencing ethnic violence similar to that which has been going on in the southeast for years.[7] Emotional funerals for Turkish soldiers killed in the war against the PKK have occurred in such cities as Izmir, Alanya, Kusadasi, and Antalya. At the funerals police and civilians shouted anti-Kurdish slogans and unfurled banners against Kurdish human rights, such as "Izmir will be a graveyard for the Kurds."

Following one such funeral in Fethiye on the southwestern coast of Turkey, many people of Kurdish origin had to flee the popular resort city in fear of their lives. In Alanya, two youths were saved by the police from being lynched after they had reportedly bothered funeral participants by shouting pro-Kurdish slogans and insulting the Turkish flag. In the northeastern town of Igdir, dozens of shops and other establishments belonging to people of both Turkish and Kurdish ethnic origin were damaged and nearly 200 arrests were made following demonstrations over the election of an ethnic Kurd to the local municipal council. People of Kurdish origin were experiencing major problems renting houses in Izmir and sometimes were not even allowed into the city. In Adana, taxis with license plates from the southeast were not allowed to wait in lines at main terminals. In June 1996, ethnic Turks shot and killed three ethnic Kurds in Kayseri who were members of the pro-Kurdish Peoples Democracy party (HADEP), the successor to the HEP and DEP parties. The murders were in retaliation for the Turkish flag being torn down and trampled upon during a HADEP party conference in Ankara a few days earlier.

Will the government authorities, confident of the support of an increasingly ill-informed, Turkish nationalistic fervor, begin to treat all people of Kurdish origin as suspects and thus exacerbate both the actual violence and the divisions between people of Turkish and Kurdish origins? Unless cooler heads prevail, it is possible that these divisions and animosities will begin to tear the Turkish state apart.

## OZAL'S INITIATIVE

Since Ozal had studied and worked in the United States on two separate occasions in his career, he presumably had been exposed to Western concepts of individual rights and pluralism. Nevertheless, he long continued Turkey's traditional policy towards the Kurds. For example, he instituted the village guards system of currently 60,000 civilian, pro-government Kurdish militia to supplement the state's military operations. In 1987, he also established a system of emergency rule (OHAL) with a regional governor for most of the Kurdish areas in the southeast. Both measures have long been considered prime examples of official state repression by the PKK and others critical of state policy.

What is more, following Ozal's meeting with the leaders of the three parties in parliament, the government issued on April 9, 1990, Decree 413 (later revised as Decree 424), which granted the regional governor in the southeast, Hayri Kozakcioglu, extraordinary powers to censor the press, exile people who present a "danger to law and order," remove judges and public prosecutors, and suspend trade union rights. Kozakcioglu was even given authority to ban or confiscate publications outside of his jurisdiction in the southeast.[8]

In September 1989, however, while still prime minister, Ozal hinted at a reassessment in his cryptic response to a question about the existence of a Kurdish minority in Turkey: "If in the first years of the Republic, during the single-party period, the State committed mistakes on this matter, it is necessary to recognise these."[9] In April 1990, he gave further hints of a new Kurdish policy at the meeting of the Turkish Industrialists and Businessmen's Association (TUSIAD). At this time he let it be known that the government was "engaged in a quest for a serious model for solving the Kurdish problem in a manner that goes beyond police measures."[10]

At about the same time, Abdullah (Apo) Ocalan, the leader of the PKK, told two Turkish reporters: "Let us declare a cease-fire and sit at the negotiating table. If Turkey abandons its oppressive policy in the region, then we will refrain from violence. . . . In fact, separating the region from Turkey immediately is out of the question. Our people need Turkey and we cannot separate, at least not for another 40 years."[11]

In the summer of 1990, the then–main opposition party in Turkey (but after the elections of October 20, 1991, the junior partner in the new coalition government headed by Suleyman Demirel), the Social Democratic Populist Party (SDPP), issued a comprehensive policy report on the Kurdish problem that went far beyond anything ever before offered by a mainstream Turkish party. Describing the ban on the use of the mother tongue as "primitive" and a "tool of assimilation," the document called for "the abolition of all restrictions on the use of the mother tongue, the enshrinement of the right of citizens to speak, write and teach their own language and use it in daily life and in various cultural activities and the establishment by the state of research centres and institutes undertaking research into different cultures and languages."[12]

Why did the Turkish authorities begin to reassess their position? Along with the demographic factors analyzed above and the PKK insurgency itself, the 1991 Gulf War and the ensuing mass exodus of the Iraqi Kurds from the wrath of Saddam acted as catalysts to their thinking and the subsequent initiatives of the new prime minister, Suleyman Demirel. Suddenly the spotlight of world attention was turned to events on the Turkish border, and Turkey quickly became an important allied associate. The Kurdish problems in Iraq and Turkey, so long segregated and obscured from world attention, suddenly burst upon the international agenda.

Although Ozal made it clear that Turkey would not tolerate a Kurdish state in northern Iraq, he was also foresighted enough to contemplate a more imaginative response than merely trying to continue Turkey's bankrupted policy of "Mountain Turks." Analyzing his country's past position on the Kurds, the Turkish president declared: "A policy of repression was adopted with the aim of assimilating them. That was a mistake."[13] Ozal proceeded in at least three ways. He presented the language bill, met with representatives of the Iraqi Kurds, and granted an amnesty which also applied to many Turkish Kurds, such as the former mayor of Diyarbakir, Mehdi Zana.

## Language Bill

In repealing Law 2932, under which the military government had banned the usage of the Kurdish language in 1983, Ozal was legalizing the use of Kurdish in a rather limited way. It could now only be used in everyday conversation and folkloric music recordings. Using the language in official agencies, publishing, or teaching would still be a crime. Asked when Kurdish could be used in newspapers, audiocassettes, radio broadcasts, and schools, Ozal replied: "In the future the use of the written language may also be allowed, but everything has its time."[14] Similarly, Metin Gurdere, the assistant leader of the ruling Motherland Party (ANAP), said that further liberalization "would depend on developments that will take place in Turkey."[15] Within the following year, however, Ozal was suggesting that the GAP (Southeastern Anatolia Project) Television Network carry 60- or 90-minute programs in Kurdish and that the appropriate schools even teach in that language: "What would happen if we do it? We should not be afraid of this at all."[16]

The response of many Turks to President Turgut Ozal's modest proposals to rescind Law 2932 illustrates how the term *Kurd* still remained a four-letter word for many of them. Suleyman Demirel, the former prime minister who was reelected to that post in October 1991 and elected president in May 1993, declared, for example: "This move is an attempt at dividing the country. . . . This is the greatest harm you can inflict on Turkey."[17]

Others expressed themselves even more strongly. In response to the query whether the new Ozal proposal would permit the manufacture of audiocassettes and the printing of books in Kurdish, the minister of justice, Oltan Sungurlu, replied: "What language is that? I do not know of such a language."[18] Illustrating the foot-in-the-door fear that yielding language rights today would lead to demands for independence in the future, the chairman of the justice committee in the Turkish parliament, Alpaslan Pehlivanli, asserted:

> If the word 'language' now in the bill stays in, we will have admitted that the Kurds are a nation. . . . If it passes this way, tomorrow there will be cafes where Kurdish folk songs are sung, theaters where Kurdish films are shown, and coffee houses where Kurdish is spoken. If this is not separatism, what is?"[19]

Other Turkish politicians, however, seemed to cautiously approve Ozal's initiative.[20] Even former president Kenan Evren, who had led the military takeover and had been the architect of the laws reinforcing the prohibition of the use of Kurdish and especially Law 2932, expressed his guarded support "as long as this does not enter the schools or appear on placards during demonstrations." Erdal Inonu, the leader of the SDPP, said that it was a positive step and that he was pleased that the government finally had accepted a policy that was originally his. Husamettin Cindoruk, the speaker of the Turkish parliament, declared the initiative was an "end of a constitutional embarrassment."

Nurettin Yilmaz, an outspoken ANAP member in parliament from Mardin and a strong supporter of Kurdish rights, however, not only called the Ozal proposal worthless but then went on to make several other declarations that served to bring out some of the latent discrimination existing on his party's right. Addressing the ANAP parliament members, Yilmaz told them: "You [Turks] are not from here [Anatolia]. You came from Central Asia. Aside from you, there are twenty million Kurds living on this land."

Yilmaz's repeated references to "you" and "we" angered the right-wing nationalist parliamentarians, and provoked strong insults and abuse. Mustafa Tasar shouted at Yilmaz, "You're a separatist. . . . Get down from there!" When

Yilmaz replied that he was a nationalist, Tasar answered, "Yes, you're a Kurdish nationalist." Yilmaz, however, continued, telling the deputies that Kurdish should be taught in the schools and that 80 percent of those killed during the battle of Gallipoli during World War I were Kurds. When he finally stepped down, the room erupted in fury, with such ANAP deputies as Ercument Konukman, Alpaslan Pehlivanli, Hasan Celal Guzel, and Gokhan Maras drumming their desktops in protest.

A number of news reporters reacted with cautious approval to the Ozal initiative. Mehmet Ali Birand, one of the more distinguished Turkish journalists, noted how this step would improve Turkey's image in Europe. Ertugrul Ozkok of *Hurriyet,* who often served in effect as an unofficial spokesman for Ozal, found the president's move "the first positive consequence of the [Gulf] war." Oktay Eksi, from the same publication, stated that "we must thus acknowledge with satisfaction the ANAP's initiative, or rather, Turgut Ozal's, to abolish this shameful prohibition of a language." He warned, however, that "there is no reason to be so naive as to believe that this new attitude is motivated only by a concern for the respect of human rights."

Even more cautiously, Ugur Mumcu of *Cumhuriyet* pointed out that there were still various other laws concerning separatist propaganda that could be used against the Turkish Kurds and their supporters. He also recalled that the political parties law still prohibited parties from asserting that any minorities existed in the country. Mumcu explained Ozal's initiative in terms of the Gulf War and the possible creation of a Kurdish state in northern Iraq. Taha Akyol of *Tercuman,* and a former member of Alpaslan Turkes's right-wing party, questioned whether "the Kurdish language will become an element of cultural enrichment for Turkey or whether, on the contrary, 'politicized' Kurdish will be transformed into a weapon in the radicalization of the processes of separation and division."

From the other side of the ideological spectrum, Ismail Besikci, the Turkish sociologist who had spent more than a decade in prison for maintaining in his scholarly work that the Kurds constitute a separate, ethnic group, responded that: "It is evident that plans for the Middle East which do not take into account the national existence and political demands of the Kurds will not be successful."[21] Former minister and parliamentary deputy Serafettin Elci; journalist and author Musa Anter; the owner of the weekly *Yeni Ulke* (New Land), Serhat Bucak; and folk singer Rahmi Saltuk all described the Ozal initiative as inadequate: "If the problem is speaking Kurdish, we were speaking it anyway. The important thing is cultural rights. It is Kurdish books, newspapers and magazines. It is Kurdish folklore being practiced freely, the ability to broadcast Kurdish radio and TV."[22]

Kendal Nezan, a Turkish Kurdish physicist who fled from Turkey in 1971 and has since become a major critic of the Turkish government's policies in his role as the director of the Kurdish Institute in Paris, reacted more positively: "The bill is a positive step towards finding a peaceful, democratic, and civilized solution to the Kurdish problem in Turkey. Turgut Ozal is the first statesman . . . to accept and recognize the Kurdish presence in Turkey."[23] Ocalan, the leader of the PKK, concurred with Nezan's judgment: "To tell the truth, I did not expect him [Ozal] to display such courage. . . . In this context, he shamed us. . . . He has taken an important step."[24] At approximately the same time, Ocalan also announced that his group "might opt for a diplomatic-political solution" and was ready to hold "conditional" negotiations with Turkey.[25] He added that the PKK no longer sought independence, just "free political expression" for Turkey's Kurds.

## DEMIREL RETURNS TO POWER

The elections of October 20, 1991 in Turkey resulted in the return to power of Suleyman Demirel and his True Path Party (DYP) in a coalition with Erdal Inonu's Social Democrats. By this time the PKK insurgency in Turkey was entering its eighth year and was escalating. Some 3,300 people had been killed since August 1984. The very month of the elections, 500 PKK guerrillas struck a Turkish border post, killing 17 and wounding many more. Turkish soldiers and foreign tourists were being kidnapped and held by the PKK, which also was issuing visas for foreigners to travel in southeastern Turkey. Finally, bloody riots in Diyarbakir followed the mysterious murder of the Kurdish spokesman Vedat Aydin in July 1991. Before the new government was even established, the Kurdish issue infringed upon the new parliament as its members were being sworn in.

## HEP

In the fall of 1989, a number of parliamentary members of Inonu's party who were of Kurdish ancestry had been expelled for attending a conference on "Kurdish National Identity and Human Rights" in Paris. These former SDPP members were the seed of the Peoples Labor Party (HEP), which was formed in the spring of 1990 to be, in effect, the legal, political organization of the Kurdish movement in Turkey. That such a party could even be formed said much about the changes occurring in Turkey's policy toward the Kurds. HEP's founding congress, however, could not be held in time for it to qualify for the 1991 elections. Therefore, in order to run for parliament, 22 HEP members rejoined the SDPP and were elected to the new parliament in October 1991.

Hatip Dicle and Leyla Zana, two of these former HEP members, caused an uproar in Turkey by their actions while being sworn in.[26] The oath they took included the words: "I swear . . . before the great Turkish nation . . . [the] indivisible integrity of the country and nation." Dicle, who held a handkerchief with the Kurdish national colors, prefaced these words by declaring that he said them under duress. Zana, wearing Kurdish national colors on her headband, added in Kurdish at the end of her oath, "I take this oath for the brotherhood of the Turkish and Kurdish peoples."

Illustrative of the ingrained nationalist fear and opposition to anything Kurdish still held by many, a number of members began to beat their desktops in the traditional form of protest for Turkey's parliament, while several members angrily approached the rostrum. Inonu himself denounced the two former HEP members and called for their resignation, while other members of parliament termed their behavior "antidemocratic, uncivilised and a great number of other things." Bulent Ecevit, the former prime minister and current leader of the small Democratic Left Party (DSP), declared: "My heart is crying tears of blood." The following morning the majority of the newspapers in Turkey carried headlines such as "Nationwide Anger," "An Ugly Show in Parliament," and "Two Terrorist MP's."

However, President Ozal simply said that Dicle and Zana had not helped the cause of the citizens in the southeast. Prime Minister-designate Suleyman Demirel further cooled the fires by adding that there was nothing to panic about. Demirel's declaration seemed to be the beginning of a remarkable opening to Turkey's citizens of Kurdish extraction.

## The Kurdish Reality

As he formally assumed office in November 1991, Demirel declared that Turkey was "a country in which people from 26 different ethnic groups live,"[27] and described the Kurdish situation as "Turkey's top problem."[28] In an exclusive interview, the new prime minister declared: "Turkey's borders, flag, and official language cannot be debated, but ethnic groups' demand to retain their own ethnic identity and culture should not be rejected. They are already using their own language. They have their own history, language, and folklore. If they wish to develop them, let them do so."[29]

His deputy prime minister, Erdal Inonu, added that one and a half years earlier, his party had issued a detailed report on the situation that recommended a number of major reforms. Now, finally in power, Inonu declared: "The Kurdish citizens' cultural identity must be recognized in full. That is, we must acknowledge the reality that some of our citizens are not Turks but Kurds who belong to the Republic of Turkey."[30] In a joint report, the new coalition government affirmed: "Diversity does not weaken a democratic and unitary state. . . . Everyone's right to research, to preserve and to develop his mother tongue, culture, history, folklore, and religious beliefs is part of his basic human rights and freedoms. These rights will be guaranteed within the framework of laws."[31]

In its first months in office, the new government actually implemented several positive steps. The notorious prison in Eskisehir was closed; 227 people who had been stripped of their citizenship for political reasons regained it; parents were permitted to give their children Kurdish names; and some films and cassettes were taken off the list of censored works. In addition, a newspaper in Kurdish was permitted, and a Kurdish Institute headed by Ismail Besikci was opened in Istanbul.

To announce their intentions and study the situation firsthand, on December 7 and 8, 1991, Demirel and Inonu journeyed to five southeastern provinces: Diyarbakir, Siirt, Batman, Sirnak, and Mardin. With them were the chief of the general staff, General Dogan Gures; state ministers Akin Gonen and Mehmet Kahraman; Defense Minister Nevzat Ayaz; Interior Minister Ismet Sezgin; and Gendarmerie Commander Esref Bitlis. The high-level nature of this delegation emphasized the importance the new government attached to the Kurdish problem.

Addressing tens of thousands of cheering Turkish Kurdish citizens in Diyarbakir, Demirel declared that "Turkey has recognized the Kurdish reality."[32] Before the building where Demirel and Inonu addressed the people of Sirnak, "Turkish flags mingled with the green, yellow and red rags symbolizing the Kurdish flag, held by Kurdish women cheering in support of the coalition."[33] By the end of the trip, the heretofore feared and distant chief of the general staff, General Dogan Gures, could not resist calling out in the once forbidden Kurdish language to a local child. "Demirel and Inonu are now our fathers. We trust them and we will support their policies," exclaimed one former HEP partisan from the Mardin township of Midyat.

In proclaiming these concessions to Kurdish rights, of course, the new Demirel government made it clear that it expected terrorism to end and loyalty to the Turkish government renewed: "Attacks against the existence and democratic authority of the state through violence and terrorism is incompatible with human rights and basic freedoms and cannot be acceptable."[34]

For its part, the PKK had asked its supporters not to try to disrupt the government's procession. Ocalan even declared that "Demirel is truly a respected politician."[35] The hardened PKK leader dampened his enthusiasm, however, when he queried whether the new Turkish prime minister could carry out his stated intentions:

We are doubtful there will be a change. For one, will Demirel be able to control the chief of [the] general staff? Will he be able to place the special warfare and counter-guerrilla [activities] under his control? . . . They are the true forces of power. . . . Will the Demirel-Inonu government be able to overthrow these forces from power? . . . As you know, Demirel was toppled from power twice [1971 and 1980] and he was not in control.[36]

## "HIZBULLAH-CONTRAS"

Demirel's initiative proved to be a false dawn. The renewed violence that occurred during the 1992 *Newroz* holiday in March 1992 illustrated that the fighting would not only continue, but escalate. In stark contrast to the official government view "that terrorists equipped with heavy arms launched an armed action against the state,"[37] the SDPP—the junior member of the coalition government—reported that "excessive use of force by security troops and provocation may have been behind the confrontation which claimed more than 70 lives in a matter of ten days."[38]

In Sirnak, where officials claimed that a PKK attack had taken place, the SDPP report quoted reliable local sources that said security forces, not the terrorists, had simply opened fire on the townspeople. The fact that the security forces suffered no casualties gave credence to this report. Similarly, a Helsinki Watch report concluded that "the Turkish military and police forces . . . were directly responsible for almost every casualty that took place during Nevroz."[39]

What is more, a series of mysterious killings of civilian Kurdish leaders by apparently right-wing, government hit squads (the so-called Hizbullah-contras)—which had begun in the summer of 1991 with the murder of Vedat Aydin, a HEP party official in Diyarbakir—continued. One report claimed that as many as 225 assassinations had occurred by the end of January 1992.[40] Another report added that there were 360 "unsolved murders" in the southeast in 1992, 140 of them in Batman alone.[41] These figures expanded to include the entire country, as well as ethnic Turks; 510 people were murdered in 1993, 423 in 1994, and 99 in 1995.[42] Yet another report pointed out that, while more than 4,000 "separatist suspects" had been detained since January 1992, not a single one of the slayings of Kurdish leaders or sympathizers had resulted in an arrest: "Many of the individual killings still go unexplained amid local claims that certain officials prefer not to pursue such cases."[43] "Executions without verdict" was a term often heard to explain what was occurring.

Many Kurds believed the killings were being perpetrated by a group associated with the Islamic Hizbullah (Party of God) to protect the unity of the Muslim Turkish state that the PKK was threatening to divide. Both ethnic

Kurds and Turks seemed to be involved. The term "contra" was in reference to its supposed official but secret connection. The government denied any involvement, long blaming the campaign of murder on the PKK.

Many observers, however, pointed out that the government had admitted that there were more than 2,500 special team (*ozel tim*) members on duty in the southeast. These counter-guerrillas were trained for close combat with the PKK, and their identities, activities, and methods were shrouded in great secrecy. When they were in uniform they often were masked. Many of them spoke Kurdish and might also wear local dress. Unlike other Turkish soldiers, they were allowed to wear long hair and grow a mustache or beard. Since the victims of Hizbullah-contras were also the targets of police harassment, arbitrary detention, ill-treatment, and torture, the belief was that these special team members either incited what was happening or actually perpetrated some of it. According to HEP's provincial chairman in Diyarbakir and Silvan, Huseyin Turhalli, in one particular incident security forces first searched the townspeople and disarmed them. "After this, the Hezbollah started its activities."[44]

The following patterns emerged. First, the victims often had similar political backgrounds and were usually of Kurdish origin. Second, they were either activists involved in campaigns for further freedoms or people who had refused to join the state-sponsored village guards. Third, most of the victims had no protection and were killed alone—while driving their cars or crossing the street, walking to the local grocer or sitting in their office. Most of the murders were committed in cold blood with the gunmen either raking their targets with bullets or simply firing a single shot into the head in an apparently professional manner.

During 1992, a number of journalists also became victims. Halit Gungen, a Kurdish reporter for *2000'e Dogru* (Toward 2000), was killed by an unknown assailant in the Diyarbakir office of the magazine on February 18.[45] That very week his journal had published a five-page article that claimed members of the Hizbullah-contras were being trained in the Diyarbakir headquarters of the police's mobile force. Six days later, Cengiz Altun, a Kurdish reporter for the pro-Kurdish newspaper *Yeni Ulke* (New Land), was killed by unknown assailants in Batman. Earlier he had been detained and allegedly given death threats by the police while researching extrajudicial executions in the neighboring province of Mardin. Hafiz Akdemir, a reporter for *Ozgur Gundem* (Free Agenda), was shot on June 8 in Diyarbakir. The previous year he had been released from prison where he had been sentenced for membership in an illegal Kurdish organization.

Yahya Orhan, also of *Ozgur Gundem,* was murdered in the street in Gercus near Batman on July 31, while Cetin Abayay of *Ozgur Halk* (Free People) died a day earlier after having been shot the previous day in Batman. On August 5, Burhan Karadeniz of *Ozgur Gundem* was paralyzed from the chest down after being shot on the street in Diyarbakir. Huseyin Deniz, of the same journal and also a member of International PEN, was shot in the head and killed on August 9.

Then, on September 20, Musa Anter—who was 74 years old and one of the most famous Kurdish intellectuals and authors of the twentieth century—was treacherously murdered by a young man who had pretended to want to rent a field from him. Naively, Anter had permitted his murderer to drive him out into the country, where the assault occurred. Anter's nephew, a witness to the shooting, was wounded in the attack.

Replying to accusations of government involvement in the killings, Interior Minister Ismet Sezgin declared that "an investigation into 55 assassinations carried out in the region had proved that at least 40 of them had been perpetrated by the PKK."[46] He added that "there is no organization named Hezbollah in our registries, and we do not know what it is . . . [or] what kind of activities it has in Turkey." Ominously, he added that while "we, too, are sorry that journalists are being killed . . . if those opinions turn into activities to destroy the state, we, as the security forces, will take our own attitude."

This official state reluctance even to admit that an organization such as Hizbullah existed ended following the brutal car-bombing assassination of the prominent Turkish journalist Ugur Mumcu in Ankara on January 24, 1993. Mumcu was a well-known defender of the secular republic, and his murder elicited a tremendous public outcry as more than 200,000 people attended his funeral.

Within days of Mumcu's death, the Turkish authorities charged that elements of the Iranian *Savama* intelligence organization and Turkish Islamic fundamentalists were responsible. In addition, this murky combination was also said to be behind the earlier unsolved murders of prominent journalists Cetin Emec and Turan Dursan, as well as Professor Muammer Aksoy.[47] All three had been noted secularists.

Yet another prominent assassination occurred on September 4, 1993, when Mehmet Sincar, the HEP MP from Mardin, was murdered in broad daylight while on a visit to Batman. Suspicions abounded concerning the culpability of the state, since Sincar's police protection had been lifted just before he was shot. Four years later, however, no one had been brought to justice for any of these murders. What is more, such prominent Turkish nationalists as the former gendarmerie intelligence officer and expert on PKK activities, Major Ahmet Cem Ersever, were also murdered during this period. Some even questioned the death in a February 1993 plane accident of the gendarmerie forces commander, Esref Bitlis.

It now seems that there were several different groups involved in the violence subsumed under the rubric "Hizbullah-contra," including an Islamic

Liberation Movement, Anatolia People's Front, Islamic Fist, and Islamic Great Eastern Raiders Front (IBDA-C). In addition, the 220-page report of the parliamentary investigation commission for unsolved political murders identified five separate organizations using some variation of the name Hizbullah: (1) an Istanbul-based Hizbullah (a.k.a. the "Islamic Movement Organization" or "Islamic Action Network"), a key figure in which was Irfan Cagrici, that was presumably responsible for Mumcu's murder; (2) a PKK-associated Hizbullah set up in the Bekaa valley under the name "Patriotic Imams Association" (presumably the PKK's Patriotic Men of Religion mentioned in Chapter 2); (3) a Hizbullah set up in Batman that later split, over whether or not to use violence against the PKK, into rival *Menzil* and *Ilim* groups; (4) an anti-PKK Hizbullah in Mardin; and (5) a pro-Iranian Hizbullah in Bingol.[48]

The anti-PKK Hizbullahs consisted of pro-Islamic Kurds who objected to the atheism of the Marxist PKK and its goal of splitting off an independent Kurdish state from Turkey. They also believed that the PKK was cooperating with the Armenians to divide the Muslim people of Turkey. A leading Hizbullah militant from Batman who was codenamed "Seyhmus" told the Turkish daily *Cumhuriyet* that his group (the Kurdistan branch of the Islamic Liberation Movement) was established in Batman in 1987 to create an "Islamic Kurdish State in Turkey."[49] Although it was as much at war with the government's secularism as it was with the PKK's communism, his group was tolerated by Turkey because it was the only solution to the PKK. The state was bound by the rules of law, while his organization had no limitations and could deal with the PKK in any way that proved effective. "Seyhmus" explained further that his group was "opposed" to the PKK because "they deny the Koran and gather women on the mountains claiming that they are guerrillas. Did men and women fight alongside each other in the wars waged by the Prophet and the Islamic warriors?"[50] "Seyhmus" also claimed that his group had "punished many people in Batman, Diyarbakir, and Nusaybin," including Musa Anter.

Similarly, the leader of the Anatolia People's Front declared that "we are the vengeance warriors implementing, under illegal conditions, what the state is unable to do under conditions of democracy."[51] He explained that his group was trying "to defend the state" and "eliminate" the PKK, but that it had no formal or informal links with the state. He also took credit for the murder of Musa Anter, and claimed that his group and the Islamic Fist were connected. Since his group was secular, however, it was "a completely different entity" from the Hizbullah.

The actions to promote Islam taken by Interior Minister Abdulkadir Aksu, before his resignation from the then-ruling ANAP government in June 1991, seem to have played an important role in this association between the security forces and the Islamists.[52] Under Aksu—a practicing Muslim and apparent member of an Islamic sect—Islamic fundamentalists nearly took over the entire police force and its intelligence organization. Senior officials walked the corridors of the General Directorate with prayer mats under their arms at prayer times, and it had become the custom to attend Friday prayers en masse. Some officials would even ostentatiously leave the doors to their offices open so that others could see them praying. Given such an atmosphere, the police became hesitant to investigate crimes committed by radical Islamic groups even after Aksu was removed and his successor, Mustafa Kalemli, launched a campaign to purge the Islamists.

Further complicating the issue was the role of such violent, right-wing groups as the *Ulkucus* (Idealists), which were associated with Alpaslan Turkes's Nationalist Action Party (NAP) in the late 1970s. Observers have commented on how many members of the current counter-guerrilla special teams are associated with Turkes's party. Their attire serves to identify them. The three-crescent flag of the Ottoman Empire, a symbol of ultra-Turkish nationalism, decorates the barrels of their guns. Pictures of gray wolves, another ultra-nationalist symbol, are etched on their muzzles. An additional touch is their mustache, which runs down from the corner of their lips. In the past allowed by the state to flourish, were such groups once again being used to accomplish covertly what could not be done openly in a democratic atmosphere?

Evidence that began to emerge following the notorious Susurluk car accident in November 1996 indicated that the state had indeed probably created a secret organization which employed such right-wing gangsters and convicted drug dealers as Abdullah Catli to kill its enemies.[53] In return, the state ignored the gangsters' drug dealing, money laundering, and other crimes. Prime Minister Ciller had also apparently paid some $8 million from a secret slush fund to such unsavory types to try to assassinate Ocalan himself sometime in 1994 and again in 1996. The interior minister, Mehmet Agar, was forced to resign after admitting he had "coincidentally" stayed at the same resort as the victims of the Susurluk incident: Abdullah Catli, the notorious gangster and drug dealer "on the lam"; Huseyin Kocadag, a top police official; Sedat Bucak, a village guards chieftain who was also a DYP MP; and Gonca Us, a gangster's "Moll." This striking evidence which suggested links between organized crime and the government in turn recalled that several different parliamentary investigations of possible corruption on the part of Ciller herself were only defeated after she agreed to join Erbakan's cabinet in July 1996.

Adding to the picture was the role of former PKK "confessants" who were given lesser sentences in return for their cooperation against the PKK and its sympathizers. The parliamentary commission that investigated the Hizbullah murders specifically mentioned Alaattin Kanat as a "confessant" who apparently carried out several assassinations while officially in prison. During his 22 months in jail, Kanat was permitted to leave on 11 different occasions "in order to assist the police."[54]

## FAILURE OF REFORMS

There are a number of explanations for the failure of the reforms instituted by Ozal and Demirel. In the first place, they were more apparent than real. On March 26, 1992, for example, Ahmet Zeki Okcuoglu, the owner of the first Kurdish-language newspaper to be published in Turkey, *Rojname* (Newspaper), was forced to discontinue publication after plainclothes police occupied and searched his office and then detained and tortured his office assistant. Three hours after Besikci opened his Kurdish Institute in Istanbul on April 18, 1992, police tore its bilingual sign down.

Although Ozal partially legalized the Kurdish language and culture in the spring of 1991, at the same time the new anti-terrorist law, as noted in Chapter 1, in effect proclaimed the further pursuit of Kurdish cultural rights to be a terrorist act. Clearly the mentality behind such legislation failed to recognize "the Kurdish reality."

Furthermore, as noted in Chapter 1, the Ankara State Security Court (DGM) prosecutor, Nusret Demiral, announced in November 1992 that he would seek the death penalty against eighteen HEP members of the Turkish parliament—including party chairman Ahmet Turk—for subversive statements they had made in their recent congress, if parliament would strip them of their immunity. HEP was closed down by the state in July 1993, but it simply reincarnated itself as the Democracy Party (DEP), which had been created the previous May. Within a few months, however, DEP's leader, Yasar Kaya, was facing a series of legal charges concerning a speech he had delivered while visiting Iraqi Kurdistan, and in March 1994, six DEP MPs were stripped of their parliamentary immunity and arrested. The mere possibility that such charges could be brought and arrests made revealed the appalling gaps in Turkish democracy and the chasms that divided the government from important elements of its Kurdish population.

The precedence of the "national security mentality" over basic human rights is another reason for the failure of the reforms. Throughout most of Turkey, "the idea of according certain guarantees even to suspected Kurdish nationalists or communists—violent or otherwise—continues to be treated as an alien concept," explained one knowledgeable Turkish source.[55] It was relatively easy for Demirel to promise democratic reforms while he was out of power. Once he again became prime minister, he saw that there were certain things regarding national security that an elected government and parliament do not have jurisdiction over in Turkey.

Illustrative of this situation was the speech given by Ismet Ocakcioglu, the president of the court of appeals, at the opening of the judicial year in September 1992: "It is entirely in keeping with the rules of the democratic State of Law for the State to use the instruments and methods used by the terrorists in order to prevent terror."[56] In regard to the judicial reform bill (CMUK) of Justice Minister Seyfi Oktay, which aimed to introduce certain basic rights for suspects in custody and thereby protect them from torture, Ocakcioglu declared: "I find the new arrangements most disturbing for the protection of unity and togetherness." Demirel himself stated that "there is no point in harping on the torture issue while ignoring the violence directed against these people [PKK victims],"[57] while Gures opined that "there is no Kurdish problem in Turkey. . . . There is a problem of assault on the Turkish Republic."[58]

Increasingly, the Demirel government chose to ignore the distinction between armed PKK fighters and civilians believing in Kurdish political and cultural rights, and acted as if any means were justified in defeating them. Thus, allegations that the Turkish state in the person of its regular soldiers, village guards, or its special team members destroyed homes, tortured, or murdered were routinely ignored. Sirnak brigade commander Mere Sayar was awarded a plaque for his "excellent service," though all the evidence indicated that he was responsible for ordering most of the property in the town to be destroyed by heavy weapons on the pretext that the PKK was hiding there during the unfortunate events of August 1992.[59] Although the new Ciller government took over in June 1993, a similar fate befell the towns of Yuksekova in August 1993 and Lice in October 1993. By 1996, more than 3,000 towns and villages had been fully or partially destroyed in an attempt to deny bases of support for the PKK.

Given the renewed violence, Ocalan declared that "the effort by the Erdal Inonu–Suleyman Demirel coalition to implement moderate measures has not achieved anything."[60] Government statements that it would recognize the Kurdish reality were "words alone."[61] "Nevruz [Newroz] has marked the beginning of a hot summer. . . . Violence may increase."[62] "The Turkish Government has to be open to the idea of a federation. If 10 million Kurds live in Turkey, they must have their own political will, national assembly, government, and culture."[63]

Trying possibly to further divide Ozal and Demirel, Ocalan also declared that the Turkish president "understands us better than anyone else. . . . If anyone is going to find a way to solve our problem, Ozal will."[64] For Demirel, however, he had only scathing words: "He has tried to destroy us. . . . From now on, we will adopt an open stand against Demirel."

In analyzing the failure of Ozal's and Demirel's initiatives, what Donald L. Horowitz, a well-known authority on ethnic conflict, has termed "the timeliness of the arrangements"[65] comes to mind. Had these reforms been instituted earlier, they might have worked better. As Horowitz pointed out: "there will generally not be the requisite determination to enact appropriate measures until ethnic conflict has already advanced to a dangerous level; but by that time the measures that are adopted are more likely to be deflected or ineffective."[66] Thus, reforms that might have worked earlier will not work now. Unfortunately, this pattern seemed destined to prevail even when the PKK suddenly declared a cease-fire early in 1993.

## CEASE-FIRE

Two major developments in Turkey's changing Kurdish problem occurred in 1993: the PKK dramatically declared an unilateral cease-fire from March 20 until the end of May; then, even more dramatically, escalated the fighting to qualitatively new stages that for a time seized the initiative and relegated the state to a mere posture of defense.

*Newroz,* the March 21 celebration of the Kurdish new year, had been the occasion for much violence between Turkey and the PKK in the past. This time, however, Jalal Talabani, the Iraqi Kurdish leader who had been at times Ocalan's bitter foe, met the PKK leader in Syria during the second half of February to discuss a new initiative. On March 8, Talabani presented Ozal and Demirel with Ocalan's surprise proposal for a cease-fire:

> (1) I am giving up the armed struggle. I will wage a political struggle in the future. (2) I am withdrawing my past conditions for holding talks to resolve the Kurdish problem. Turkish officials can hold talks with Kurdish deputies in the national Assembly. (3) We agree to live within Turkey's existing borders if the necessary democratic conditions are created to allow us to do so.[67]

On March 17, Ocalan followed up this message with a formal declaration of "unilateral and unconditional" cease-fire at a press conference in the Bekaa valley town of Zahlah, some six miles from the Syrian border. Symbolically, the PKK leader doffed his guerrilla fatigues and put on a suit and tie for the occasion.

In an interview, Ocalan made the following conciliatory points:[68] "Turkish-Kurd brotherhood is about 1,000 years old, and we do not accept separation from Turkey, even if they [the Turks] force us to do so." The Turkish Kurds "want peace, dialogue, and free political action within the framework of a democratic Turkish state." He added that "we hope that the Turkish authorities will understand that this question cannot be resolved militarily and that the Kurdish people, their existence, their language, their identity, and their rights cannot be ignored." Again he stressed that "we are not working to partition Turkey. We are demanding the Kurds' human rights (cultural, political, and so on) in the framework of one homeland." After praising Talabani's role "in bringing this initiative to fruition," the PKK leader then demanded that "we want guarantees, because we cannot be betrayed, as happened with our historic leaders like Shaykh Said and the Badrakhaniyyin."[69] Flamboyantly, he concluded: "if the Turks are willing to take one step, we will take ten. And if they begin with one initiative, we will make ten initiatives in political action."

Two days later, Talabani again moved to facilitate the cease-fire process by bringing together Ocalan and his longtime enemy Kemal Burkay, the moderate general secretary of the Kurdistan Socialist Party (PSK) in Turkey. Their meeting took place in Damascus. Because of its potential importance in helping to bring about some type of united front of Kurdish parties in Turkey, as well as for its outline "for a peaceful resolution of the Kurdish question," it is useful to cite parts of the resulting statement in some detail.[70]

The document consisted of two sections: (1) several general statements and recommendations, and (2) nine specific steps. The first part began with the Kurds themselves by declaring that "the national parties and organizations throughout Kurdistan must respect each other's existence and settle all questions and problems through dialogue and peaceful means." Then, "in the future, there should be an endeavor to set up a front grouping the national factions."

Attention next turned to the Turkish-Kurdish relationship: "The Kurdish question could be resolved by achieving equality between the two peoples." Unfortunately, "although it has recently recognized the existence of a Kurdish people, the Turkish Government does not accept the rights and freedom of this people, rendering such recognition meaningless." The PKK and PSK "believe that the two peoples could coexist under a democratic regime and could live side by side in a fraternity provided this regime is a federal and democratic system."

The second part of the statement then listed nine steps that "if the Turkish Government has a serious desire for peace, democracy, and equality, it must embark on . . . speedily and without delay."

1. The two sides must declare a cease-fire. The PKK's recent step provides an appropriate and historic opportunity.
2. The extraordinary situation in Kurdistan must end, attempts to empty the region of its inhabitants must stop, and the special troops and village guards—the militia—must be disbanded.

3. A new democratic constitution for the country, guaranteeing the existence and rights of the Kurdish people, must be drafted and all antidemocracy laws and regulations must be abrogated.
4. A general pardon must be declared.
5. All rights and freedoms of thinking, expression, publishing, and organization must be granted.
6. All outlawed parties, including our two parties, must be permitted to operate and advertise themselves legally.
7. The ban on the Kurdish language, culture, and civilization must be lifted. The Kurds must be permitted to study in their own language at schools and freedom of radio and television transmission for the Kurds must be granted.
8. All those forced to immigrate and those evicted from the region as a result of the fighting and burning of homes as well as those exiled in recent years must be permitted to return to their areas of residence and be compensated.
9. In view of the increasing economic deterioration in the past few years, the economy must be consolidated, an appropriate program to promote Kurdistan's economy must be devised, and agriculture and trade must be developed.

## Failure

A truly historic opportunity, the cease-fire failed for two basic reasons: (1) the attitude of the Turkish authorities, who interpreted Ocalan's move as a sign of weakness and therefore their chance to finish his movement off, rather than as a way to achieve a permanent solution to the Kurdish problem, and (2) the sudden death of Ozal, the Turkish leader who was probably most receptive to some type of compromise that might have ended the struggle.

Apparently the Turks believed that the PKK's back had been broken the previous October during their joint operation with the Iraqi Kurds in northern Iraq. (See Chapter 4.) Thus, when Ocalan announced his cease-fire, "all were agreed that the PKK was in a position of weakness."[71] Specifically listed were "military setbacks . . . the changing international environment . . . and possibly too a loss of prestige among the mainly Kurdish population of the Southeast itself caught in a web of poverty, unemployment and terror and oppression on all sides."[72]

Although there were offers of partial amnesty and an end to the state of emergency in the southeast, an independent Turkish post-mortem on the cease-fire's failure argued that "Ankara's response . . . had never gone further than words. While the PKK ceased its raids, reports of mystery killings, torture and the burning of villages in the region persisted."[73] Even more, this source maintained: "The State authorities have chosen to act as if they believed that the PKK would refrain from terrorism unconditionally and simply allow itself to be mopped up by the security forces, and that the sufferings, suspicions and views of the mainly ethnic Kurdish population of the region would somehow evaporate as a result." Indeed, Ocalan justified the killing of some 33 unarmed Turkish recruits along the Bingol-Elazig highway at the end of May—the event that effectively ended the cease-fire—in precisely this manner: "The state has maintained its attacks ever since the PKK declared a cease-fire. The operations and attacks on the guerrilla forces and the people have given us the right to retaliate."[74]

Another independent Turkish source went on to explain that "the balances of power in Ankara are dramatically against any [overall] solution" to the Kurdish issue. "There is still a tendency to treat the PKK as a dominant part of the Kurdish question and to index any reform or step for democratization to an end to terrorism. . . . This is . . . saying in general, the people aren't regarded any differently than the PKK."[75]

Explaining further the Turkish reluctance to respond more positively to Ocalan's initiative, the independent Turkish source cited above criticized Demirel for "always bowing down" to those "who regularly oppose efforts towards democratisation, whether by rejecting judicial reform legislation or by banning concerts and demonstrations, closing down trade unions, protecting torturers, etc. in complete disregard of the Constitution."[76] Therefore, concluded this source: "Not having put an end to oppression and injustices already, it is hard to see how Demirel and his colleagues can take liberal steps in the Southeast in the wake of Apo's initiative." Indeed, in response to Ocalan's initial cease-fire offer, Demirel declared that "it is out of the question for the state to negotiate with those who shed blood," adding that "there are no two sides to the issue but it [the state] is only trying to repel an attack."[77]

As for Ocalan's proposal for a federation, Demirel declared: "Turkey is a unitary state; its flag carries a star and crescent. The country is an indivisible whole and its official language is Turkish. . . . It would be wrong to debate the concept of federation."[78] Similarly, General Dogan Gures, the chief of staff, asserted: "That is impossible because . . . the borders were established by Ataturk. It is impossible. Otherwise, the people will kill us. We would be unable to walk in [Ankara's] Kizilay Square."[79]

While the cease-fire hung in the balance, the sudden death of President Turgut Ozal on April 17 dealt it a fatal blow by removing the Turkish official most receptive to bold, imaginative thinking on the issue. Citing "very senior sources within the security apparatus,"[80] for example, Ismet G. Imset claimed that if Ozal had lived, "everything would have been different. A major reform package would have been underway and even the hawks (hard-liners) would have fallen in line."

Apparently, an important meeting of the National Security Council (the joint military-civilian body that effectively sets Turkish policy toward the Kurdish problem) had been scheduled for a week after Ozal's death. The president had ordered a special group within the Council to be set up "to seek political solutions to the crisis, to brainstorm and produce ideas, and to carry them out." In the words of one official, "it would have been [just] short of a revolution." After Ozal unexpectedly died, however, the meeting was postponed.

For several weeks, Turkish policy drifted until Demirel finally emerged as the new president and Ciller as the new prime minister. When the meeting was finally called, Demirel, who was unwilling to take bold steps, was now in charge. "What happened is that Ozal was a momentum, a political one, that was thrusting us out of a vicious cycle. Now, we have fallen back into orbit again. We are part of the vicious cycle," declared a senior officer.

During an interview at the end of 1993, Jalal Talabani agreed with this interpretation when he argued that "in the past, when I acted as a mediator, there was a good person like Ozal," and that "Ozal was making [an] enormous effort for this problem. Ozal's death was a great loss for democracy and peace."[81]

Even before Ozal's death, Ocalan himself seemed to have had similar sentiments. In an interview with a Turkish newspaper, the PKK leader was asked, "How do you assess Turkish politicians?"[82] He cautiously responded that Ozal "seems to be open to progress. He seems to be open to change. He has confirmed this in his statements and in the concepts he has put forward." Following Ozal's death, Ocalan even declared that "a solution to the problem could have been reached had the late President Turgut Ozal lived."[83] The PKK leader also claimed that Talabani had told him that Ozal had intended "to put some radical changes on Turkey's agenda."

For the other Turkish authorities, however, Ocalan had nothing positive to say: "Demirel is not a reformist. He supports the status quo. He is a great demagogue on the concept of democracy."[84] Comparing Demirel to Bulent Ecevit, a former Turkish prime minister, Ocalan said, "I do not believe they think about the need to solve the problem." As for Demirel's then deputy prime minister, the PKK leader declared: "Expecting Inonu to draw up a policy is absurd. Who would expect him to achieve anything?" And regarding Interior Affairs Minister Ismet Sezgin, Ocalan sarcastically declared that "they plan to treat me like they treated Shaykh Sait, who was arrested at about this time of year."[85]

## ALL-OUT WAR

As mentioned above, the cease-fire effectively ended when the PKK killed some 33 unarmed Turkish soldiers along the Bingol-Elazig highway on

May 24, 1993. Evidence indicates, however, that the deed was not specifically sanctioned by Ocalan, but perpetrated by Semdin Sakik (a.k.a. "Parmaksiz" Zeki), his hard-line field commander in the Amed (Diyarbakir) area. Ocalan himself, for example, called the incident "unfortunate. I did not plan it. I see no sense in the way it developed. I assessed it as somewhat premature and excessive. Had I known about it, I would have prevented it."[86] After hesitating for a number of hours, however, Ocalan came out in support of the action, rather than split his organization.

Despite the breakdown of the cease-fire, the new Turkish prime minister, Tansu Ciller, at first appeared to be conciliatory. She broached the idea of a "Basque model," which implied a substantial degree of autonomy for the Kurdish provinces, and also specifically mentioned the possibilities of Kurdish language lessons in the schools and Kurdish broadcasts on television. When these proposals were denounced by much of the Turkish establishment including members of her own True Path Party, however, she quickly withdrew them.

Increasingly, she then abandoned the Kurdish issue to the military to the extent that the phrase "as good as thirty men" was reportedly being used to describe her.[87] For his part, the new president, Suleyman Demirel, already the victim of two previous military coups, seemed to be reduced to "merely murmuring platitudes."[88] The old Turkish proverb "If you give your hand, you could lose your arm" was increasingly cited as the rationale for not making reforms that might look like concessions. Justifying its refusal to grant any concessions, the Turkish military argued:

> The PKK intends first to raise the debate of cultural and social reforms for the Kurds. If this is tolerated, the PKK will raise the issue of autonomy or a federation. If this is tolerated, it will create an independent Kurdish state. And, again if nothing is done, Kurds living in four countries will unite and create the true Independent Kurdistan. Thus, even pursuing language rights for the Kurds in Turkey—let alone Kurdish radio and television broadcasts—is to be regarded as serving the PKK's interests. Period.[89]

As a result, concluded one astute observer, "the only solution that comes to mind is to increase the use of force in the southeast region."[90] Under heavy pressure from the military, army enlistments were extended for three- to five-month periods in January 1994.

Once the cease-fire ended, the renewed fighting quickly reached unprecedented heights of intensity and casualties. By the end of 1993, more than 4,100 people had been killed in that year alone, making it the bloodiest twelve-month period yet.[91] Even more died the following year. By the summer of

1996, more than 21,000 people had been killed since the PKK insurgency had begun in 1984.

As 1993 drew to a close, the crisis for Turkey was clearly worsening, with the PKK beginning to exercise its own de facto sovereignty by enforcing a ban on Turkish political party activity and the press in certain areas of the southeast. In mid-October, for example, PKK officials simply kidnapped a number of journalists from the center of Diyarbakir and took them off into the countryside to hear the closure orders. Those who still wanted to file reports were required to obtain a "PKK visa." In Diyarbakir, now a city of over a million people, Turkish newspapers for a while could not be sold anywhere except in police stations.[92]

Cemil Bayik, the head of the ARGK, or military arm of the PKK, and often referred to as the number two man in that organization, cautioned foreigners "not to visit Turkey" unless they had obtained permission from the PKK first.[93] In a statement to the press, the PKK also warned that it had decided to take "action against the tourist economy. . . . This includes tourist areas, hotels, beaches and other facilities."[94] Since Turkey's struggling economy earned a much-needed $4.5 billion a year in hard currency from foreign tourism[95] (while spending between $6-8 billion a year on the war against the PKK),[96] this threat seemed very serious. Although several Western tourists were captured and held as hostages during the summer of 1993, scattered bombings took place in tourist spots, and tourism itself fell off considerably for a time, in the long run the threat failed to close down Turkey's tourism industry.

Attempting further strikes against the economic underpinnings of the Turkish state, Ocalan claimed that "no oil pipelines can be laid without an agreement with us, and if they are laid it will not be possible to operate them."[97] Turkish officials themselves admitted that revenue losses due to PKK attacks and threats against the tourism industry had contributed to the worsening economic situation,[98] while by 1996 the struggle itself was involving as much as 75 percent of the huge 530,000-strong Turkish military.[99]

Despite all the official talk over the years about solving the problems of the southeast through economic measures, reports indicated that because of the security problems the economy had "pulled out" of the troubled region.[100] The United Nations embargo on trade with Iraq and the PKK trade embargo between Turkey and northern Iraq during the summer of 1992 dealt further body blows to the economy. Local migration within and out of the region is accelerating, while the sales organizations of major firms have pulled out completely because their staff do not want to locate there. Little business activity occurs anyway because of the lack of cash, while those few who still do have resources prefer not to risk them, lest they be lost or damaged by the recurring violence.

Prices of real estate have fallen dramatically, banks are closing down branch offices, and the tourism industry has dried up. Even public sector operations have been closed or trimmed. Projects which were being constructed stand half-finished, were imaginary in the first place, or have been abandoned. Overnight transport has come to a virtual halt. During the economic crisis of April 1994, work on the much-publicized GAP project itself came to a halt. Although usually criticized for increasing the problems of the region, the village guard system of some 60,000 local residents at least still pumps money into the local economy, since the guards receive relatively generous wages.

In reaction to the PKK's campaign of "total war," the "majority of citizens [of Turkish ethnic heritage] spent Republic Day [on October 29, 1993] in a highly nationalistic and anti-Kurdish mood."[101] This growing ethnic tension between Turks and Kurds was well illustrated in Erzurum, a Turkish city in the northeastern part of the country, when mass anti-Kurdish demonstrations took place at the end of October during a funeral for victims of a PKK raid and then at the end of a football game. Mobs numbering some 10,000 to 15,000 had to be restrained from assaulting Kurdish targets and then bought off by an offer from the provincial governor to arm them with 1,000 kalashnikovs.

When asked what the state would do if the PKK was not finished off by the following spring of 1994, as promised by the military, Demirel speculated, "We could do what Kuyucu Murat Pasha did, what Mustafa Muglali did."[102] The commentator explained that "what Kuyucu Murat Pasha did is obvious: He threw those whom he slaughtered into a well [hence his nickname Kuyucu, which means well man]." The other individual apparently distinguished himself by building execution platforms made of severed heads. The commentator then closed this discussion by declaring that although he knew Demirel did not think along these lines, "an overwhelming section of the public and even some of those who administer the country are." This belligerent, anti-Kurdish mood was further illustrated at the beginning of March 1994, when, as noted in Chapter 1, the Turkish parliament finally voted to lift the immunity of six of the pro-Kurdish DEP MPs.

As the insurgency continued, the PKK began to murder elementary school teachers in the southeast whom they denounced as "government agents." For its part, the government stepped up its campaign to evacuate and in many cases destroy villages seen as offering support to the guerrillas. As noted above, more than 3,000 settlements had suffered this fate by the summer of 1996. Replying to criticism, the government claimed that the PKK had torched the villages, in part with helicopters flown in from Armenia, a patently ridiculous proposition.

In March 1994, Ocalan called for a cease-fire in a message he sent to the "International Northern Kurdistan Conference" held in Brussels, Belgium. In a letter sent to leaders of Western states near the end of the year, he repeated this call. The appeal was ignored, however, as a propaganda ploy from a terrorist organization.

## TURKEY REGAINS THE INITIATIVE

Although the PKK's fifth congress in January 1995 proclaimed that "our national liberation struggle has entered the period of victory"[103] and Ocalan himself vowed that "1995 will be a year of major steps for our part,"[104] by the spring of 1994 the enormous Turkish military effort had begun to show results, and the state's forces gradually regained control of most of the countryside. This was accomplished by a number of tactics, not the least of which was the assumption of supreme authority for the conduct of the war against the PKK by the Turkish military's chief of staff, after August 1994 General Ismail Hakki Karadayi. The theoretical civilian chain of command, consisting of the president, prime minister, interior minister, supra-governor for the emergency region, and provincial governors, was marginalized. Given the preeminent role of the National Security Council detailed above, this was not surprising.

The full or partial destruction of some 3,000 villages dried up a considerable amount of the PKK's logistical base among the rural population, negatively affecting both the supplies and militia system of part-time fighters and sympathizers feeding the insurgency. The *ozel tim* (the gendarmerie's special forces) and *ozel hareket tim* (police special forces)—also known collectively as the counter-guerrillas—began to carry out more efficient search-and-destroy operations in the mountains and other rural areas. As noted above, these counter-guerrillas were highly trained in their tactics and well motivated ideologically to accomplish their mission. According to a former Turkish officer interviewed by Human Rights Watch, these counter-guerrillas were recruited from Turkey's ultra-nationalist movement and "really hate Kurds and the PKK. Their primary motivation in life is to kill the PKK."[105] The elite members of these government forces were "so scary that even we Army officers were frightened of them. We never get in their way, and always try and remove ourselves if they are in the area."

Given the altered situation, the counter-guerrillas could now simply occupy the abandoned mountainous regions that formerly offered havens to the PKK guerrillas and wait for them to reveal their position when hunger forced them out of their hiding places. Once this happened government planes could also pound the rebel concentrations with increased efficiency both in the mountains of southeastern Turkey and former ARGK safehouses in northern Iraq. And instead of simply waiting for the PKK's annual spring offensive, in March 1995 the

Turkish military launched the largest foreign operation in the history of the Turkish Republic against the PKK in northern Iraq.

Previously, the government forces had simply waited for the ARGK guerrillas to run into them, a tactic that allowed many of the ARGK guerrillas to slip by and infiltrate into the interior. A new tactic involved flooding the mountainous areas along the Turkish-Iraqi border in the southeast with government troops, which then moved north and west in the same direction as PKK guerrilla-infiltrators did. Moving along southeastern Turkey's valleys and mountain ranges together made it easier for the government's troops to locate and destroy their enemy. Employing this tactic, by the fall of 1994 the government was able to compress some 2,500 ARGK guerrillas in Tunceli province, where supposedly they could then be eliminated, especially given the troops' new willingness to operate in altitudes up to 10,000 feet.

By the spring of 1995, the PKK no longer ruled the nights or was forcing civilians in small settlements to stage demonstrations in the streets. Shops in such cities as Diyarbakir, Silopi, and Cizre were staying open until midnight, no longer shut on orders from the PKK. Unable to repeat its spectacular operations of 1993 against army posts and heavily defended towns, the PKK returned to its earlier, lower-key ambushes, raids on remote, lightly protected villages, and highway minings.

Illustrative of his weakened position, Ocalan's attempt to repeat his highly publicized press conferences of 1993 failed when Syrian and Lebanese officials refused to permit one in October 1994. Intercepted communications between Ocalan and his commanders in the field showed further frustrations.

> Who are you anyway? The tragic thing is that you are pitiable. You wet your pants when you are threatened. If you took half an hour to think things out, you could win victories. Instead you get your units destroyed by taking time to sleep. . . . Are you cows? Are you donkeys? If not, how do you get yourselves in these situations?[106]

The PKK leader also complained of all kinds of misbehavior, lack of discipline, idleness, shirking, corruption, and immorality, declaring that when he saw such things, he wanted to "hit out and smash people's brains."

## ERBAKAN GOVERNMENT

Another idea the state seemed to be considering was encouraging a pan-Islamic solution to the Kurdish problem. This increasingly appeared to be taking the form of encouraging Necmettin Erbakan's Islamic Welfare (Refah) Party when it competed for votes in the southeast. Indeed, in reply to a correspondent's inquiry of whether "you will be replacing the Turkish-Kurdish conflict with Islamic unity,"[107] Erbakan himself declared: "We have bonds of brotherhood. There is nothing more absurd than ethnic differentiation among Muslim brothers." When the Refah Party finally did enter the government as the head of a coalition that was formed in July 1996, Abdullah Gul, its deputy chairman, reiterated this idea: "We lived together without any problems until the end of the Ottoman Empire. Why? Because a common religion unites us as brothers. This might again be possible."[108] He added that "the problem is the state ideology, the assimilation efforts," and concluded that "if they want to speak Kurdish, let them speak Kurdish."

Such an approach, of course, was really an extension of the old Ottoman principle that Islam took precedence over nationality among Muslims and that only non-Muslims could hold some type of officially recognized minority status.[109] It ran headfirst into the secular concepts of Ataturk upon which the Turkish republic supposedly was constructed and for which the Turkish military had always stood. The secular state was clearly playing with fire by encouraging Erbakan in the southeast while opposing him in the rest of the country. Additionally, Ocalan vowed to "expose Erbakan and demonstrate that he will not be able to trick people by misusing the Islamic unity."[110]

In spite of these problems, Erbakan's Refah Party did indeed emerge as the biggest apparent winner in the local elections held throughout Turkey on March 27, 1994, and the national elections held on December 24, 1995.[111] To what extent its ability to carry votes among the Kurds in Turkey's southeast was based on its own merits, however, was not completely clear. Due to intense harassment of its candidates ranging from beatings and threats to outright murders, DEP had decided to withdraw from the 1994 local elections one month earlier. And in the national elections at the end of 1995, the new pro-Kurdish party HADEP was still able to draw considerable support in the southeast despite the fact that as many as one million of its potential supporters had been disenfranchised due to the destruction of their villages and resulting forced displacement.

Despite the apparent successes on the battlefield and Turkey's admission into the European Customs Union in December 1995, the national elections produced a hung parliament that resulted in a weak, short-lived minority coalition government between the bitter rivals Mesut Yilmaz of the ANAP and Tansu Ciller of the DYP. Paralyzed politically and able to do little about Turkey's continuing economic malaise, Yilmaz was forced to resign within a few months, thus allowing Erbakan to become the new prime minister, with Ciller as his deputy prime minister and foreign minister.

For the first time in the history of the secular Turkish republic established by Ataturk in 1923, an avowedly Islamist party headed the government. If its past positions were any indication of its present policy, Refah seemed poised to turn Turkey away from the United States, NATO, and the European Union and return it to its Islamic roots. In the United States, some observers even began to ask "who lost Turkey?"[112] They pointed to Erbakan's $23 billion deal with Iran to purchase gas and construct a natural gas pipeline between Turkey and Iran—reached just one month after he assumed office—that flew in the face of the new U.S. Iran-Libya Sanctions Act, or D'Amato Law, sanctioning any state investing more than $40 million in Iran's oil and gas industry. What is more, Erbakan's call for Turkey, Iran, Syria, and Iraq to deal with the Kurdish problem in northern Iraq seemed an open bid to replace the U.S.-led OPC, when its latest renewal expired at the end of the year, with a local Muslim force manned in part by two states the United States considered "terrorist" and was trying to isolate and contain. Erbakan's protestations that he was not trying to overthrow Turkey's secular institutions were dismissed as *takiyye,* an Islamic term meaning "deception" or "concealment of real intentions to protect Islamic believers."

For a number of reasons, however, it seemed unlikely that the new Erbakan government would dramatically reorient Turkey's overall policies. In the first place, Erbakan was not a fire-eating, fundamentalist radical lacking any practical governmental experience. He first had been elected to the Turkish parliament as far back as 1969. During the 1970s he had served as deputy prime minister in a coalition government headed by Bulent Ecevit and later as an important participant in the Nationalist Front cabinets headed by Suleyman Demirel. These years of experience and knowledge of Turkish political realities made Erbakan sensitive to the responsibilities of government. Upon assuming power, for example, he promised to discuss national security questions with his "noble generals" and defer to the advice of the "heroic Turkish military."[113] Accordingly, he made a quick U-turn as soon as he became prime minister and supported a renewal of OPC. When the military demanded, he dutifully signed an expulsion order for 28 officers and 30 NCOs for religious fanaticism. He also agreed to continue all Turkey's existing international agreements including the recent one allowing Israel to train its jets in Turkish airspace. Indeed, less than two months after he assumed office, Erbakan signed another agreement with the Jewish state exchanging technical information and paving the way for Israel to refurbish Turkey's aging F-4 Phantom jets.

Given the fact that Erbakan's party had received only 21 percent of the vote, political realities also forced him to give the ministries of foreign affairs and defense to his coalition partners in the DYP. Even without the military, president, and DYP acting as honest brokers, however, it was unlikely that Refah would attempt to reverse Turkey's overall world position as indicated by the agreement with Israel. An analysis of its policy positions, for example, suggested that Islam often served as a means for the assertion of the Turkish national identity, which the party feared was being lost to westernization. Thus, Refah's opposition to NATO and the European Customs Union was based more on the belief that those western organizations hurt Turkey's multilateral relations with Muslim states and were bad for Turkey's unskilled laborers, rather than a visceral opposition to the West in the manner of Iran.

In addition, evidence showed that many Turks supported Refah because they were looking for an alternative to the other parties, which they perceived to be corrupt, inefficient, and insensitive to their needs. Indeed, Refah's record on the local level was one of providing compassionate, efficient, and honest services, in contrast to the other parties. Islam was more an appeal to a common Islamic heritage shared by 99 percent of Turkey's population, than a militant call to arms against Turkey's 70-year-old, secular heritage. Without denying its important emphasis on Islam, Refah's assumption of power seemed more likely to integrate Turkey's Islamists fully into a new, broader understanding of what Turkish secularism allowed than to return Turkey to some sort of atavistic Islamic past.

Initial experiences also indicated how intractable the Kurdish problem would remain. Although Erbakan made moves upon coming to power to repopulate some Kurdish villages in the southeast and announced that GAP-TV would begin broadcasting daily up to two hours in Kurdish, Refah's Turkish nationalism made it a strong foe of Kurdish nationalism and separatism. What is more, initially promising attempts to begin indirect negotiations with the PKK itself soon foundered.

Almost as soon as he had become prime minister, Erbakan and Refah ministers Fethullah Erbas and Fehim Adak met twice with Ismail Nacar, an Islamist author with close links to the PKK and spokesman for the think tank Peace Brotherhood and Solidarity Committee. Nacar also visited Murat Bozluk, the pro-Kurdish HADEP leader, imprisoned along with most of his party's senior leadership following an incident at the party's congress in Ankara on June 23, 1996, in which the Turkish flag was torn down and replaced with the PKK banner and a portrait of Ocalan. As soon as word of Nacar's initiative was leaked, however, Turkish nationalistic elements including the military, president, Refah's coalition partners, and others, all raised the hue and cry. Like his predecessor, Ciller—she tried to suggest reforms upon first assuming power in 1993—Erbakan was forced to retreat.[114]

Similarly, when Refah parliamentary deputy Fethullah Erbas visited a PKK camp in northern Iraq to arrange the release of 14 Turkish soldiers held for over a year, the closely watched effort ended in failure. Encouraged initially by the PKK, Erbas had hoped to parley the visit into exploring grounds for indirect negotiations. Ocalan apparently reneged because he wanted to deal with a more official governmental representative. Several months later, however, the PKK finally did release the soldiers.

In addition, Erbakan's opening to Iran and Syria to join Turkey and Iraq as a four-power substitute for OPC failed to convince Iran and Syria to drop their support for the PKK. Indeed, by the beginning of September 1996, this proposal had been overcome by events, as Iran and Iraq were drawn into opposite sides in the renewal of the Kurdish civil war in northern Iraq. In addition, Erbakan's attempt to pursue further Islamic unity and a more independent foreign policy by journeying to Libya in October 1996, backfired badly when his mercurial host, Colonel Muammar Gaddafi, called for the creation of an independent state for Turkey's Kurds. Although it managed to survive a resulting vote of confidence in the Turkish parliament, Erbakan's government had been badly shaken.

The events of Erbakan's first months in office illustrated how elusive a solution to the Kurdish problem remained. And, of course, although the recent military offensives had contained the PKK, they had certainly not defeated it. Given its reserve of hard-learned experiences and remaining cadres, the PKK was likely to remain a force to be reckoned with for the future. Indeed, the forced migration of so many Kurdish civilians to the cities in the west may have simply added to the problem geographically. As long as the state denied basic cultural and linguistic rights to the Kurds, the PKK or its successors would still possess fertile ground for growth and support. In the end, the situation required a political, as well as a military, solution.

**4**

# The Foreign Factor

Until recently, most scholars have analyzed Turkish foreign policy with scarcely a mention of the Kurdish factor.[1] In so doing, of course, these academics were implicitly mirroring the official Turkish position that Turkey had no Kurdish population living within its borders (only "Mountain Turks") and thus no Kurdish problem. It is the contention of this chapter, however, that shortly after the establishment of the modern Turkish republic in 1923, the Kurdish factor became an important, albeit latent factor in Turkish foreign policy and, much less controversially, has become one of the most important factors influencing it today. Indeed, it is now obvious that the Kurdish problem is challenging the very future of the unitary Turkish state as it has existed since 1923, as well as its foreign policy.

## THE EARLY YEARS

In his enlightening analysis of the consequences of the Sheikh Said Kurdish rebellion in Turkey of 1925, Robert Olson has made a number of very interesting points challenging the traditional paradigm, which ignored the Kurdish factor.[2] After pointing out how the suppression of the rebellion (1) facilitated the resolution of the Mosul question between Britain, Iraq, and Turkey and thus limited Turkey's access to the oil of Mosul; (2) reduced the potential for Turkey to use Islam as a foreign policy means of challenge or access to the other states in the Middle East; (3) forced Turkey to emphasize Turkish nationalism and state secularism; and (4) helped bring about the treaty of friendship between Turkey and Iran in 1926 and the signing of a definitive border treaty between them in 1932; Olson insightfully maintained that "the rebellion had the consequence of Turkey's eschewing interference in the internal affairs of other countries and contributed to the Turkish motto: peace at home and peace abroad."[3] Thus, he concluded, "the Sheikh Said rebellion forced Turkey to abandon any hopes it may have nursed for an assertive foreign policy, and to form a non-interventionist foreign policy."[4]

Elsewhere, Olson continued to emphasize the Kurdish factor in Turkish foreign policy by pointing out that most of the military engagements carried out by the Turkish armed forces since the mid-1920s have involved the Kurds.[5] Thus, he again concluded—with relevance for this analysis—that "the struggle against Kurdish nationalism, in which certain patterns of policies were implemented and against which certain nationalist, ideological, and psychological premises and attitudes were initially adopted in 1925, continued to play an important role in Turkey's policy decisions more than fifty years [later]."[6] Indeed, looking to the future, Olson even argued that "Kurdish nationalism, articulated and symbolized by the Sheikh Said rebellion, will also continue far into the next century."[7]

Given their common interest in suppressing Kurdish nationalist aspirations, as well as their suspicions of communist infiltration associated with minority demands, Turkey, Iran, and Iraq (as well as Afghanistan) concluded the Middle Eastern Pact—better known as the Saadabad Pact, for the palace in Tehran where it was signed—on July 8, 1937. Under the terms of this treaty, the parties agreed to cooperate against any subversive activities that might occur against them. Although the Saadabad Pact made no specific mention of the Kurds and amounted to little more than a weak non-aggression pact that soon was overcome by World War II and its aftermath, with some justice the Kurds believed that it was directed against them.

The Baghdad Pact of 1955 between the same three states plus Britain and Pakistan was again with some validity viewed in a similar vein, although once again no specific mention was made in it of the Kurds. Officially, this new treaty was supposed to extend the NATO doctrine of the containment of communism to the Middle East. Clearly, however, there was a latent Kurdish factor also influencing Turkish foreign policy in these early days.

## RECENT YEARS

The rebirth of Kurdish nationalism in Turkey since the 1970s has brought the Kurdish factor to the forefront of current Turkish foreign policy. By August 1993, for example, Ocalan had gone so far as to claim that "the Kurdish problem has blocked [Turkish] foreign policy,"[8] and that Tansu Ciller had defeated Ismet Sezgin to become the new Turkish Prime Minister "because Sezgin failed on the Kurdish issue."[9] As evidence, Ocalan cited the breakdown of the ceasefire between the PKK and Ankara in May and June 1993, while Sezgin was still minister of the interior.

Striking at the economic underpinnings of the Turkish state, the PKK recently warned that it would target any projected pipeline across the Caspian

Sea to carry oil from central Asia to the Mediterranean through Turkey "unless it [the PKK] is counted as a negotiation partner. Just as they conclude agreements with other states for the pipeline, they have to reach an accord with the authority representing the Kurdish people and with us."[10] Until Turkey was finally admitted in December 1995, Turkish membership in the highly valued European Customs Union was partially made dependent on its making progress toward solving its Kurdish problem.[11] As noted in Chapter 3, recent estimates indicated that Turkey was spending as much as $8 billion per year to combat the PKK and engaging as much as 75 percent of its military. Kemal Kirisci, a Turkish professor at the University of the Bosporus in Istanbul, concluded that "as a result, the politics associated with ethnicity and nationalism has come to affect Turkish foreign policy behavior in a profound manner."[12]

Because Turkey chose so long to refuse to admit that it had a Kurdish problem, the sudden resurgence of the situation since the 1970s helped give rise to conspiracy theories involving various foreign influences. Many Turks, and the government, feel that the PKK has been receiving aid from various states and groups which desire a weakened Turkey. Turkish Prime Minister Tansu Ciller declared in November 1993 that "we know that the PKK is being nurtured and trained in our neighboring countries such as Syria, Iran, Iraq, and Armenia."[13]

Ciller's statement was a bombshell because for a long time there was a tradition in Turkish foreign policy to avoid using the names of neighboring states when making such accusations, even though everyone always knew who was meant when the government complained about "outside support and shelter for the PKK by certain states." Although the first break with this custom had already come in 1989, Ciller's declaration clearly caught the Turkish foreign ministry off-guard and surprised others with its scarcely veiled threat to intervene against this perceived support of the PKK. She added that "an intensive diplomatic process has been started. . . . If our neighbors are our friends, then this is the time to show their friendship. If they are not our friends, we must know this and act accordingly."

Those Turkish officials who took Ciller's position undoubtedly have been influenced by their historical memories of European imperialist schemes to weaken and divide the Ottoman Empire in the nineteenth and early twentieth centuries.[14] Even after the establishment of the Turkish republic in the 1920s, the Turks suspected that the British had backed Sheikh Said's Kurdish rebellion during 1925 in order to weaken the Turkish claim to the vilayet of Mosul, which was largely inhabited by Kurds. A Kurdish revolt against Turkey would vitiate Turkey's claim that it could best represent the Kurds who inhabited the oil-rich territory of what became northern Iraq.

The Turks, however, were never able to produce any serious evidence to substantiate their suspicions. Winston Churchill, for example, declared: "We have not been able to liquidate all the promises given or alleged to have been given to the Arabs during the war. I am entirely opposed to creating similar difficulties with the Kurds."[15] As a result, concluded Olson: "By 1 December 1921, there was, then, unanimous disapproval of proposals . . . to instigate Kurdish rebellion against the Turks outside of the British mandate in Iraq." Indeed, the Sheikh Said rebellion was crushed in part because the French gave the Turks permission to use the Baghdad railroad that passed through Syria for troop transport.[16] Similarly, during the Kurdish revolt around Mount Ararat in 1930, Iran allowed Turkish troops to pass through its territory and surround the insurgents. Iran and Turkey later legalized their understanding by making minor border adjustments in 1932.[17]

Not everyone, however, shared Ciller's position concerning foreign support for the insurgents. Her foreign minister, Hikmet Cetin, who was of Kurdish ancestry, associated himself with the following view, expressed by a high-level government official:

> It is nonsense to establish a belt of hostility and insecurity around the country with declarations and remarks accusing some of the eastern neighbours of sheltering and harbouring separatist terrorists, particularly if there is no concrete evidence against those countries. It is not in the interest of Turkey to have so many enemies around it.[18]

In partial explanation of Ciller's accusations, some have speculated that they were uttered for domestic or even party consumption as she faced a congress of her own party for renewal of her leadership position. A tough foreign policy position on the Kurdish issue would help take some of the pressure off her for perceived policy failures on other issues. Be that as it may, the following analysis will illustrate the depth and breadth of the Kurdish factor in Turkish foreign policy.

## THE MIDDLE EAST

### Syria

Ismet Cheriff Vanly, a prominent Kurdish academic and activist, summed up the role of Syria well when he wrote that Assad's regime has given the PKK "what may justifiably be called a strategic alliance."[19] As noted in Chapter 1, even before the Turkish coup of 1980 Syria provided a haven for Ocalan, the leader of the PKK. After the military finally took power, the Syrians permitted the remnants of the PKK to reassemble and reconstitute themselves on Syrian territory and in the parts of Lebanon they controlled. All five of the PKK congresses also took place there. Until April 1992, the PKK was permitted to maintain the Mahsun Korkmaz Military Academy as a training camp in the Bekaa valley. To this day, Ocalan spends at least part of his time living in Damascus, while the nucleus of the PKK forces remains encamped in or near the Bekaa valley. There are probably a number of reasons for the PKK-Syrian connection. Smoldering animosities concerning the Turkish annexation of Hatay (Alexandretta) province in 1939 and problems concerning the waters of the Euphrates River, which flow through Turkey before reaching Syria, have long kept Turkish-Syrian relations cool. As Ankara's *Guneydogu Anadolu Projesi* (GAP), or Southeast Anatolia Project of harnessing the Euphrates and Tigris Rivers nears completion, Syria has unsuccessfully sought an annual guaranteed quota from Turkey.[20]

In addition, disagreements have existed over Cyprus, Israel, and the PLO leadership. Some Turks have argued that the PKK has helped keep Syria's own Kurds from making problems for Assad in return for its Syrian safehouse. The memories of the harsh Ottoman rule that lasted into the early years of the twentieth century, as well as the fact that each was on opposite sides during the cold war, also probably play a background role. Finally, one might mention the grandiose ambitions of the Syrian leader Hafez Assad to occupy a dominant position in the region.

Over the years, a dialogue of the deaf has occurred between Turkey and Syria over the situation. Turkey periodically has complained about the PKK presence in Syria, and Syria has denied it, at the same time bringing up its own grievances concerning water. In July 1987, then–Turkish Prime Minister Turgut Ozal signed a security protocol with the Syrians in Damascus. Under its terms, Syria agreed to stop permitting the PKK to raid Turkey from across its borders and to remove the PKK camps from its territory. For its part, Ankara agreed to supply Damascus with no less than 500 cubic meters per second of water per month. Further Syrian intransigency soon became evident, however, as the PKK camps were simply moved to the Syrian-controlled parts of the Bekaa valley, which were supposedly within Lebanese territory and thus beyond Syrian legal control.

In April 1992, Turkish Interior Minister Ismet Sezgin met Assad in Damascus and presented him evidence[21] that: (1) Ocalan was still living in Damascus near the Selahaddin Eyyubi Mosque, and he was guarded by the Syrian intelligence services, or the *Mukhabarat*; (2) the *Mukhabarat* had provided money, materials, and false identifications to the PKK; (3) Syria had permitted PKK meetings, congresses, and conferences to be held within its territory at various dates; (4) Syria had permitted PKK camps and training centers to exist in the Bekaa valley and had also provided SAM-7 missiles to protect them; (5) Syria had given the PKK assistance from its arsenals established near its border with Turkey; and (6) Syria had allowed the PKK to make radio transmissions to a distance of 72 kilometers (approximately 44 miles) from Damascus; among other items.

Initially, the Sezgin mission seemed to result in success. Syria reportedly promised to close down PKK camps within the Bekaa valley, declare the PKK a "terrorist organization" that was "illegal in Syria," arrest and try PKK members when apprehended, and even oust such other Turkish terrorist groups as *Dev Sol* (Revolutionary Left).[22] Sezgin declared, "I do not believe Syria will be behind PKK terrorism after this," and described his agreement with Assad as "the best protocol ever obtained."[23]

Within months, however, it became clear that Syrian duplicity was continuing, as a new PKK camp was simply established some 20 kilometers west of the Bekaa valley near the Lebanese town of Barr Ilyas. Turkish complaints about serious PKK incidents originating from Syria continued. In the spring of 1996, Turkish Prime Minister Mesut Yilmaz denounced "this blackmail policy" and asserted that "the Syrian Government has embarked on a dangerous path . . . by using the PKK terrorism as a trump card against the water issue."[24] Yilmaz's deputy prime minister, Nahit Mentese, even threatened to give Syria a "lesson."[25] In the summer of 1996, the usually more cautious Turkish President Demirel unequivocally added that "Syria's support for the PKK is clearly evident" and that "Turkey has irrefutable evidence that this organization's leaders are still in Syria and the neighboring areas under Syrian control."[26]

The rift between Turkey and Syria grew as Syria reached a vague understanding with Greece concerning military cooperation that was clearly directed against Turkey. Partially in reply, the Turks reached a more explicit agreement with Israel regarding military cooperation. The "strategic alliance" between Syria and the PKK, as well as "a dialogue of the deaf" between Turkey and Syria, continued.

## Iran

Despite the profound ideological differences between pro-American, secularized Turkey and anti-Western, Islamic Iran, the two states were long able to maintain surprisingly friendly relations. This was because both had calculated that such a policy would serve their respective interests.[27] As a result, Iran has never played the role of PKK safehouse to the extent Syria has. Nevertheless, problems existed and have recently escalated.

In the summer of 1989, for example, a Turkish source charged that there were some 25 PKK militants under the command of Ocalan's brother, Osman

Ocalan, in Iran.[28] Supposedly, some 80 PKK guerrillas had infiltrated into Turkey over the Iranian border the previous April. Further data indicated an "extensive PKK force deployment from camps in Iranian territory to the . . . buffer zone between Iran and Iraq."[29]

In October 1991, a Greek-Cypriot–registered ship, *Cape Maleas,* loaded with arms, munitions, and base heroin, was seized in Istanbul. The vessel had been hired by Iran two years earlier and reputedly had already made four previous trips carrying arms from the Bulgarian port of Burgas to Syria, where its cargo was then allegedly transferred to the PKK, among others, supposedly supported by Iran and Syria. Although Iran denied the charges, the incident caused much Turkish ill-will toward the Islamic republic.

In September 1992, Turkish Interior Minister Sezgin journeyed to Iran in an unsuccessful attempt to get that state to prevent PKK infiltrations into Turkey. Iran simply rejected the accusations and countered that it wanted the halting of activities in Turkey of the *Mojahedin-e Khalq,* or Peoples Holy Warriors—an Islamic socialist organization violently opposed to the Iranian government. The assassination of the prominent, secularist Turkish journalist Ugur Mumcu in January 1993, reputedly by Islamic extremists trained and supported by Iran, added further fuel to Turkish suspicions concerning Iran's role.

During the combined Turkish-Iraqi Kurdish drive to uproot PKK bases in northern Iraq in October 1992 (see below), the PKK apparently was able to transfer some of its guerrillas to Iran. One report indicated that as many as 1,500 of them were based in six PKK camps in Iran's Orumiyeh province in the summer of 1993.[30] The same report added that "in addition to logistics support, Iran provides arms, ammunition, provisions, and clothing to the militants."

In August 1993, a Turkish delegation presented Iran with photographs, cassette tapes, and files containing revelations by captured PKK militants on PKK links with Iran's intelligence and *pasdaran* (revolutionary guards) units, as well as data on the locations of PKK arms depots, training centers, liaison offices, and the names of PKK members who were in charge of the camps and cell houses in Iran.[31]

One theory to explain Iran's behavior is that it seeks to weaken Turkey's position in the struggle over influence in the former Soviet Caucasus and Central Asian republics.[32] Another possible explanation is that by encouraging the PKK to carry on armed struggle from Iraqi Kurdistan, Iran seeks to expand the Turkish-PKK and PKK-Iraqi Kurdish conflict there, in hopes of destabilizing the de facto Iraqi Kurdish state and government created after the 1991 Gulf War. Iran sees this de facto Kurdish state as an intolerable model of autonomy for her own Kurds and a tool for the United States to intervene in Iranian affairs. Indeed, beginning in the spring of 1993 and continuing through the summer of that year,

Iran itself shelled the Iraqi Kurdish countryside in a declared intention to hit Iranian Kurds who were supposedly sheltering there. Then in late July 1996—with the permission of Jalal Talabani's Patriotic Union of Kurdistan (PUK)—Iranian troops penetrated deeply into northern Iraq in an effort to strike the Iranian Kurds. The Islamic Republic followed this action with blatant support for Talabani's PUK in its civil war against Massoud Barzani's Kurdistan Democratic Party (KDP). The intention in this action also seemed to be to take advantage of Baghdad's inability to control what were still legally its northern provinces.

On the other hand, Iran has cooperated with Turkey to oppose Russian influence from being reasserted in central Asia and the Caucasus. The Islamic Republic has also worked with both Turkey and Syria to the extent that the three have met in each other's capitals since the Gulf War on a semi-regular basis to consider how to meet the common threat of a Kurdish state in northern Iraq. Thus, meetings were held in Ankara in November 1992, Damascus in February 1993, Tehran in June 1993, Damascus in July 1994, and Tehran in September 1995. The most recent tripartite meetings, however, have been called less frequently. The one in 1995 was postponed for several months because of the Turkish invasion of northern Iraq in March 1995. Moreover, in October 1993 Iran rejected a Turkish request to allow Turkish forces to enter its territory to pursue PKK guerrillas, as the Turks have done repeatedly in northern Iraq.

At the end of 1993, Iran supposedly agreed to crack down on PKK operations within its territory and to allow the Turks to observe any actions taken to enforce this understanding. For its part, Turkey agreed to reciprocate Iran's actions in regards to the *Mojahedin-e Khalq*. For a while, the resulting joint security committee established by the two seemed to be bearing positive results, as it held numerous meetings to exchange information on terrorism and border security. In the spring of 1994, for example, Iran turned over 14 PKK guerrillas to the Turks and did not allow the Turkish bombing of the PKK's Zaleh camp near the Iranian border, which also killed some 20 Iranians, to upset Iranian-Turkish relations. For its part, Turkey did not support U.S. President Bill Clinton's call in May 1995 for his country's allies to join the United States in cutting off all trade and investment with Iran.

In June 1995, however, new reports of PKK activity in Iran surfaced. Some eight camps were supposedly established by the PKK after it fled the Turkish invasion of northern Iraq in March 1995.[33] According to the well-connected Turkish reporter Ertugrul Ozkok, the Turks did not take any military actions because "attacking a camp in Iran would be a very risky and dangerous initiative. Bombing Iran is quite different from bombing northern Iraq."[34] Furthermore, in the spring of 1996 relations between the two were further attenuated by Iran's claim that Turkey had allowed a group of *Mojahedin-e Khalq* members to stage an anti-Iranian demonstration on the anniversary of the victory of the Islamic revolution. This was followed by mutual accusations about diplomatic spies in each other's country.

Shortly after assuming office in July 1996, however, the Islamist government of Necmettin Erbakan moved to soothe these difficulties by reaching an important agreement with Iran about the purchase of natural gas and constructing a pipeline to carry it. Erbakan also called for talks among Turkey, Iran, Syria, and Iraq whose goal would be to replace the forces of the U.S.-backed Operation Provide Comfort enforcing the no-fly zone over Iraqi Kurdistan. This attempted opening to Iran foundered, however, amid fresh Turkish accusations about PKK infiltrations from Iran made by the new foreign minister, Tansu Ciller, who seemed to be working at cross-purposes with her coalition partner, Erbakan. The rewewal of the Iraqi Kurdish civil war in August—in which Iran supported the PUK, while Turkey sided with the KDP and thus implicitly Iraq—also worked against a Turkish-Iranian agreement.

## Iraq

During the Iran-Iraq war of 1980-88, Iraq permitted Turkey to pursue PKK guerrillas into its territory on a number of occasions. Such cooperation served the interests of both states at that time, as Baghdad had its hands full with the Iranians and thus had difficulty in controlling its northern provinces where the Iraqi Kurds were permitting the PKK to enjoy safehouses. Thus, although the PKK maintained bases in northern Iraq, they did not have the permission of the host government as they did in Syria and to a much lesser extent in Iran.

The understanding between Ankara and Baghdad against both the PKK and the Iraqi Kurds began to unravel upon the conclusion of the war in 1988, when Iraq chased some 60,000 Iraqi Kurds over the border into Turkey, where they were reluctantly received as refugees. The 1991 Gulf war led to even more dramatic changes in Turkish foreign policy as Turkish President Turgut Ozal moved quickly to support the U.S.-led coalition against Iraq by shutting down the oil pipeline between Iraq and Turkey and cooperating in various other ways that facilitated the coalition's victory.

At the end of the war, Turkey was suddenly faced with the incredibly difficult situation of some half a million Iraqi Kurdish refugees on its border fleeing from Saddam. To handle this crisis, Turkey continued its cooperation with the U.S.-led alliance against Saddam by (1) housing Operation Provide Comfort (OPC)—also known in Turkey as Operation Poised Hammer—which provided air cover for the Iraqi Kurds against the threat of renewed attacks from Baghdad and (2) entering into a de facto alliance with the emerging Iraqi Kurdish state and government in northern Iraq. Both positions represented major changes in

Turkey's traditional foreign policy of scrupulous neutrality on the one hand and visceral opposition of Kurdish nationalism on the other.

Operation Provide Comfort began on April 5, 1991, at the direction of U.S. President George Bush, following suggestions from Turkish President Turgut Ozal, French President Francois Mitterrand, and British Prime Minister John Major.[35] Its "original mission was to provide immediate humanitarian assistance to Iraqi refugees who had fled to the mountains of northern Iraq and across the border into southern Turkey to escape repression from Saddam Hussein" at the end of the 1991 Gulf War and upon failure of the subsequent Kurdish uprising. At one time or another, coalition forces from thirteen different states participated. At its peak in May 1991, the United States had more than 12,000 military personnel committed to relief efforts, and they themselves were part of an overall coalition force of nearly 22,000 people. Subsequently, OPC continued until the end of 1996 in the form of 80 combat and support aircraft stationed at the Incirlik Air Base in Turkey's southern Adana province; they were making daily patrol flights over Iraqi Kurdistan to deter incursions from Baghdad. Turkish permission thus was a *sine qua non* for OPC's continuance and had to be renewed at increasingly shorter intervals. A small Military Coordination Center (MCC) team was also stationed in Zakho, Iraqi Kurdistan, to monitor conditions, and several thousand local Kurds were employed in relief and intelligence operations. The United States, Britain, and France were the main Western participants.

The continuance of OPC became a major political issue in Turkey, because many Turks believed it was facilitating the vacuum of authority in northern Iraq that enabled the PKK to enjoy sanctuaries there. Some even argued that OPC was the opening salvo of a new Treaty of Sevres[36] that would lead to the creation of a Kurdish state in northern Iraq. Thus, went the argument, Turkey was facilitating its own demise by housing it. In addition, an accidental airdrop that resulted in supplies falling into the hands of the PKK led to further suspicions in the Turkish public, which was already irritated by the presence of a foreign military force in the Turkish midst.

However, there was a variety of reasons why Turkey now sought to protect and, in effect, promote the Iraqi Kurds. For one thing, if the Iraqi Kurds were dependent on Turkish goodwill, Turkey might be able to influence them not to establish their own state, which could conceivably be a dangerous example to the Turkish Kurds. Additionally, an unfriendly Iraqi Kurdish state might begin aiding the PKK, or even make territorial claims on Turkey's Kurdish region. On the other hand, by supporting the Iraqi Kurds, Turkey might influence them to be pro-Turkish and thus help to solve its own Kurdish problem more readily. What is more, if Saddam were to crush the Kurds again, Turkey might have to face hordes of destabilizing Kurdish refugees once more. Finally, being looked upon as the protector of the Iraqi Kurds would win Turkey respect and support in the West, where Turkey still sought eventual membership in the European Union. In explaining his state's position toward OPC, then–Turkish Prime Minister (since May 1993, President) Suleyman Demirel declared: "This . . . is a force which says, 'I am here' in order to prevent the people who have been subjected to Saddam Hossein's tyranny in the past from falling into new difficulties."[37] He then added: "We cannot watch another Halabja" (the site of one of Saddam's most notorious chemical gas attacks against the Iraqi Kurds in March 1988).

Others explained the Turkish position in a more realistic manner as a "no-win situation,"[38] since by allowing OPC to continue, Turkey in effect was reinforcing de facto Iraqi Kurdish statehood. To abandon the force, however, would simply lead it to regroup elsewhere and strip Ankara of any influence whatsoever over the course of events. At best, some argued, "Turkey appears to have been selling support for the multilateral force against silence on its own Kurdish question."[39]

Accordingly, the Turkish parliament voted in favor of renewing OPC whenever it came up for its frequent renewals until the end of 1996, although it always added the proviso that the territorial integrity of Iraq had to be respected. This meant, of course, that Turkey opposed the creation of a Kurdish state in northern Iraq. This opposition was unanimously reiterated in the series of tripartite conferences held among Turkey, Syria, and Iran from November 1992 onwards, as mentioned above. For the same reason, these three states also opposed the Iraqi Kurdish elections of May 1992, which resulted in the creation of a de facto Iraqi Kurdish government in July 1992 and the proclamation of a federated state in October of that year.[40] Moreover, following Barzani's alliance with Saddam in August 1996, the small military mission in Zakho was withdrawn to Turkey and OPC's relief efforts in northern Iraq terminated.

Many Turks also argued that Turkey deserved some kind of compensation for all the financial sacrifices she had made since Saddam's invasion of Kuwait. In the summer of 1993, for example, Turkish President Suleyman Demirel estimated that the sanctions against Iraq had cost Turkey up to $5 billion in direct and indirect losses.[41] Three years later this figure had risen to almost $30 billion. Turkey thus began to encourage the Iraqi Kurds to reach an understanding with Saddam so that trade could resume. Islamic Iraq, argued the Turks, had been punished enough, especially since the Christian Armenians and Bosnian Serbs (until 1995 at least) had gone unpunished for similar acts of aggression. At a minimum, some way ought to be found to reopen the lucrative oil pipeline to bring crude from Kirkuk in Iraq to Yumurtalik on Turkey's Mediterranean coast. Repeated attempts to accomplish this finally seemed successful in the summer of

1996 when United Nations Security Council Resolution 986 permitted Iraq to sell up to $2 billion in oil every six months to pay for humanitarian supplies. This permission was temporarily withdrawn, however, when Saddam entered the Iraqi Kurdish civil war by taking Irbil at the end of August 1996. Once again Turkey seemingly would have to pay the price for Saddam's misdeeds as the oil pipeline remained closed. In December 1996, however, the pipeline was finally opened under the provisions of the UN resolution. In addition, Turkey was supposed to begin receiving money from the UN compensations committee established to distribute 30 percent of the revenue Iraq earned from the sales.

For their part, the Iraqi Kurds long felt dependent on Turkey. Hoshyar Zebari, a member of the politburo responsible for foreign policy in Barzani's KDP, explained: "Turkey is our lifeline to the West and the whole world in our fight against Saddam Husayn. We are able to secure allied air protection and international aid through Turkey's cooperation. If Poised Hammer is withdrawn, Saddam's units will again reign in this region and we will lose everything."[42]

When he journeyed to Turkey in late 1991, Talabani—the leader of the other major Iraqi Kurdish party, the PUK—concluded that "Turkey must be considered a country friendly to the Kurds."[43] By the time he met with Demirel in June 1992, the Turkish prime minister was referring to the PUK leader as "my dear brother Talabani,"[44] while the Iraqi Kurdish leader declared that "the people in northern Iraq will never forget the help of the Turkish Government and people in their difficult days." Talabani even went so far as to suggest that the Iraqi Kurds might want to be annexed by Turkey.[45] As will be explained fully in Chapter 5, however, Turkish relations with Talabani began to cool soon afterwards because of his apparent support for the PKK.

The civil war that broke out between Barzani's KDP and Talabani's PUK in May 1994 shattered the unity of the de facto Iraqi Kurdish state and plunged it into increasing anarchy. In August 1996, after Talabani began receiving aid from Iran, an increasingly desperate Barzani shocked many by allying with Saddam to oust Talabani from Irbil and most of his other strongholds in Iraqi Kurdistan. Since Turkey had long been encouraging the Iraqi Kurds to reach an understanding with Saddam, this alliance presumably met with some approval in Ankara. In addition, Barzani's alliance with Saddam and apparent victory over Talabani called into question the rationale for continuing OPC, a situation Turkey seemingly would also favor. Iran's support for Talabani, however, could not have pleased the Turks, especially coming as it did just after Turkey's new Islamist government had reached a lucrative deal for natural gas with Tehran.

By mid-October 1996, however, Talabani had regained most of the territory he had lost the previous month, and the situation seemed to have returned to where it had been the previous summer. At the end of 1996, the Turkish

Parliament renewed for another six months the mandate for a scaled-down OPC renamed the Surveillance Force or the Northern Watch. The renamed operation continued to enforce the no-fly zone over northern Iraq, but the French no longer participated in it and the relief role in northern Iraq was terminated.

## WESTERN EUROPE

In recent years a Kurdish diaspora of some 600,000 has formed in western Europe due to a variety of political, economic, and sociological factors.[46] Of the estimated 1.8 million citizens of Turkey living in Germany, at least 400,000-450,000 are believed to be Kurds. By 1993, maybe 40,000 of these Kurds in Germany could be regarded as PKK sympathizers, while activists numbered some 4,800.[47] In addition, some 200,000 Turkish Kurds lived elsewhere in western Europe, including Scandinavia, the Benelux states, and Britain. In France, where the wife of the late President Francois Mitterrand had long supported the Kurdish cause, there were about 60,000 Kurds and 400,000 Turks.

Clearly, the potential numbers were present to export the Kurdish factor in Turkish foreign policy to western Europe. Indeed, Turkish sources had long complained that "various extremist organizations and the PKK have used European territory as their play-ground, recruiting new militants, establishing liaison with the East Bloc, transferring militants to Turkey, etc."[48] Prophetically, Siyamend Othman, an official at the time in the Kurdish Institute in Paris, wrote in March 1987: "It is my personal opinion (and fear too) that this [traditional Kurdish quiescence] might not remain the case for much longer since the interviews I have conducted with the leaders and cadres of Kurdish organizations incline me to think that the Kurds, particularly those of Turkey, are beginning to get desperate for attention."[49]

As far back as June 1987, the West German Interior Ministry issued a report which stated: "The orthodox communist Kurdish Workers' Party (PKK) was in 1986 by far the most active and most militant extremist organization among the Kurds."[50] The report added that in a publication in West Germany the previous year, the PKK had referred to itself as "the force that has taken up the struggle against the fascist Turkish occupation" and declared that it was committed to "revolutionary violence" in pursuing its goals.

Six months later, the Federal Criminal Office in Wiesbaden called the PKK "a dangerous organization" and declared that in West Germany during the previous year (1987) it had been "involved with carrying out at least one murder, two attempted murders, three cases of assault, and four other serious incidents, including robbery, blackmail and coercion." The office also stated that there were at least 1,000 Kurdish extremists in West Germany trying to overthrow the Turkish government. "Although their primary targets are the Turkish government and fellow Turks [Kurds], West German citizens and institutions who cooperate with the Turkish government . . . are also in danger."

By the late 1980s, the PKK was publishing a sophisticated review in Cologne, West Germany, called *Serxwebun* (Independence), while the ERNK was producing another one in Dusseldorf called *Berxwedan* (Defense). During the early 1990s, these activities grew to include more than thirty related organizations in Germany alone, including Kurd-A, a Kurdish news agency operating out of Dusseldorf, and in May 1995, MED-TV, a PKK-affiliated television station broadcasting out of Britain and Belgium back to the Middle East.

The Kurdish factor has presented further difficulties for Turkish foreign policy in its relations with Germany and western Europe. It offered, for example, one of a number of pretexts for the European Community to put off consideration of the Turkish application for full membership in 1987.[51] It also led to a German arms embargo against Turkey for two months following the *Newroz* (Kurdish New Year) fighting in March 1992 and allegations that weapons provided by Germany had been used against the civilian population in southeastern Turkey.

As noted in Chapter 3, a tremendous increase in fighting occurred in southeastern Turkey during the summer of 1993. Mirroring this situation, a totally unprecedented outbreak of PKK-led violence also struck western Europe on June 24 and again on November 4 of that year. The situation has remained volatile ever since.

In the June 1993 instance, Kurds attacked Turkish consulates, banks, airlines offices, and travel agencies in some 20 different cities in Germany, France, Sweden, Switzerland, Britain, and Denmark. Even better-coordinated and more violent attacks occurred during the November round of violence when Kurdish militants smashed and burned Turkish consulates and businesses in Germany, Switzerland, Austria, Britain, France, and Denmark.

The European attacks in June led to what one Turkish source called (with, at the time, understandable exaggeration) "the worst diplomatic problem Ankara has ever faced."[52] The crisis began when a group of Kurdish demonstrators attempted to enter the Turkish embassy in Bern, Switzerland. Apparently overreacting, staff from the embassy fired on the demonstrators, killing one and wounding nine others. The Turkish Ambassador, Kaya Toperi, was initially quoted as declaring that the Turkish guards had simply fired into the air to ward off a crowd of hundreds that the Swiss authorities were slow in responding to.

The Swiss, however, claimed they had reacted promptly to the threat. The demonstrators had numbered only about 30, and they were armed just with stones. What is more, Toperi himself was accused of waving a gun, if not actually using it, while the gunshots had not been fired merely into the air—indeed they had continued after the Swiss authorities had arrived.

Given their version of the events, the Swiss announced that they "could not tolerate random gunshots being fired at people from a foreign embassy, even if they were taking part in an unauthorized demonstration"[53] and demanded that the diplomatic immunity of four Turkish embassy staff be waived so they could be charged with causing grievous bodily harm, endangering life, and accidental homicide.

The Turks refused to comply, arguing that the Swiss had not taken adequate security measures to protect the embassy from a terrorist organization operating within their borders, as international law obligated them. If they had, the incident would not have occurred in the first place. To the Turkish public in general, the Swiss position amounted to an open expression of support for the PKK—which had organized the attacks throughout Europe, including the demonstration in front of the embassy in Bern—and a denial of the right of the Turks to defend themselves.

After a furious row that lasted for over a month, the incident closed with both states expelling each other's ambassador. As one perceptive Turkish source noted, however, "the prospect of Ankara coming under pressure to relinquish the diplomatic immunity of its diplomats in Switzerland . . . was not a pleasant one. As things stand, enough harm has been done to Turkey's image."[54]

The European reaction to the November 1993 PKK violence proved much more favorable from the Turkish point of view. By the end of the month, both Germany and France—hosts to the two largest concentrations of Kurdish emigres in western Europe—had taken the potentially momentous step of banning the PKK and many of its front organizations.

German Interior Minister Manfred Kanther declared that "foreign extremism must be fought with determination. Germany must not become a battlefield for foreign terrorists."[55] The ban also applied to 35 PKK fronts, including such important ones as the ERNK and the Kurdish news agency Kurd-Ha. Immediately, German police raided Kurdish centers across the country, seizing documents and equipment and taking control of bank accounts and post office boxes. At the Kurdistan Committee headquarters in Cologne, the authorities removed desks, files, closets, wastepaper baskets, and even the venetian blinds.

In France, the government banned two PKK fronts, the *Comite du Kurdistan* (Kurdistan Committee) and the *Federation des Associations Culturelles et des Travaileurs Patriotes du Kurdistan en France* (Federation of Kurdistan Cultural Associations and Patriotic Workers). French Interior Minister Charles Pasqua declared that "these associations are the legal front of the PKK, which in France as in other European countries carries out terrorist or criminal actions which we cannot tolerate on our territory."[56] Pasqua added that the banning followed earlier arrests that month of 101 suspected Kurdish supporters of the PKK, 24 of whom were charged with terrorist conspiracy and extorting money from Kurdish businesses in France.

The German and French actions led to initial "rejoicing"[57] in Ankara, and a Turkish diplomat in Brussels described the situation as "a major breakthrough."[58] However, although other west European states declared that they would punish violations of their laws, none followed the German and French examples. On the contrary, Belgium and Turkey exchanged harsh words after Turkish immigrants staged violent anti-Kurdish protests in Brussels at the beginning of 1994. The Turks were responding to a pro-PKK "freedom march" from Germany into the Turkish quarter of the Belgian capital. Belgian Interior Minister Louis Tobback blamed the Turkish ultra-nationalist Gray Wolves for instigating the violence, warned them "not to export this dirty war to Belgian territory," and expressed "understanding for the Kurdish drive for autonomy from Turkey."[59]

In reaction to the bans, thousands of Kurdish protesters demonstrated in Germany and France during December 1993. In Paris, they carried banners reading "If the PKK is banned, we all belong to the PKK,"[60] while in such German cities as Cologne, Frankfurt, Bonn, Hanover, and Berlin, they occupied cultural centers and social clubs that the police had closed, eventually forcing them to be reopened. In France, Ali Sapan, the European spokesman for the ERNK, threatened that "now Germany and German interests are going to attract the Kurdish people's anger,"[61] while the Kurdistan Committee in France warned that French and German interests could be harmed.[62]

Earlier, Germany's domestic intelligence agency, the Office for the Protection of the Constitution (BfV), had already noted in its annual report that some PKK publications had referred to Germany as "enemy number two" for supplying weapons to Turkey that then were used against the Kurds.[63] Given German Interior Minister Kanther's doubts about the legality of such a widespread ban, and the possibility of uncovering the numerous other shadowy groups around the PKK,[64] one wondered what the long-term effect of the ban would actually be.

Kanther's apprehensions were not misplaced. During *Newroz* celebrations in March 1994, militant Kurds blockaded German roads and fought with police. March 1995 saw firebombings in dozens of German cities against Turkish businesses, travel agencies, homes, mosques, and meeting centers. The attacks coincided with Turkey's massive invasion of northern Iraq and had occurred despite Germany's not implementing its earlier decision to deport Kurds found guilty of acts of violence back to Turkey. Kanther said the attacks "bear the signature" of the PKK,[65] while Foreign Minister Klaus Kinkel told a meeting of his colleagues in the European Union that "the Kurds are acting in a way that we cannot accept."[66]

In the summer of 1995, a hunger strike by some 170 Kurdish men and women in Germany sparked more violent clashes between police and Kurdish protesters. Turkish businesses continued to be targets for firebomb attacks as estimates of the over-all damage rose to several billion dollars.[67] The war between Turkey and the PKK had opened a "second front,"[68] and the PKK, according to the Office for the Protection of the Constitution in Lower Saxony, even threatened to attack German police and property.[69]

Clearly the German ban against the PKK was not working. Indeed, authorities estimated that by the summer of 1996 the number of PKK activists had grown to 8,300, while the number of sympathizers had increased to 50,000.[70] Undercover leaders, using code names and changing their jobs every few months, made police surveillance almost impossible. To facilitate its activities, the PKK had even divided Germany into five operational regions split into 17 separate areas. If anything, Germany's policies against the PKK had helped drive moderate Kurds into the PKK fold. Mustafa Kisabacak, for example, the chairman of Germany's moderate *Komkar* Kurdish association, declared that the Kurds "feel cheated by the German government's policies which see an arsonist in every immigrant Kurd, and which send weapons for Turkey's dirty war."

During October 1995, Heinrich Lummer, a member of Chancellor Helmut Kohl's Christian Democratic Party (CDU) and former senator, journeyed to Damascus to talk with Ocalan about the situation. Shortly afterwards, Germany dispatched a high-ranking intelligence advisor from the BfV to meet with Ocalan. Although the PKK leader admitted that he made "mistakes"[71] and regretted that "our actions have caused problems to the German legal system," he pointed out that "Germany is giving a lot of weapons to Turkey for free." He argued that "a German Government that supports the Turkish Army and the secret service is, of course, a threat to us," and maintained that "we have a right to ask why there is such a great deal of German support for Turkey." Disingenuously, he asserted that the firebombings in Germany were provocations by the Turkish MIT "to harm the PKK," and he claimed that "the Turkish secret service has staged a drugs conspiracy against the PKK. In fact, it is Turkish right-wing extremists who are the drug mafia." He concluded his remarks by asserting that "the Germans have not kept the promises that they gave me," a point he reiterated a few months later: "Germany has taken a negative stand against the PKK. . . . If Germany is insistent on these issues, it might be faced with an extreme Kurdish reaction."[72]

Further PKK-inspired violence indeed continued in Germany during the spring of 1996, climaxing in reputed death threats against German Chancellor

Kohl and Foreign Minister Kinkel.[73] Ocalan, however, denied that threats had been made, and he explained that he had simply meant German economic interests in Turkey could be targeted. He also admitted that he had not had as much control over the situation as he wanted. Despite Ocalan's concessions, as noted in the previous chapter, Germany joined a European-wide crackdown against the PKK and its various fronts in September 1996.

Despite continuing Turkish claims that Europe was still not doing enough, with the partial exception of Germany, one would conclude that the bigger European states such as Britain, France, and Italy have been less likely to allow the Kurdish factor to influence negatively their relations with Turkey because of their mutually important economic and security interests. Smaller states such as Belgium, Denmark, the Netherlands, and Switzerland, on the other hand, whose relations with Turkey are less important, have found it easier to take the high moral ground on the Kurdish issue.[74]

## OTHERS

### The United States

Since the days of the Truman Doctrine in the 1940s and Turkey's adhesion to the NATO alliance in the 1950s, the United States has been Turkey's main ally. Illustrative of this close relation, a study by the U.S. Department of Commerce in 1995 found that the United States supplied Turkey with 80 percent of its foreign military hardware.[75] Of all its Western allies, the United States proved most understanding of Turkey's invasion of northern Iraq in the spring of 1995. General John M. Shalikashvili, the chairman of the U.S. Joint Chiefs of Staff, declared in the summer of 1995 that the Turkish military was "moving forward with new measures aimed at enhancing Turkish democracy and human rights,"[76] and he reminded the U.S. Congress of the crucial role played by Turkey as a U.S. ally in NATO, Korea, the Gulf War and OPC, and Somalia.

Such aid and support for Turkey has not gone unnoticed by the PKK. In the summer of 1994, for example, Kani Yilmaz, a leading PKK official, ranked the United States alongside Germany as "the most negative and reactionary country as regards the Kurdish problem."[77] A year later, Ocalan lashed out at the United States for concocting "unfair and distorted views for the international public about our party."[78] By claiming that the PKK was "the principal representative of international terrorism," the United States had manifested an "enormously unfair assessment" that "could only be an imperialistic view." The following year, Ocalan declared that "the United States has won the enmity of the Kurds through the support it extended to Turkey"[79] while criticizing it for arresting his "friend" (representative) in the United States, Kani Xulam, on passport charges.

Nevertheless, the Kurdish issue has created problems between the two allies, as witnessed in the annual outrage in Turkey at the U.S. State Department's Country Reports that criticize Turkey for its human rights violations concerning the Kurds. In recent years, the U.S. Helsinki Commission—an independent government agency established to monitor the implementation of the human rights standards listed in the Final Act of the Helsinki Conference on Security and Cooperation held in 1975 and its subsequent initiatives—also has served as a platform for public and private criticism of Turkey's Kurdish policy by sponsoring hearings and distributing information. In 1996, for example, the Helsinki Commission sent a "Dear Colleague" letter to U.S. Congressmen asking their support for House Congressional Resolution 136 which, among other things, requested that Turkey declare a cease-fire, allow Kurdish-language schools, radios, and television, and repeal the state of emergency in the southeast. Although only 25 of the needed majority of 218 signed the measure, Turkey did not appreciate what it felt was undue interference in its domestic affairs.

Rep. John Porter (R-IL) and his wife, Kathryn, have lashed out at Turkey's policy toward the Kurds at every opportunity. As chair of the Congressional Human Rights Caucus, Porter has played an instrumental role in trying to cut the annual military aid the United States supplies Turkey. Kathryn Porter claimed she was tailed by Turkish agents when she visited Turkey in 1994 to monitor the trial of some Kurdish lawyers accused of separatism. Although the Porters' efforts usually have been canceled out by the U.S. executive and the plenary congress, they still cause ill will and misunderstanding for the United States in Turkey.

Moreover, in November 1996, angered by the delays and attached conditions, Turkey finally did cancel its $150 million order for ten U.S. super cobra helicopter gunships. Human rights advocates had successfully stalled the sale for more than a year by claiming that the helicopters could be used in southeastern Turkey against the Kurds. The Turks also expressed dismay over delays caused by pro-Greek lobbies in the delivery of three U.S. Perry-class frigates for which they had already paid. Such actions recalled the U.S. arms embargo against Turkey in the 1970s over the Cyprus issue and the still-continuing pro-Armenian resolutions in the U.S. Congress that also berated Turkey.

Given the widespread sympathy in the United States for the plight of the Kurds, and the resulting Turkish conspiracy theories concerning foreign intentions toward Turkey, such Turkish politicians as Necmettin Erbakan and Bulent Ecevit have made something of a career in recent years of criticizing the U.S.-sponsored OPC. The fear is that OPC is tantamount to an invading force, with the secret aim of establishing an independent Kurdish state in northern Iraq that will then make territorial claims on Turkey's southeastern provinces. Some even claimed that OPC had dropped supplies to the PKK or helped PKK wounded,[80] an assertion given partial credence by accidental drops that had fallen into PKK hands.

In October 1996, a U.S. court furthered these Turkish-American misunderstandings, when it declined to expel Kurdish activist Kani Xulam on passport fraud charges, instead sentencing him to 400 hours of community service with the very PKK-associated office he had been heading in Washington, D.C. Clearly, despite the United States being a staunch ally and friend of Turkey, the Kurdish issue has created problems in their normally close relations.

## Armenia

In speculating on a possible Armenian-PKK link, a "high-ranking Turkish intelligence officer" was recently quoted as stating that it would be "naive" not "to assume that the Armenians, as traditional and bitter enemies of the Turks, would waste an opportunity to help other enemies of the Turks."[81] Unconfirmed reports in 1993 concerning PKK camps in Armenia and military training provided by the Armenians to the PKK did claim that there were at least six PKK camps in Armenia.[82] Three of them were near the Turkish border between the villages of Okcuoglu and Gullubudak in Leninakan province, one was three kilometers away from the town of Mazdaian, another two kilometers from the town of Mislis, and the sixth near the town of Colga.

In addition to the revenge factor, others have argued that the Armenians are cooperating with the PKK as a way to block a possible oil pipeline between Azerbaijan and Turkey.[83] In 1993, Armenian forces did occupy large areas of Azerbaijan bordering on the Arax River with Iran, through which such a pipeline would have run. During the same year, Turkish officials produced as evidence of Armenian support for the PKK the claim that some of the guerrillas they had killed on the mountains were uncircumcised.[84] They also claimed that the PKK had at that time one camp in Armenia which it used to train guerrillas and then infiltrate them into Turkey. In addition, the Turks asserted that the Armenian Writers Union had given Ocalan an award for the books he had written on popular and guerrilla war.

Another report declared that Osman Ocalan, the brother of the PKK leader Abdullah Ocalan, had visited Yerevan in September 1992 and asked Armenian officials to provide a camp for the PKK in Armenia.[85] Reportedly, this was the second such visit by PKK officials. The Armenians, however, turned the PKK request down, while Armenian President Levon Ter-Petrosyan declined even to meet with the visitors. Indeed, the PKK delegation was reported to have been invited by the discredited, right-wing Dashnak Party opposition, which had a history of attempting to cooperate with Kurds rebelling against Turkey that went back at least to the 1920s.

Allegedly, Abdullah Ocalan himself visited Armenia in April 1993 at the invitation of the Dashnaks to discuss the possibility of the PKK being permitted to establish a camp in the Lachin region of Azerbaijan currently occupied by the Armenians.[86] Ocalan supposedly sought such a safehouse because of the recent pressures by Turkey on Syria and Iran to end their support for him. It is almost certain, however, that Ocalan actually did not visit Armenia. Furthermore, since the report cited here did not make it clear whether or not a camp site was specifically permitted, given the unsettled conditions in this war-torn area of Azerbaijan, and the fact that it was the opposition Dashnaks, not the Armenian government itself, that supposedly had tendered the invitation for Ocalan to visit—it is difficult to conclude from this report that the Armenian government is supporting the PKK.

Casting further aspersions on the reputed Armenian-PKK link was the ludicrous claim by Turkish Minister of the Interior Mehmet Gazioglu that "the PKK is an Armenian organization," and Ocalan himself "an Armenian,"[87] an assertion also made by the longtime Turkish ultra-nationalist leader Alpaslan Turkes who, as mentioned in Chapter 2, once declared that Ocalan was an Armenian whose real name was "Agop Agopian."[88] General Dogan Gures, the chief of the Turkish general staff, even claimed that the Armenian church was behind the PKK,[89] declaring that the PKK "are telling people that 'there used to be churches here when our ancestors were here.' This makes it clear with whom they are in cahoots. . . . These are savages; these are infidels."

Similarly, another report maintained that the PKK had received funds and arms from Armenia through Armenian priests in Lebanon.[90] As "proof" of this assertion, photographs were said to exist showing Ocalan meeting with some Armenian priests at his sanctuary in Barr Ilyas in the Bekaa valley. The same account also asserted that Armenians made up one-third of the PKK's mountain forces, a patently impossible situation, supposedly confirmed by the many uncircumcised guerrillas killed by the Turks. Yet another allegation was that ASALA, the Armenian terrorist organization that had ceased operations a decade earlier due to internal strife within its own ranks, was cooperating with the PKK.[91] More than ten PKK camps were said to have been established in Armenia.

In assessing such wild claims, the objective scholar must agree with the pro-Kurdish publication in Turkey *Ozgur Gundem* that: "By trying to depict the PKK as an Armenian organization, the Turkish Republic is trying to provoke the chauvinistic feelings of the Turkish people and instigate the anti-Armenian feelings that exist in the . . . people, thus redirecting these feelings against the PKK."[92] Interestingly, however, *Ozgur Gundem* admitted that the PKK does maintain transnational contacts: "the participation of internationalist fighters of various nationalities in the PKK is not a weakness. . . . Our brothers from Turkish, Arab,

Persian, Armenian, Azerbaijani, German, Circassian, and other peoples, who are fighting side by side with the Kurds, are living examples of the international character of our national liberation struggle."[93] A report more credible than some of those cited earlier did indicate that as a result of the Turkish invasion of northern Iraq in March 1995, some PKK forces had fled through Iran into Armenia.[94] From there they were beginning to infiltrate into Turkey.

## Greece

The Turkish-Greek enmity may be just as great as the Turkish-Armenian enmity and has existed for much longer. Even today Greeks lament the loss of their polis "Constantinople" to the Turks in 1453. In modern times, both peoples won their wars of independence against each other, the Greeks in the 1820s, and the Turks a century later when they rolled back the *Megali* Idea of a greater Greece. Today their problems continue due to a number of reasons: (1) the Aegean continental shelf, (2) the Greek decision to regard the Aegean flight information region as the border between the two states, (3) Greece's insistence on claiming a territorial sea of twelve miles for each of its Aegean islands, a situation that would largely turn the Aegean into a Greek sea, (4) Greece's arming of the eastern Aegean islands, (5) the Turkish minority in Thrace and the Greek minority in Istanbul, (6) Cyprus, and most recently (7) the Kardak (Imia) rocks off the coast of Turkey.[95] As Ocalan told a Greek journalist: "We love the Greeks. We are together because of the common [Turkish] enemy."[96]

In a front-cover article on foreign support for the PKK, *Nokta,* a leading Turkish weekly, recently cited "a high-ranking Foreign Ministry official, who wished to remain anonymous," as claiming that "Greek aid to the PKK amounted to $1 billion over 12 years."[97] Retired Greek Lt. General Dimitris Matafias and retired Greek Navy Admiral Antonis Neksasis had visited the PKK's Mahsun Korkmaz base camp in the Bekaa valley in October 1988 along with parliamentarians from the Panhellenic Socialist Movement (PASOK). At that time it was reported that Matafias assumed responsibility for training some of the PKK guerrillas. The Greeks also had dispatched arms to the PKK through the Greek Cypriot administration.

In the summer of 1993, the Turkish scholar and subsequent foreign minister Mumtaz Soysal claimed that it was "common knowledge" that "the terrorist PKK established itself in south Cyprus many years ago . . . [and] that the Greek Cypriot side has provided funds and arms to that organization and allowed it to establish small camps for training."[98] Mumtaz went on to allege that "Greece has allocated at least $10 million to the PKK every year," and that "the Greek Cypriot side has allowed 700 PKK militants to be based in south Cyprus." He also asserted that "travelers from Athens to Lavrion [a town on the coast in central Greece hosting a Kurdish refugee camp] will notice a road sign which says: 'To the PKK Camp.'" Giving voice to a popular Turkish belief, Mumtaz concluded by noting that Armenian terrorism and the Kurdish movement against Turkey only began in 1974, after Turkey occupied northern Cyprus. The implication, of course, was that Greece and the Greek Cypriots helped start these two anti-Turkish movements in revenge.

In 1993, a lengthy file of 25 items concerning Greek support for the PKK was supposedly submitted to then–Turkish Prime Minister Tansu Ciller.[99] This file claimed that Greece was paying a monthly salary of 30,000 drachmas (some $900) to the PKK's ERNK front members, had previously paid $10 million to them under former foreign minister Andonios Samaras, and also had supplied Aris antitank missiles and other types of arms and explosives to them. Further allegations included: (1) PKK members and retired officers in the Greek secret service drew up a plan in 1992 to sabotage tourism in Turkey, which plan they put into effect in 1993; (2) three PASOK deputies appeared on Channel 19 calling for support for the PKK against Turkey, which they called the "common enemy"; (3) a refugee camp at Lavrion was given to the PKK; (4) an account numbered 129/62639077 was opened for PKK members in Lavrion at the Greek National Bank branch; (5) the PKK operated a radio station in Greece known as "Voice of Kurdistan" (*Foni tou Kurdistan*); (6) the Greek Ministry of Foreign Affairs provided scholarships for 33 PKK members in Greece; and (7) one of Prime Minister Papandreou's advisers, Mikhalis Kharalambidhis, (who worked for the Greek national intelligence organization and was a member of the PASOK central committee) met with Ocalan in the Bekaa valley and promised him that a maritime agency would be established in Athens to facilitate the PKK's arms trade, that an import-export company would be established as a cover, and that forged passports would be supplied, among other things.

In December 1993, Greek European Affairs Minister Theodore Pangalos was quoted as saying that "we must be supportive of the Kurdish people's struggle to be free," and that "Greek foreign policy must be a direct opposition to Turkish aggression and the horrible violation of human rights exercised by the Turkish government on the Turkish population and the Kurds."[100] Greek Prime Minister Andreas Papandreou declined to join Germany and France in moving against the PKK when those two west European states banned the Kurdish militants in late November 1993. Indeed, a German source claimed that Greek objections prevented the European Union from announcing a joint ban on the PKK when the other eleven members of the community were on the verge of doing so.[101]

In the succeeding years, similar reports continued to appear in the Turkish press concerning both Greece and the Greek Cypriots. In the summer of 1995, for example, it was asserted that the deputy speaker of the Greek parliament, Panayiotis Skouridhis, had held talks with Ocalan in Syria and presented him with the Greek state award, the Shield of Macedonia.[102] Apostolos Kaklamais, the speaker of the Greek parliament, supposedly had sent a note professing support for the PKK. Other reports claimed that PKK agents trained in Greece had infiltrated into Turkey to bomb economic and tourist sites.[103] Based on the above evidence, however, it would seem that Greek and Greek Cypriot support for the PKK, as distinguished from sympathy, is marginal. Compared to such states as Syria, it has been insignificant.

## Russia

Russia and Turkey have been enemies for centuries. Until its collapse in 1991, the Soviet Union was considered by some the main support behind the PKK.[104] Despite such speculation, the intensity of the PKK's insurgency did not decline subsequent to the Soviets' demise, but, as noted above, it escalated tremendously. Obviously the Soviets were not the main instigator some believed. Indeed, during the final years of the Soviet Union economic relations between it and Turkey grew considerably largely because of Ozal's economic liberalization policies. This cooperation has continued between Russia and Turkey in the 1990s.

In the immediate post-Soviet era, the main competition between Russia and Turkey has been over the new Turkic states in central Asia and the Caucasus, their oil, and Russia's failure to implement the Conventional Forces Reduction Agreement (CFRA), under which it had agreed to reduce its forces on NATO's northern and southern flanks. The Kurdish issue was a useful card for the Russians to play in this game, particularly to counter the Turks' interest in such sensitive Russian domestic issues as Chechnya. Accordingly, the Russians permitted the PKK to stage conferences in Moscow in February, September, and October 1994[105] and, as noted in Chapter 2, hold a session of the Kurdistan Parliament-in-Exile there at the end of October 1995. After the first PKK conference, the Turks sent a special envoy to conduct talks with Russian officials and voiced their dissatisfaction. Following the second conference on September 24, 1994, which brought together some 85 representatives claiming to speak for more than 10,000 Kurds in the former east bloc states, the Turks displayed even more dismay.

The third conference met for three days at the end of October 1994 and brought together 80 delegates representing 35 Kurdish organizations. It was entirely financed by the PKK. Ocalan sent it a message, and his portrait was displayed in the conference hall. Yuri Nebiev, a Kurd from the Lachin area of Azerbaijan, was elected to head the "Kurdish Union" formed at the meeting's end. He declared that the PKK was "the leader of the Kurdish national liberation movement" and "the nucleus of our future national state." The conference also decided to establish a Kurdish university in Moscow, as well as Kurdish-language schools and cultural centers in various parts of the Commonwealth of Independent States (CIS).

On December 25, 1994, at least 150 Kurds sympathetic to the PKK, as well as some Russians including Li Olega, the president of the Congress of Russian Minorities, were present at the opening of a new "Kurdish House" in Moscow. It replaced a smaller House that had been opened in Moscow three months earlier. The new House's 680 square meters allowed it to host the Kurdish Committee, Kurdish Association, Kurdish Cultural Center, Kurdish Press Center, and Confederation of Kurds living in the CIS. All were affiliated to the PKK. The building was draped by flags of the PKK, ERNK, and ARGK. A large portrait of Ocalan and the pictures of some 80 PKK martyrs killed in the insurgency were also displayed.

Turkish Interior Minister Nahit Mentese and several high-ranking national security officials hurried to Moscow the following month in an effort at damage control.[106] The two sides signed a "Protocol to Prevent Terrorism," and the Russians promised that the PKK would "not be a legal organization in Russia." In late February 1995, the Russians sent two important intelligence officials to Ankara: Yevgeny Primakov, head of the foreign intelligence service and subsequently foreign minister, and Sergei Stepashin, head of the counter-intelligence service. Russia promised not to permit the PKK to establish itself in its territory in return for Turkish support for Russian policies in Chechnya. The subsequent intensification of the war in Chechnya and Turkish protests on behalf of their Turkic co-religionists there, however, prevented the two sides from implementing their agreements. Although the meeting of the Kurdistan Parliament-in-Exile was not officially recognized by the Yeltsin government, the entire matter showed how Turkish foreign policy with Russia had become hostage to its Kurdish problem.

## CONCLUSIONS

Although it has been and will continue to be concerned with a host of factors exogenous to the Kurdish issue, it is the main contention of this chapter that over the years Turkish foreign policy has been surprisingly influenced by the Kurdish factor in many different ways. The ending of the Cold War can only be expected to increase the influence of this Kurdish factor, as the Soviet threat that long dominated Turkish foreign policy concerns has disappeared and a host of national and irredentist claims have arisen. The Kurdish issue is one of the chief examples.

The Kurdish factor has not only been playing an important role in Turkish foreign policy toward its immediate Middle Eastern neighbors, but has also influenced relations with western Europe. During 1995, it came close to blocking Turkish admission into the European Customs Union, a major foreign policy and economic goal of Turkey. To win eventual approval, Turkey had to countenance foreign pressures to liberalize and change its laws and constitution on matters relating to human rights and the Kurdish issue. The Kurdish factor has also curtailed Turkey's ability to play a stronger role in the Balkans crisis unfolding on its western door, as well as restricting severely the opportunity to make gains in the Caucasus and central Asia by taking advantage of Russia's problems in Chechnya.

Even foreign policy issues involving the United States have come under the influence of the Kurdish factor, as witnessed in the annual outrage in Turkey at the U.S. State Department's yearly Country Reports that criticize Turkey for its human rights violations concerning the Kurds. Recently, problems concerning Operation Provide Comfort have also involved the Kurdish factor in U.S.-Turkish relations. Given the increasing strength of the Kurdish movement in Turkey as well as elsewhere, the Kurdish factor can be expected to become even more important in Turkish foreign policy in the coming months and years.

# 5

# The PKK and the Iraqi Kurds

At first glance it might be expected that, given the oft-quoted maxim "The Kurds have no friends," the various Kurdish groups, at least, would be natural allies. A brief survey of the numerous and at times bitter divisions in Kurdish society, however, would quickly disabuse one of this notion.[1] Since 1994, for example, the two main Iraqi Kurdish parties, Massoud Barzani's Kurdistan Democratic Party (KDP)[2] and Jalal Talabani's Patriotic Union of Kurdistan (PUK)[3], have been locked in an on-again, off-again struggle that has cost some 3,000 lives, while bringing chaos and ruin to much of their domain. In addition, of course, the divide-and-rule strategies of the neighboring states containing Kurdish populations have reinforced these differences.

On August 26, 1995, yet another dimension of this Kurdish divide erupted. With the tacit cooperation of Syria, Iran, and the PUK, the PKK was able to mass up to 2,500 fighters and suddenly attack some 20 KDP bases and offices in the KDP's Bahdinani homeland in northern Iraq. Sporadic but bitter fighting led to hundreds of deaths during the fall of 1995, until the PKK finally declared a cease-fire early in December 1995. The purpose of this chapter is to analyze the checkered and often obscure relationship between the PKK and the Iraqi Kurdish parties that has led to the present situation. In so doing, further light will be thrown upon yet another element concerning the Kurdish problem in Turkey.

## EARLIER ALLIANCES

Ironically, the PKK and KDP were once allies. In July 1983, the two signed an accord termed "Principles of Solidarity," under which they each agreed upon a unified commitment against "every kind of imperialism, with American imperialism at the top of the list, and the struggle against the plans and plots of imperialism in the region."[4] The two also committed themselves to "cooperating with other revolutionary forces in the region and the creation of new alliances."

Another provision of their protocol emphasized that the struggle "should depend on the force of the Kurdish people." Article 10 of the agreement stated that neither party should interfere in the internal affairs of the other or commit actions that could damage the other. The eleventh and final article declared that if one of them made a mistake in implementing their alliance and ignored a warning from the other, then the alliance could be terminated.

At first the accord worked well for both parties. PKK militants being trained in Syrian and Lebanese camps were slowly moved to northern Iraq, where new camps were established. PKK leaders apparently traveled mostly through Tehran and then to northern Iraq, while the foot soldiers moved as armed groups from Syria over the Turkish border near Silopi and Cizre. From there they traveled on foot over the Silopi-Sirnak-Uludere path into northern Iraq.

Soon the Lolan camp, located in the triangle of land where Turkey, Iran, and Iraq meet, became the PKK's largest base in its newfound sanctuary. This camp also contained the PKK press and publications center, as well as the KDP's headquarters and clandestine radio stations. It was at this time in 1984 that Barzani and Ocalan actually met each other in Damascus for the first and apparently only time.[5]

Relations between the two groups began to cool in 1985, however, because of the PKK's violence against women and children and even members of the KDP itself, who were considered by the PKK as collaborators with Turkey. In May 1987, the KDP issued a warning to the PKK, as required under their accord of 1983. In this caveat, the KDP declared that "it is clear they [the PKK] have adopted an aggressive attitude towards the leadership of our party, towards its policies and the friends of our party."[6]

Barzani's KDP denounced what it termed "terrorist operations within the country and abroad and their actions to liquidate human beings. . . . The mentality behind such action is against humanity and democracy and is not in line with the national liberation of Kurdistan." Turkish pressures also played a role in ending the PKK-KDP alliance, which was severed completely by the end of 1987.

A little more than a year later, the other major Kurdish party in Iraq, Talabani's PUK, signed a "Protocol of Understanding" with the PKK in Damascus[7] that called for strengthening Kurdish unity and for cooperation and joint action by Kurdish groups. Talabani even threatened to give overt support to Ocalan if Turkey repeated its earlier military incursions into northern Iraq in search of PKK guerrillas hiding there.[8] Within a year, however, Ocalan declared the protocol with Talabani "null and void."[9]

## TURKEY'S ROLE

In May 1988, shortly after the KDP and PKK formally ended their alliance, the KDP and PUK officially announced the creation of the Iraqi Kurdistan Front

(IKF), made up of their two parties and at one time or another six other, smaller groups in Iraqi Kurdistan. As the results of the Gulf War in 1991 began to bring the Turks and Iraqi Kurds together, a situation analyzed in Chapter 4, the IKF declared on October 7, 1991, its intention to "combat the PKK."[10] Although the Turkish bombing of PKK camps in northern Iraq—which also killed some Iraqi Kurds—momentarily caused Barzani to consider rescinding this decision, the logic of the Turkish connection prevailed.

At regular intervals Turkey has renewed the mandate of the U.S.-supported Operation Provide Comfort (OPC), based in southeastern Turkey, to enforce the no-fly zone that protects the Iraqi Kurdish enclave from Saddam. Although by so doing Turkey has been supporting the emergence of an embryonic Iraqi Kurdish state that was anathema to its interests, abandoning the OPC would simply lead it to regroup elsewhere and thus strip Ankara of any influence over the course of events. Begrudgingly, therefore, Turkey continued to play its new role as part-time protector of the Iraqi Kurds.

For their part, the Iraqi Kurds felt dependent on Turkey. Given the catch-22, double economic blockade imposed on them by both the United Nations and Saddam, the Habur (Ibrahim al-Khalil) border crossing point with Turkey just north of Zakho was the only legal entry point for commerce and customs revenues, which amounted to approximately $150,000 per day. Hoshyar Zebari, a foreign policy spokesman for the KDP, explained: "Turkey is our lifeline to the West and the whole world in our fight against Saddam Husayn. We are able to secure allied air protection and international aid through Turkey's cooperation. If Poised Hammer [OPC] is withdrawn, Saddam's units will again reign in this region and we will lose everything."[11] As noted in Chapter 4, Talabani concluded that "Turkey must be considered a country friendly to the [Iraqi] Kurds."[12] Given the PKK's longstanding struggle against Turkey, this pro-Turkish position of the Iraqi Kurds began to cause Ocalan increasing difficulties.

In October 1991, Talabani apparently made one last attempt to bring Ocalan around by arguing that the "PKK must respond positively to Turkish President Turgut Ozal's statement [on Kurdish rights] by halting its armed activities and by looking for a dialogue with the Turkish Government."[13] Late in November 1991, the PUK leader reported that the PKK had agreed to a four-month cease-fire so long as Turkey did not initiate any further hostilities: "Ocalan will not resort to armed activities until Nawroz [March 21]."[14]

The purported offer came after a month of direct contacts between the PKK and the Iraqi Kurds who, in effect, were acting for the Turks. One of the PKK negotiators was even quoted as declaring: "The PKK no longer pursues a claim of independence and does not want any further bloodshed."[15]

## PKK-IRAQI KURDISH POLEMICS

In the middle of December 1991, Ocalan reportedly crossed into northern Iraq from his safehouse in Syria to meet Talabani at his headquarters. Their meeting took place amid reports that Talabani's *peshmergas* (guerrillas) had arrested seven members of the PKK Central Committee. Although no statement was issued by the two Kurdish leaders, presumably they failed to come to an agreement. Shortly afterward, Ocalan sarcastically declared that Talabani had written him from Ankara to "lay down your arms unilaterally, accept a cease-fire, come to Ankara and sit at the table with obscure people, and be thankful and grateful for whatever you are given."[16] Defiantly, Ocalan declared: "I am allergic to such letters," adding that "if they try to make us collaborate, we will react with more fervor than they could muster to defend that policy." Talabani was then told "to forget about the 'new world order,' 'U.S. support,' and 'freedom to the Kurds' slogans" and instead "join the militarization and resistance effort" and "not act as a minor broker in dealing with the people." For Barzani, Ocalan had even worse remarks: "Barzani does the same job in a more pompous manner."[17] The KDP leader "had made very bad business dealings in Kurdish blood. His is the policy of a broker."

In February 1992, the IKF issued a warning to the PKK that "if it failed to cease activities against Turkey, it would be purged from the region."[18] Talabani declared that "his party does not approve of activities directed against Turkey by the terrorist organization active in southeastern Anatolia,"[19] while Barzani maintained that "the behavior of the . . . [PKK] has led to the ruin of the reputation of Kurds everywhere."[20] Barzani also denounced the PKK actions during *Newroz* in March 1992 as "savagery" and "terrorist."[21]

In return, Ocalan called Barzani a "collaborator . . . reactionary, feudal person and a primitive nationalist."[22] He accused both Barzani and Talabani "of trying to stab the PKK in the back by cooperating with Turkey" and noted that the two leaders "have signed their own death warrants."[23] The PKK leader added that "the first thing we must do is remove these leeches [because] . . . they espouse the views of the fascist Turks. These two leaders are now our enemies."

Ocalan went on to claim that he would challenge Barzani and Talabani both militarily and politically in northern Iraq and would isolate them.[24] Indeed, earlier Ocalan had already questioned the very support Barzani and Talabani had among their followers: "These organizations and leadership, which have little support among the people, are . . . a narrowly based clique."[25] Now the PKK leader claimed that his party had "a sister organization"[26] in northern Iraq, the Kurdistan Liberation Party (PAK), which would be able to challenge Barzani and Talabani on their own grounds.

## HOSTILITIES

Finally, in the summer of 1992, these intra-Kurdish diatribes began to break out into actual hostilities, following the killing of the Sindi tribal leader Sadik Omer in Zakho on June 29.[27] Reportedly, Omer had abandoned the KDP after having supported it for the previous 21 years and had become associated with the PAK, the new pro-PKK organization mentioned above. The PKK claimed that the assassination of Omer had been carried out by Sadun Mutni, the local KDP chief in Dohuk. In apparent retaliation, the PKK then killed KDP "Commander Mehmet Sefik" and three of his comrades in a rocket ambush in Dohuk.

In response, the KDP launched large attacks on the Sindi tribe that resulted in some civilians being taken hostage and others fleeing to the mountains. The KDP carried out further operations against the PKK's urban network in July, detaining "Tirej," a senior member of the PAK central committee, and blockading the PKK camps along the Turkish border.

On July 24, the PKK responded by successfully placing an embargo on trade between Turkey and northern Iraq. This PKK-imposed ban threatened to cut the Iraqi Kurds' economic lifeline, as local drivers, in fear of the consequences, stopped taking supplies to northern Iraq. Soon a shortage of foodstuffs and medicine resulted, and prices doubled and tripled. The PKK asserted that it would lift the trade ban only if Barzani would remove his blockade of the PKK camps.

Barzani declared that the PKK was challenging the very sovereignty of the new Kurdistan Regional Government (KRG), which had been established that very summer in 1992.

> Ocalan's men acted as if they were the authorities and started to control roads and collect taxes. . . . Ocalan's men threatened to expel the government and parliament from Irbil, [the seat of the KRG]. They said they would hang all those "who sold out the homeland." They even threatened to expel us from Dahuk and al-Sulaymaniyah and started to form espionage, terrorism, and sabotage networks inside cities. It has unequivocally been proven that they are conspiring and planning to undermine the existing situation in Kurdistan and its experiment [the KRG].[28]

Talabani supported Barzani by charging that the PKK "intended to establish a revolutionary authority . . . a state to replace the [Iraqi Kurdistan] front."[29]

The KRG added that the PKK "has seized over 30 border villages and has prevented farmers from returning to their homes."[30] Furthermore, by making northern Iraq a base against Turkey, "the villages, from where they [the raids against Turkey] are staged, are bombed on the pretext that PKK forces and bases are located there." The KRG even charged that "the PKK is collaborating with Iraqi officials," adding that "the Iraqi, Iranian, and Syrian governments help the PKK against the Iraqi Kurdish movement . . . because they do not want our parliamentary and governmental experiment to be successful."[31]

To meet the perceived threat and retain Turkey's support, the Iraqi Kurds, on October 4, 1992, launched major assaults against the PKK at its main base in the Khwakurt region where northern Iraq meets Turkey and Iran, and further to the west in the Zakho area across the Turkish border at Habur and Silopi. Since this was the very day that the Iraqi Kurds also declared a federated state, a proclamation which the Turks viewed unfavorably, the importance of retaining Turkey's trust was obvious as heavy fighting between the Iraqi Kurds and the PKK ensued.

Some 12 days later the Turks also entered the battle in force. By October 29, the fighting supposedly had forced the PKK to surrender to the PUK, a situation that gradually helped lead to a detente in their relations, while those between the PKK and KDP remained hostile.

Initially, the Turks claimed that "more than 2,000 Turkish PKK separatist guerrillas have been killed."[32] Several months later the Turkish chief of staff, General Dogan Gures, still claimed that "Ocalan's legs have been broken" and that the PKK had "lost 4,000-5,000 men."[33] It gradually became clear, however, that the actual figure was probably no greater than 300.[34] Based on the tremendous escalation of the PKK guerrilla war against Turkey in June 1993, it became obvious that its supposed near destruction the previous October had been greatly exaggerated.

## NEW DEVELOPMENTS

Many Turkish commentators began to accuse Talabani of having provided a new base and safehouse for the PKK in the Zaleh camp northeast of Sulaymaniya, where some 1,700 PKK fighters had been forced into supposed internment after surrendering at the end of October 1992.[35] Accordingly, the Turkish air force destroyed the camp in January 1994, but again it appeared that its occupants largely had melted away before the blow fell.

Further illustrating the emerging PKK-PUK detente, Talabani and Ocalan met in Syria during the second half of February 1993 to discuss a new cease-fire proposal between the PKK and Turkey. A month later, praising Talabani's good offices, Ocalan actually proclaimed one, but the death of Turkish President Ozal in April and the Turkish belief that Ocalan had been defeated the previous November (1992) eventually led to a renewal of the hostilities at the end of May 1993.

The outbreak of civil war between the KDP and PUK in May 1994 and the resulting anarchy created new opportunities for the PKK to establish bases in the Bahdinani area of northern Iraq that bordered on Turkey. This area, of course, lay within Barzani's territory, as Talabani's writ ran further to the south and east. Thus the reestablished PKK bases only presented a threat to the KDP and indeed could be seen by the PUK as a second front against the KDP, which was now its enemy.

In March and again in July of 1995, Turkish troops once again crossed into Iraqi Kurdistan in attempts to destroy the PKK units camped there. The March incursion entailed some 35,000 soldiers, the largest foreign expedition in the history of the Turkish republic. Although both the KDP and PUK officially opposed these Turkish actions, the KDP partially cooperated with the Turks, since the PKK presence in Barzani's portion of Iraqi Kurdistan was what had called forth the Turkish incursions in the first place. Inevitably, the Turkish incursions furthered the ill will between the PKK and the KDP.

## PKK-KDP HOSTILITIES

When the U.S.-brokered Drogheda (Dublin) talks in early August 1995 appeared to be leading to a settlement of the KDP-PUK fighting in Iraqi Kurdistan, as well as security guarantees for Turkey in the form of the KDP policing the border to prevent PKK infiltration from northern Iraq into Turkey, the PKK struck out at the KDP in an attempt to derail the truce that would constrain its freedom of maneuver. The PKK also sought to build on its "pilot regions" in Iraqi Kurdistan by establishing some type of government-in-exile or Kurdish federation.

The PKK claimed that two leading members of the KDP politburo, Nechirvan Barzani and Sami Abdal Rahman, had called the PKK a "terrorist" organization over Turkish TV in early August 1995.[36] Cemil (Cuma) Bayik—often referred to as the number two person in the PKK hierarchy and then-commander of its military wing, the Kurdistan Peoples Liberation Army (ARGK)—personally visited Barzani in an attempt to have the KDP repudiate the accusation that the PKK was "terrorist." When Barzani refused, the PKK retaliated.

In its weekly paper *Welat* (Motherland)—published in the PUK-held Iraqi Kurdistan capital Irbil—the PKK explained that it was attacking the KDP because it refused to join the fight for "a greater Kurdistan" and added that Barzani's party had "to be wiped out because it was backing Turkey's bid to crush PKK rebels."[37] Ocalan himself condemned as an "act of treason" the Drogheda agreement between the KDP and PUK, which was aimed at preventing the PKK from launching cross-border attacks from Iraqi Kurdistan against targets in Turkey.[38]

In a lengthy interview, the PKK leader termed Barzani's *peshmergas* "primitive nationalist forces"[39] who "have for 40 years slaughtered Kurdish patriotic forces for their own narrow tribal interests and in league with the Turkish intelligence services." Barzani's "collaborationist forces" were guilty of a "betrayal of the people of the north [the Turkish Kurds]" and had committed "an unforgivable crime" by developing "relations with Turkey" and putting "themselves under the command of its special forces." In reference to Turkey's village guard program of some 60,000 Turkish Kurdish supporters of Ankara, Ocalan also accused the KDP of having "played a key role in the development of the village guard system in Botan [the area in Turkish Kurdistan that borders Iraq]" and of having "tried to set up a village guard party . . . to strangle our struggle."

The PKK leader maintained that these actions had "prevented many areas becoming liberated zones" and "killed many [PKK] patriots and our most respected fighters." By attacking the KDP now, the PKK "will play a significant role in putting an end to this" and "open the way for the people of south [Iraqi] Kurdistan to move towards a federation." He also added that "we do not expect the PUK to oppose these developments very much."

In another interview on MED-TV—the pro-PKK TV channel that began broadcasting to Kurdistan from Britain in the spring of 1995—Ocalan further developed his theme of how "the notorious collaborationist policy of the KDP was the most basic internal reason why, during the past 40 years, the Kurdish national liberation movement failed to develop."[40] The PKK leader asserted that his conflict with the KDP "started in the 1970's" when "patriotic revolutionaries from Turkish Kurdistan went there—we can include the Faik Bucak incident of 1965[41] in that, too—and asked for support and solidarity." The KDP, however, "has considered the elimination of contemporary and patriotic policies and their leaders as one of its main missions."

Ocalan then explained that "of course, it was impossible for us to accept this because we wanted to take progressive steps." Not only did the KDP reject the PKK's position, but it also "wanted to implement Turkey's demands in northern Kurdistan as well. In 1985, Barzani asked us to stop. He said: 'Your armed struggle is not timely.'" Ocalan further maintained that "recently the KDP wanted to implement against our forces in the south the policy it had implemented against patriots earlier. With difficulty, we managed to save our forces from this danger." Ocalan's reference was to the proposed KDP role in policing the Turkish-Iraqi border to prevent PKK infiltration into Turkey.

The Atrus UN refugee camp near Dohuk and the Turkish border in KDP-controlled territory also played a significant role in the outbreak of conflict between the PKK and KDP. In May 1994, at the same time that serious fighting broke out between the KDP and PUK, the PKK encouraged some 20,000 Turkish Kurds to flee the strife raging in Turkey for sanctuary in northern Iraq. Not only was this viewed as a propagandistic ploy against Turkish repression, but also a chance to establish shelters for PKK fighters amidst the thousands of women and children protected by the United Nations. In the long run, moreover, these Kurdish refugees from Turkey could serve as the first step in establishing a Kurdish federation in northern Iraq under PKK control. Reports at the time indicated that Barzani was wary of the refugee influx, while Talabani favored it.[42]

Once fighting broke out between the PKK and KDP, Turkish Kurds took eight UN and other humanitarian workers in the Atrus camp hostage against possible attack from the KDP. Eventually, however, Barzani's *peshmergas* managed to search the camp and supposedly uncovered some PKK fighters, arms, and equipment.

The KDP declared that "it is high treason to aim weapons at the legitimate Kurdish administration in the region, the KDP,"[43] and that the PKK attacks "confirmed that Ocalan is the enemy of Kurds"[44] and constituted "terrorist and criminal behavior."[45]

Barzani himself claimed that, contrary to Ocalan's accusations of KDP betrayal in the past, "had it not been for the party's [KDP's] assistance, the PKK would not have managed to stand on its feet."[46] However, "no sooner had they [the PKK] sensed that they are once again standing on solid ground than they broke their promise and disavowed values." The "ungrateful PKK has forgotten all the support and assistance the party [KDP] offered them in 1980 when they fled from Turkey following the military coup."

Turning to the present situation, the KDP leader maintained that the Drogheda agreement of August 1995 used by the PKK "as an excuse to justify their aggression" was "a peace agreement the Kurdish people and all their friends have welcomed." As to the specific PKK charges that the KDP was supporting Turkey, Barzani maintained that he had "not asked for any Turkish assistance despite the Turkish Government's offer. . . . We are committed to safeguarding only our people's security and not that of others." He added, however, that "we respect relations with all neighbors and we do not permit that their security be threatened from our territory."

## CONCLUSIONS

While Turkey implicitly at least supported the KDP against their common PKK enemy, it seemed likely that both Iran and Syria were supporting the PKK because neither wanted to allow Turkish influence to expand in northern Iraq. What is more, neither Iran nor Syria wished to see the U.S.-brokered peace talks between the KDP and PUK succeed, because this would extend U.S. influence in the region. Supporting the PKK would be a way to sabotage the U.S.-sponsored peace process. Finally, the PUK could not help but see the

PKK-KDP struggle as, in effect, a second front against its KDP enemy. Given this almost Byzantine background of implicit alliance politics, as well as more than 20 years of intra-Kurdish rivalry between the different actors, the PKK-KDP fighting came as little surprise.

Although by late October 1995 the KDP was claiming that most of the Dohuk region and Khwakurt to the east had been cleared of the PKK,[47] it was difficult to believe that Barzani's *peshmergas* could have crushed in a few short months an organization that Turkey had been unable to eradicate in more than 12 years of warfare. A future reckoning between the two Kurdish enemies seemed likely.

Nevertheless, on December 10, 1995, the PKK announced a cease-fire brought about, in part, through the mediatory efforts of Daoud Baghistani, the permanent UN representative of the International Committee for European Security and Cooperation (OSCE). The central committees of the two parties then held talks from December 12 to 18, 1995, while early in February of the following year Ocalan met with high-level officials of the KDP. His brother Osman Ocalan even attended the KDP's fiftieth anniversary celebrations in the summer of 1996.

Pulling significant numbers of its fighters out of southeastern Turkey due to the relentless Turkish pressure, and positioning them in northern Iraq, it was clear that the PKK had emerged as a third force in northern Iraq. Barzani no longer referred to it as a "terrorist organization." Speaking over MED-TV in June 1996, Ocalan concluded that "we are currently experiencing a certain detente with the KDP."[48] Referring to a clash between the KDP and the Surci tribe that had just occurred, however, he warned that "certain frictions have arisen. . . . It is not right to trick and undermine those who wish to develop ties with us." Ominously, he threatened that "if they insist on continuing the clashes of the past, we will exercise our power." He concluded that "for the time being, we are exercising our power in the field of mediation," and added that "with time we may exceed this political framework; call for the unity of all the patriotic forces, the tribes, and the various parties; and try to reach a solution in that manner."

This was a reference to his rather vague goal of somehow establishing a "revolutionary democratic federation"[49] in northern Iraq that would lay the groundwork for a federation in Turkey. The PKK leader declared that the two main Iraqi Kurdish parties had led to a "dead end" and had become "obstacles."[50] To their supporters, he advised: "Go beyond the old classical diplomatic approach and the method of war or the so-called solution based on the narrow interests of the two parties." It was clear that although the PKK supposedly had renounced its goal of Kurdish independence in Turkey, it was at the same time thinking about leading some type of a pan-Kurdish federation.

During the summer of 1996, the situation again deteriorated in Iraqi Kurdistan as Iran began to support the PUK in its civil war against the KDP. As noted in Chapter 4, this eventually led to the KDP turning to Saddam for support at the end of August. Saddam's involvement then provoked U.S. missile strikes against Iraqi air defenses in the south. These heightened tensions at first caused Turkey to consider proclaiming a temporary buffer or security zone up to nine miles into Iraq along their joint border, in which Turkish soldiers would threaten to shoot anyone who entered. Only vehement Arab and Iranian opposition convinced Turkey not to implement such a zone. Unless cooler heads prevailed, northern Iraq was threatening to degenerate into a free-for-all involving everyone, including Turkey and the PKK.

In October 1996, however, Talabani managed to regain most of the territory he had lost to the KDP the previous month. A new U.S.-brokered cease-fire backed by the Turks then seemed to be taking hold in which, among other items, the KDP and PUK promised not to support the PKK. Having earlier suggested that the PKK might position itself between the KDP and PUK "as a peace force,"[51] Ocalan now declared that unless the two Iraqi Kurdish parties at least declined to support Turkey against the PKK, they would both "be eradicated."[52] "We say enough is enough. The people of southern Kurdistan [northern Iraq] must get rid of these parasites and build a modern leadership."[53] It was clear that the original PKK insurgency in Turkey had now taken root in northern Iraq, where it found itself in a basic conflict of interest and ideology with the KDP and, to a lesser extent, the PUK. Whether Turkey would be able to take advantage of this intra-Kurdish divide or the various Kurdish groups would be able to reach a pan-Kurdish understanding, remained to be seen.

# 6

# Prospects

The Kurdish problem is the main source of political instability in Turkey today and has become the biggest challenge to the future of the Turkish Republic since its creation in 1923. As illustrated in the preceding chapters, the Kurdish problem now affects practically all of Turkey's domestic and foreign policies. Its annual expense, for example—currently estimated at some $8 billion per year—is one of the main reasons for the weakness of the Turkish economy. The Kurdish problem also impacts negatively upon the economy by affecting tourism, direct foreign investments, and foreign credits. Politically, the Kurdish problem stands in the way of improving democracy and human rights, and it is helping the military preserve its special influence over the authority of the elected civilian government. What is more, the hard-line pursuit of a military solution without any political reforms simply wins more sympathy for the PKK from Turkey's Kurdish population. The Kurdish problem also limits foreign policy by giving foreign states a powerful opening with which to pressure Turkey, while alienating the democratic west Turkey aspires to join. Unless dealt with adequately, it ultimately threatens Turkey's very territorial integrity. Moreover, even if it is solved within the confines of the existing Turkish borders, it will necessitate major constitutional and legal changes.

## THE TOBB REPORT

The 168-page TOBB report illustrated both the importance of the Kurdish problem to the future of Turkey and the country's bitter, almost paranoid fear of compromising its Turkish identity. It was issued in August 1995 by Turkey's Chamber of Commerce and Commodity Exchange (TOBB), the country's main business federation, and was formally entitled "The Southeast Problem: Diagnoses and Observations." Professor Dogu Ergil, the head of the political science branch of the faculty of political sciences at Ankara University, was the main researcher, while Yalim Erez—the chairman of TOBB, a close political adviser of then–Prime Minister Tansu Ciller, and himself an ethnic Kurd—authorized it.

The report was based on interviews with 1,267 people, all but 3.6 percent of whom were Turkish Kurds.[1] Slightly more than 90 percent of them were male. All were either residents of the southeastern provinces of Diyarbakir, Batman, and Mardin, or were recent immigrants from the southeast now living in the southern Mediterranean cities of Adana, Mersin, and Antalya. The report analyzed their demographic, economic, religious, ethnic, linguistic, and political characteristics. Among its principal findings were that although 96 percent spoke Kurdish as their mother tongue, 75 percent did not believe that the state could defeat the PKK, and 43 percent backed some sort of a federation as the best solution—still, 85 percent did not demand a separate Kurdish state. Professor Ergil concluded from these findings that most Turkish citizens of Kurdish ancestry would be satisfied by the legal and constitutional guarantee of their Kurdish cultural identity. Since it constitutes the most thorough and recent survey dealing with the beliefs and opinions of Turkish Kurds, a detailed analysis of the report would be valuable.

In response to the question, "What is your mother tongue?" 89.8 percent replied Kurdish, 6 percent Zaza,[2] 3.5 percent Arabic, and only 0.007 percent Turkish. Almost 88 percent did reply, however, that Turkish was their second language, while only 3.7 percent said that they did not know any second language.[3] When asked what language they used in their homes, 65.1 percent said Kurdish, while 15.1 percent said Turkish. Outside the home, 52.5 percent spoke both Turkish and Kurdish together, while 23 percent spoke only Turkish, and 21.5 percent spoke only Kurdish. In regard to the official language of the state, 63 percent wanted both Turkish and Kurdish, 32 percent wanted only Turkish, and 5 percent wanted only Kurdish. By cross-referencing the answers to the questionnaire, the report found that 42.5 percent of the Kurds identified themselves with their ethnic origin, 21.8 percent as Turkish citizens, and 9.3 percent with their religious identity.

The vast majority of the respondents (97 percent) were Muslims, 1.4 percent were atheists, and 0.002 percent were Christian. Divided by Muslim "sects," 83.3 percent were Sufi, 13.5 percent Hanefi, and 1.7 percent Alevi.[4] Ergil found that 76 percent had regular jobs, while 23.3 percent were unemployed. To illustrating the destruction wrought in the countryside: less than 5 percent had agricultural jobs,[5] and less than 20 percent owned their own land.

Slightly less than half responded to the question, "What do you think the PKK cannot achieve?" Among those who did respond, 27 percent declared that the PKK could not form a Kurdish state, while 10 percent stated that it could not divide the country. Almost 77 percent believed that the state would not be successful in battling against the PKK, while only 20.3 percent believed that it would be. Among those who declared that the state was not going to be successful against the PKK, 24 percent asserted that the PKK enjoyed popular support, 18 percent felt that the state was applying force and authority, and 10 percent said the state was using the tactics of terrorism as much as the PKK.

Slightly more than 46 percent approved of the PKK's current policies and tactics. This support was higher in the cities, seemingly indicating that Kurdish immigration to urban areas was radicalizing those involved, rather than solving the problem for the state. A huge 89.7 percent wanted to have political and administrative structural change in the state. Only 10.3 percent were satisfied with the current situation. Among those who favored a structural change, 13 percent wanted autonomy, while 19.4 percent proposed reforms of local administrations and an increase in participation in the local administration. A striking 42.5 percent wanted a federation. Among the urban respondents, 71 percent wanted a Kurdish state, while 58 percent favored a federation. More than 70 percent of those who favored an independent state were illiterate or only primary school graduates. Thus, the report states, "it is not a coincidence that the large majority of the fighting staff of the PKK are uneducated village boys."

When asked whether they had any relatives associated with the PKK, 34.8 percent of the respondents replied "yes." Among these, 40.3 percent believed that the PKK's main goal was to establish a state, while 17 percent declared that democracy and the recognition of the Kurdish identity were its main aims. Interestingly, 75 percent of those who had family members in the PKK did not want a Kurdish state to be established, stressing that they favored a solution within the boundaries of the existing Turkish state.

Further indicative of support for the state was the finding that only 2.7 percent demanded that the emergency rule regime, village guards, and special forces be lifted. The report interpreted this as meaning that "the solution does not lie with the PKK. An agreement should be reached with the people of the area." In addition, of those who proposed an independent Kurdish state, only 9.4 percent supported talks with the PKK. This was interpreted as meaning that even the most radical do not want the PKK to be seen as the representative of the people of the area. The report also concluded that this meant that "if the question is well understood, and a healthy approach taken, it can be solved without the involvement of the PKK." In other words, "the PKK is not the reason for the problem but a product of it. If the problem is solved, [the] PKK might either disappear or become a marginal organization that engages in unregistered business."

Although barely one-third of those polled replied to the question about what they did not support among the PKK's activities, of these, almost half complained about the PKK's extreme acts of violence and obliteration of any environment for democratic debate. The report concluded from this that "the overwhelming majority of the Kurdish people do not believe that the organization [PKK] is either a peaceful one or one which is waging a legal struggle for human rights." Thus, if the Kurds can "achieve their expectations without the organization, then there is no reason why the PKK should not be marginalized and pushed outside of politics."

The Kurds "see the PKK as a multifaceted means of expressing their requests despite all the difficulties it is imposing on them and their belief that it will not be able to realize much of its aims." The report compared the PKK to a train. Its leaders "aim at arriving at the station of complete independence." The vast majority of the Kurds, however, "are ready to step out of the train when they arrive at the stops of more independence in regard to their daily lives, income, job, education, health, respect for their identity and daily and cultural lives." The report recommended that "social, cultural, and educational reforms should be carried out so that the individual is free of traditional control mechanisms." This meant that "the base of politics should be enlarged and all kinds of political programs and organizational movements should be encouraged except separatism. If these are not done, the East will continue its bloody fight within its traditional underdeveloped structure."

On the other hand, the report also argued that "sooner or later" the PKK would move its struggle onto "the political plane." Since "the Turkish Republic has based its struggle with the said organization [PKK] wholly on military strategy," such a change would create serious difficulties: "If the organization all at once declares that it is laying down its arms and is entering politics, then Turkey could be caught unawares as it gains the support of world public opinion." Since the struggle against the PKK was "only one aspect of the Eastern question," the report maintained that "there is an advantage to continuing economic, administrative and cultural initiatives independent of the armed struggle."

## Reactions

To one unaccustomed to the fears, passions, and suspicions aroused by the Kurdish problem in Turkey, the contents of the TOBB report seemed rather innocuous and prosaic. Much of the Turkish establishment, however, was outraged, lambasting Ergil, the main author of the report, as "an opportunist, a left-wing extremist, a CIA agent and a PKK sympathizer."[6]

Mesut Yilmaz, the leader of the main opposition ANAP party, dubbed it a "CIA report" that was "prepared according to the requests of the [Ciller] government." Bulent Ecevit, the leader of the leftist DSP, criticized it as "rife with contradictions." Alpaslan Turkes, the head of the ultra-nationalist NAP, characterized it as "devoid of scientific content," and in effect termed it "rubbish." Unal Erkan, the emergency rule governor in the southeast, at least substantively criticized the report's findings by faulting its discussion of a federation and language, and he charged that Ergil did not understand the region about which he was writing. He added that the report's recommendations "harm the unitarian nature of this state, its single flag, and its territorial integrity." Coskun Kirca, a DYP MP, wrote that the report "had no scientific value and was written with the arguments used by the PKK." Emin Colasan, an ultra-conservative columnist, wrote in *Hurriyet* that Ergil was "an opportunist who would sell his soul for money" and "a traitor who serves the separatists." Eventually, Ergil was even called to testify before the Ankara State Security Court. Legal charges were not immediately brought against him, but Nusret Demiral, the chief prosecutor, declared that inquiries were still continuing, thus holding out the possibility that Ergil could be charged under the provisions of the Anti-Terrorism Law.

The unwillingness of many members of the Turkish establishment to read the TOBB report seriously, instead of resorting to *ad hominem* attacks on its author, illustrated well the inability of Turkey to come to grips with the problem threatening its very future. It was as if the policy of the Turkish republic toward the Kurds had made it functionally illiterate on the issue. Ergil himself confessed that "I am very disappointed. If this is how the major—I don't say all—part of Turkey's media and politicians are, Turkey is in real trouble. It is obvious why Turkey fails to solve its problems."[7]

## Other reports

Despite the flack it aroused, the TOBB report soon spawned at least two other reports. On November 7, 1995, the large Turk-Metal union issued a report that warned of unrest in western Turkey after years of Kurdish migration from the southeast.[8] Many of these Kurds had developed a radical brand of Kurdish nationalism, due to the discrimination and alienation they were suffering from in their new, more western-oriented environment. "It will soon be difficult to talk of the 'Kurdish problem' [only] in the southeast, but . . . we can see that the elements of the problem are even more valid in the west." This new report was based on 10,600 mainly Kurdish respondents in the ten southeastern provinces under emergency rule and six western provinces where many Kurdish immigrants from the southeast were now living.

A few weeks later, Sakip Sabanci, one of the leading businessmen in Turkey, also released a report on the Kurdish problem. His analysis, however, dealt almost exclusively with economic policies for reducing the backwardness of the region.[9] These prescriptions included setting up new private and public sector organizations to "teach the people how to fish." Businessmen who had moved out of the region would establish industrial and agricultural "centres of attraction," industrial zones, and mass housing projects under the supervision of a special ministry or under-secretariat. Some argued that Sabanci had ignored any political recommendations due to official pressures. Sabanci himself, however, maintained that "as a businessman, I cannot write a prescription to solve the problem as a whole. I can only make suggestions in my own field."

## POSSIBLE SOLUTIONS

Based on their claims and statements over the years, both the Turkish government and the PKK are in favor of expanding and further developing democracy in Turkey. The beginnings of the solution to the Kurdish problem lie along these lines. Many Turks fear, however, that any such movement here will lead inevitably to Kurdish secession. For them, "political solution" has become a code term for such a result. Those who use the term are suspected of disloyalty to Ataturk's principles of a strong, unitary Turkish state and of conniving at foreign plots to weaken and divide Turkey, as was done historically. The recent controversy over the TOBB report well illustrated this situation.

On the other hand, those who suggest a political solution along the lines of greater democracy are not necessarily the enemies of Turkey. Indeed, the argument that is to be made here is that they are its friends in that these suggestions have in mind solving Turkey's Kurdish problem within the confines of the pre-existing unitary state structure. As Cem Boyner, the former leader of the New Democracy Movement, recognized when asked about the Kurdish problem: "We must start to establish democratic conditions in our country. This is the solution to all our problems."[10]

What then, specifically, does a solution entailing the expansion and further development of democracy mean? In the end, of course, these specifics are for the Turkish people themselves, including those of Kurdish ethnic heritage, to decide. What is offered here are only suggestions that have grown out of a long analysis of the problem.

In the present situation, what is called for are constitutional and legal guarantees recognizing and protecting the Kurdish cultural existence. There should also be a corresponding deletion from the constitution and legal system of all those provisions mandating the exclusive Turkishness of the state. Consideration might then be given to a new constitutional provision describing Turkey as "the common homeland of the Turks and Kurds." Without denying the necessity of maintaining the forces of state security, such non-military or political options should be taken *now,* not in some hypothetical future when the PKK has been defeated and terrorism ended. Given the nature of the Kurdish problem and the contemporary international climate, such a time is unlikely to come without political initiatives.

Although the specifics of such constitutional guarantees are for the people of Turkey to decide, surely they must include cultural, educational, linguistic, and publishing rights, among others. Without necessarily making Kurdish the second official language of Turkey, as French is in Canada—although such action should not necessarily be vetoed—bilingual signs and official dual names for geographical locations in the southeast can easily be implemented and would demonstrate enormous goodwill and commitment to positive change. Primary and possibly even secondary education options in Kurdish for those who want it, radio and television broadcasting, as well as rights to publish freely in Kurdish should also be absolutely guaranteed.

That these are not treasonous ideas was demonstrated by Mesut Yilmaz when he was briefly prime minister of a right-wing coalition government during the first half of 1996.[11] At that time he "promised a political solution." After asserting that he first would lift the state of emergency and promote economic development in the southeast, he also declared that he would strengthen "the individual cultural rights of the Kurdish citizens." He then noted that "among other things, that means the use of the Kurdish language, and perhaps a television station for the Kurds." A year earlier Yilmaz also said that "there can be education in Kurdish in the form of elective courses. That is not separatism."[12] He added that "if our citizens wish to develop their cultures in their mother tongue, that is in Kurdish, then the state must ensure that these citizens have that right." He even maintained that "doing that would elevate the stature of the state in the eyes of these people and provide a better guarantee for Turkey's integrity."

For his part, Abdullah Ocalan seemingly has indicated that he would be satisfied with such genuine democratization.[13] In reply to the question, "Where does the solution rest?" the PKK leader declared: "In a free democratic atmosphere! There should be an opportunity for the free exchange of views and political choice by removing the shadow of coercion. . . . If you guarantee this security throughout Turkey, I will have no other demand concerning the Kurdish problem." He then added that "the use of political rights depends on particular guarantees," and he asserted that "I will seek security in the Constitution and the law." In other words, Ataturk's famous dictum: "Happy is he who can say he is a Turk," should be updated to read "Happy is he who can say he is a Turkish citizen."

In implementing Kurdish language reforms, advocates of the Turkish language have little to fear, since clearly a continuing knowledge of Turkish will be necessary for anyone of Kurdish ethnic heritage who wants to succeed in the larger Turkish state or the outside world. Even now, for example, Ocalan and the other PKK leaders communicate in Turkish, not Kurdish. Indeed, historically

Turkish had shown an amazing ability to assimilate and absorb other languages in Anatolia. Once given the right to use Kurdish, how many Kurds will really want to educate themselves exclusively in a medium that would only lead to a dead end? Moreover, such language and cultural rights are nothing more than what Turkey demanded in the 1980s for the Bulgarian Turks, who constituted only some 10 percent of the total Bulgarian population, and still demand for the Cypriot Turks, who make up approximately 20 percent of the population of Cyprus.

By satisfying the demands of the more moderate Kurdish population on these issues, Turkey could gradually co-opt, and even end up partially leading, the Kurdish movement as a trusted and valued ally, instead of regarding it as a debilitating and mortal enemy. And if the PKK is not being forthright in its intentions regarding genuine democracy and simply ups the ante to full independence, a Turkish policy of promoting and defending Kurdish cultural rights would have a better chance of ultimately winning the allegiances of its citizens of Kurdish ethnic heritage and defeating the PKK than would a hard-line, exclusively military strategy.

After constitutional guarantees for the protection of genuine democracy and the Kurdish identity, a federation is the other major demand most often made by the PKK and many of the more moderate Kurds such as the longtime leader of the Kurdistan Socialist Party, Kemal Burkay. Again, such demands are nothing more than what Turkey insists upon for the Turkish minority on Cyprus. To most Turks, however, a federation would be an anathema, a major way station along the road to separatism.

It is interesting, therefore, to realize that since the inception of the Turkish republic in 1923, Turkish Kurdistan for most of the time has already been ruled by various special regimes such as martial law, state of seige, and currently a state of emergency complete with a supra-governor. Moreover, until 1950 the region was under an inspector general for the eastern provinces. In addition, the government's recent willingness to deal separately with "loyal" tribes in the region illustrates a tacit admission that a strict unitary solution is difficult to maintain. Few Turks from the western part of the country have ever even traveled to the east, let alone expressed a desire to do so. It is almost as if in their minds the region already was somehow different and separate from the rest of the country. Without realizing it then, a separate regime for the region already exists! Would it not be better if this regime had the support of the local population, instead of what is currently the case?

Given the migration of some 60 percent of Turkey's Kurds to the western part of the country, many now feel that a federation between the Turks and the Kurds would be unworkable, short of massive population shifts that presumably many Kurds would be unwilling to undergo given their better lives in the west. Accordingly, what Turkey might consider is the maintenance of its overall unitary structure, but the devolution of more real powers to the provincial and local governments. Such reforms not only might help solve the Kurdish problem, but also create positive new economic and social possibilities.

While prime minister in 1996, Mesut Yilmaz made just such a suggestion when asked how he wanted to solve the Kurdish conflict: "We will strengthen the local administrative bodies in the southeast and give them greater self-administration. It is no longer possible to force everything through the bottleneck of Ankara."[14] For his part, Ocalan has indicated some possible flexibility on his demand for a federation by asserting that "the rigid conception of forms of state in terms of extreme unitarianism or decentralization does not suit the realities of our times."[15] In addition, recognizing that the government could not simply agree suddenly to negotiate with those it for so long had denounced as "terrorists" and "mass murderers," Ocalan has also offered to step aside in favor of Kurdish parliamentarians in discussions with Ankara.

One such politician who has been mentioned is Serafettin Elci, a former minister in Bulent Ecevit's government during the 1970s and the chair of the new Democratic Mass Party (DKP) that was created in January 1997. According to Elci,[16] the DKP was created to avoid the past "mistakes" of DEP and HADEP's "Marxist tradition" and to find a "better solution . . . through a more cautious approach" that stresses federalism and democracy. Elci emphasized that "the people can share the power in matters concerning themselves without harming the country's integrity." He suggested that local and regional administrations be "authorized to have their own legislative and executive bodies, make their own laws, be elected by the regional occupants, collect their own taxes, and exercise their own education, health and internal security policies."

Given the preeminence of the military in Turkish politics, however, it is unlikely that a civilian will be able to take the required steps for a political solution. The utter failure of President Demirel to move beyond his mere admission of a "Kurdish reality" to a real solution is a case in point. After all, on two separate occasions the military removed him from office when he was deemed unsuitable. What may well be needed, therefore, is a military leader like Kemal Ataturk, Charles de Gaulle, Yitzhak Rabin, or George Marshall who can complement his impeccable martial credentials with the necessary political acumen and courage to reach a political solution.

No such military leader has yet appeared. In December 1996, however, the current Turkish chief of staff, General Ismail Hakki Karadayi, may have taken the first cautious step when, in discussing the situation, he declared, "the military has fulfilled its obligations and will continue to do so, but terrorism will never be eradicated by military means alone."[17] Such an assessment clearly implied that it was time for the civilian government to implement political, social, and economic[18] solutions. To the extent that such solutions would lead to a more democratic and stronger Turkey, the Kurdish problem would begin to be solved with positive results for all those concerned. This in turn would be a fitting tribute to all those who have suffered and died because of it.

# NOTES

## INTRODUCTION

1. See the figures listed in *Turkish Daily News* (Ankara), June 10, 1995; *Yeni Yuzyil* (Istanbul), July 6, 1995; and Human Rights Watch Arms Project, *Weapons Transfers and Violations of the Laws of War in Turkey* (New York: Human Rights Watch, 1995), pp. 1, 23; citing Turkish Interior Minister Nahit Mentese's public briefing to the Turkish parliament on June 27, 1995. Citing the Turkish Human Rights Foundation (TIHV), Ismet G. Imset, a most knowledgeable source, listed a total of 3,000,000 displaced Kurds and 3,000 torched villages at the end of 1995. "The PKK: Terrorists or Freedom Fighters?" *International Journal of Kurdish Studies* 10 (nos. 1 & 2, 1996), pp. 48, 69. By the beginning of 1997, reports indicated that more than 21,000 had been killed in the continuing struggle.
2. "The Kurdish Problem in Turkey," *Middle East Journal* 42 (Summer 1988), pp. 380-406.
3. *The Kurds in Turkey: A Political Dilemma* (Boulder: Westview Press, 1990).
4. See the reviews of my book in *Middle East Journal* 45 (Autumn 1991), pp. 684-85; and *Turkish Studies Association Bulletin* 16 (April 1992), pp. 103-06.
5. For a sample, see Ismet G. Imset, *The PKK: A Report on Separatist Violence in Turkey (1973-1992)* (Istanbul: Turkish Daily News Publications, 1992); Philip Robbins, "The Overlord State: Turkish Policy and the Kurdish Issue," *International Affairs* 69 (October 1993), pp. 657-76; Henri J. Barkey, "Turkey's Kurdish Dilemma," *Survival* 35 (Winter 1993), pp. 51-70; Henri J. Barkey and Graham E. Fuller, "Turkey's Kurdish Question: Critical Turning Points and Missed Opportunities," *Middle East Journal* 51 (Winter 1997), pp. 59-79; Robert Olson, ed., *The Kurdish Nationalist Movement in the 1990s: Its Impact on Turkey and the Middle East* (Lexington, KY: University Press of Kentucky, 1996); and David McDowall, *A Modern History of the Kurds* (London: I. B. Tauris, 1996), pp. 395-444. My earlier work owes a particular debt of gratitude to the articles and insights the Turkish journalist Ismet G. Imset published in the 1980s. Also see the two early pieces by Martin van Bruinessen, "The Kurds in Turkey," *MERIP Reports* no. 121 (Feb. 1984), pp. 6-12; and "Between Guerrilla War and Political Murder: The Workers' Party of Kurdistan," *Middle East Report* no. 153 (July-August 1988), pp. 40-42, 44-46, 50.
6. Cited in Ihsan Akdemir, "Restoration in Southeast," *Milliyet*, Dec. 2, 1991, p. 17; as cited in *Foreign Broadcast Information Service—West Europe*, Jan. 8, 1991, p. 58.
7. Cited in "Late Ozal's letter to then PM Demirel," *Turkish Daily News*, Nov. 16, 1993.

**CHAPTER ONE**
1. Adda B. Bozeman, *The Future of Law in a Multicultural World* (Princeton, NJ: Princeton University Press, 1970), p. 78.
2. *Ibid.*, p. 61. Also see Bozeman's *Politics and Culture in International History* (Princeton, NJ: Princeton University Press, 1960); and Nevzat Soguk, "A Study of the Historico Cultural Reasons for Turkey's 'Inconclusive' Democracy," *New Political Science* no. 26 (Fall 1993), pp. 89-116.
3. The classic but now dated analysis of modern Turkey is Bernard Lewis, *The Emergence of Modern Turkey* (2nd ed.; London: Oxford University Press, 1968). Two excellent new studies have recently appeared. See Feroz Ahmad, *The Making of Modern Turkey* (London: Routledge, 1993); and Erik Zurcher, *Turkey: A Modern History* (London: I. B. Tauris, 1993). All three books proved very useful to me in my following discussion and contain useful bibliographies that will refer the interested reader to many other worthy sources.
4. The classic study of Ataturk in English remains Lord Kinross [Patrick Balfour], *Ataturk: A Biography of Mustafa Kemal, Father of Modern Turkey* (New York: William Morrow and Company, 1965). More recently, see A. L. Macfie, *Ataturk* (Harlow: Longman, 1994). Ali Kazancigil and Ergun Ozbudun, eds., *Ataturk: Founder of a Modern State* (London: C. Hurst & Co., 1981) consists of a series of articles on Ataturk's ideas and legacy. One of Ataturk's famous reforms was the law in 1934 mandating that all Turks adopt a surname. His, "Ataturk," means "Father of the Turks." Such last names are placed in parentheses in the text when referring to individuals before 1934.
5. Ahmad, *Making of Modern Turkey*, p. 17.
6. Kinross, *Ataturk*, p. 323.
7. "Prosperity Party Leader Interviewed," Ankara Show Television in Turkish, 2030 GMT, Jan. 31, 1994; as cited in *Foreign Broadcast Information Service—West Europe*, Feb. 3, 1994, p. 41. Hereafter cited as *FBIS-WEU*.
8. On the first major Kurdish rebellion in the Republic of Turkey, see Robert Olson, *The Emergence of Kurdish Nationalism and the Sheikh Said Rebellion, 1880-1925* (Austin: University of Texas Press, 1989); and Martin van Bruinessen, *Agha, Shaikh and State: The Social and Political Structures of Kurdistan* (London: Zed Books Ltd., 1992), pp. 265-305.
9. Erik J. Zurcher, *Opposition in the Early Turkish Republic: The Progressive Republican Party, 1924-1925* (Leiden: E. J. Brill, 1991).
10. Walter F. Weiker, *Political Tutelage and Democracy in Turkey: The Free Party and Its Aftermath* (Leiden: E. J. Brill, 1973).
11. On this point, see Lewis, *Emergence of Modern Turkey*, pp. 1-5.
12. Ismet Cheriff Vanly, *Le Kurdistan irakien: entite nationale* (Neuchatel: Editions de la Baconniere, 1970), p. 54; as cited in George S. Harris, "Ethnic Conflict and the Kurds," *Annals of the American Academy of Political and Social Science* 433 (Sept. 1977), p. 115.
13. See Ismet G. Imset, "The PKK: Terrorists or Freedom Fighters?" *International Journal of Kurdish Studies* 10 (nos. 1 & 2; 1996), p. 53; and Robert Olson, "Kurds and Turks: Two Documents Concerning Kurdish Autonomy in 1922 and 1923," *Journal of South Asian and Middle Eastern Studies* 15 (Winter 1991), pp. 20-31.
14. Derk Kinnane, *The Kurds and Kurdistan* (London: Oxford University Press, 1964), pp. 32-33; and Ismail Besikci, *Kurdistan & Turkish Colonialism: Selected Writings*

(London: Kurdistan Solidarity Committee and Kurdistan Information Centre, 1991), p. 34.

15. National Foreign Assessment Center (U.S. Central Intelligence Agency), *The Kurdish Problem in Perspective* (Aug. 1979), p. 25.

16. On this period see Feroz Ahmad, *The Turkish Experiment in Democracy, 1950-1975* (London: C. Hurst & Company, 1977); Kemal Karpat, *Turkey's Politics: The Transition to a Multi-Party System* (Princeton, NJ: Princeton University Press, 1959); and Richard D. Robinson, *The First Turkish Republic: A Case Study in National Development* (Cambridge, MA: Harvard University Press, 1963).

17. On the role of the military in Turkish politics, see William Hale, *Turkish Politics and the Military* (London: Routledge, 1994); and Mehmet Ali Birand, *The General's Coup in Turkey: An Inside Story of 12 September 1980* (London: Brassey's Defense Publishers, 1987).

18. "55 Landowners 'Exiled' from Towns," *Christian Science Monitor,* Dec. 5, 1960, p. 14.

19. Cited in Kendal [Nezan], "Kurdistan in Turkey," in *People Without a Country: The Kurds and Kurdistan,* Gerard Chaliand, ed. (London: Zed Press, 1980), p. 97.

20. This and the following citation were taken from "Turkey: Defense Minister on Foreign Policy Issues, Coalition," *Türkiye* (Istanbul), April 7, 1996, p. 9; as cited in *FBIS-WEU,* April 11, 1996, pp. 22, 23.

21. "Military: We're Against Lifting of Article 8," *Turkish Daily News,* July 1, 1995.

22. See Paul J. Magnarella, "The Legal, Political and Cultural Structures of Human Rights Protections and Abuses in Turkey," *Journal of International Law and Practice* 3 (1994), pp. 439-40.

23. U.S. Department of State, "Turkey Human Rights Practices, 1995," March 1996, received via the Internet. The following citations were taken from this source.

24. See Amnesty International, *Human Rights and U.S. Security* (New York: Amnesty International, 1995), pp. 48-50; Amnesty International, "Turkey: A Policy of Denial," Feb. 1995; and Amnesty International, "Turkey: Unfulfilled Promise of Reform," Sept. 1995.

25. Amnesty International, "Turkey: Human Rights Defenders at Risk," Sept. 1994; and Amnesty International, "Turkey: Dissident Voices Jailed Again," June 1994.

26. Human Rights Watch Arms Project, *Weapons Transfers and Violations of the Laws of War in Turkey* (New York: Human Rights Watch, 1995); Helsinki Watch, "Free Expression in Turkey, 1993: Killings, Convictions, Confiscations," Aug. 1993; and Helsinki Watch, "The Kurds of Turkey: Killings, Disappearances and Torture," Mar. 1993. In October 1996, the Turkish translator and publisher of the 1995 Arms Project study cited above were charged with "defamation and belittling the state's security and military forces" under article 159/1 of the Turkish Penal Code.

27. This and the following citation were taken from "Human Rights Report 1994," *Turkish Daily News,* Oct. 25, 1995. Also see Human Rights Association Issues Monthly Report, *Turkish Daily News,* Oct. 31, 1995, p. A3; as cited in *FBIS-WEU,* Nov. 3, 1995, p. 27; and "Human Rights Report 1994," *Turkish Probe,* Oct. 27, 1995.

28. "Hacaloglu on Conditions of Kurds in Southeast," *Turkish Daily News,* July 24, 1995, p. A3; as cited in *FBIS-WEU,* Aug. 1, 1995, pp. 28-29. Azimet Koyluoglu, Hacaloglu's predecessor as Turkish Human Rights Minister, called the government's burning of villages, "state terrorism." Cited in Human Rights Watch

Helsinki, "Turkey: Forced Displacement of Ethnic Kurds from Southeastern Turkey," October 1994, p. 3.

29. Cited in Kemal Balci, "Unsolved Killings Report Paints a Picture of Horror," *Turkish Daily News,* April 18, 1995.

30. Orya Sultan Halisdemir, "Reactions to Unsolved, Political Killings Draft Report Reflect Rifts in Parliament," *Turkish Probe,* April 28, 1995, p. 5.

31. Nazlan Ertan, "Minister's Remark on EU Officials Causes Discord," *Turkish Daily News,* June 12, 1995, p. A2; as cited in *FBIS-WEU,* June 16, 1995, p. 40.

32. "Chief Prosecutor Discusses Antiterror Measures," *Turkish Probe,* Aug. 26, 1994, pp. 2-5; as cited in *FBIS-WEU,* Sept. 12, 1994, p. 56.

33. The *Halkin Emek Partisi* (HEP) or Peoples Labor Party had been formed in 1990 as a legal Kurdish party and entered the Turkish Parliament as members of Erdal Inonu's Social Democratic Party (SHP) in the national elections of October 1991. When it was closed down by the Constitutional Court in July 1993, it simply reincarnated itself as DEP.

34. "Sezgin on PTP [HEP] Congress, 'Enemies of Humanity,'" Ankara Turkiye Radyolari Network in Turkish, 2000 GMT, Sept. 22, 1992; as cited in *FBIS-WEU,* Sept. 23, 1992, p. 45.

35. "Ankara Security Court Seeks Trial of Kurdish Deputies," *Turkish Daily News,* Nov. 25, 1992, pp. 1, 11; as cited in *FBIS-WEU,* Dec. 7, 1992, p. 58.

36. The following excerpts in translation were provided by the Institut Kurde de Paris in Paris, France.

37. Cited in John Darnton, "Outspoken Turkish Author Faces Trial," *International Herald-Tribune,* Mar. 16, 1996.

38. Cited in "Reuters Reporter Charged Over Article on Kurds," *Turkish Daily News,* Sept. 18, 1995.

39. The following translation was provided by the International Committee for the Liberation of the Kurdish Parliamentarians Imprisoned in Turkey; Paris, France.

40. "Turkish President Signs the Legal Reform Bill," Press Release, Turkish Embassy, Washington, D.C., Dec. 1, 1992.

41. Magnarella, "Human Rights Protections and Abuses in Turkey," p. 453.

42. The following argument owes a debt to "The Drift to Nationalist Totalitarianism," *Briefing* (Ankara), Nov. 13, 1995, pp. 6-7.

## CHAPTER TWO

1. Unless otherwise noted, the following analysis is based largely on Ismet G. Imset, *The PKK: A Report on Separatist Violence in Turkey (1973-1992)* (Istanbul: Turkish Daily News Publications, 1992), hereafter referred to as *The PKK;* Ismet G. Imset, "The PKK: Terrorists or Freedom Fighters?" *International Journal of Kurdish Studies* 10 (nos. 1 & 2; 1996), pp. 45-100; Mehmet Ali Birand, *Apo ve PKK* (Istanbul: Milliyet Yayinlari, 1992); Ahmet Cem Ersever, *Kurds, PKK and A. Ocalan,* accessed from the Internet, [1992]; and interviews with knowledgeable Kurds. In my opinion, Imset is the single most knowledgeable source on the PKK. A Turkish journalist, he eventually became so close to the PKK, however, that he was forced into exile in Britain during 1995. For detailed descriptions of many of the following groups I mention, see Imset, *The PKK,* appendices 6-7, pp. 379-450.

2. In addition, Duran (Abbas) Kalkan and Halil (Abu Bakir) Atac, two high-ranking members of the PKK since at least the early 1980s, were also said to be members

of these two top PKK organs. The sixth and final member of the Leadership Council, Mustafa Karasu, had been imprisoned for many years following the military coup in 1980. Sabri (Hassan) Ok, still another longtime PKK leader, was also named to the new Central Committee, while other sources have listed Riza Altun too as a member, indicating an amazing continuity, claims by many outside observers to the contrary notwithstanding.

3. This and the following citations were taken from Martin van Bruinessen, "Between Guerrilla War and Political Murder: The Workers' Party of Kurdistan," *Middle East Report,* no. 153, (July-Aug. 1988), pp. 40, 41, and 42.

4. The following is based largely on Ismet G. Imset, "PKK in Syria: Burden for Ocalan, Trouble for Turkey," *Turkish Daily News* (Ankara), Nov. 11, 1993; hereafter cited as *TDN.*

5. Pir, an ethnic Turk present at the first meeting of the AYOD in 1974, was captured and killed by the Turks shortly after the coup in 1980.

6. Later, Ocalan for a time wrote articles under the pseudonym "Ali Firat" for newspapers distributed in Turkey.

7. Ersever, *Kurds, PKK and A. Ocalan.*

8. Cited in Imset, "PKK in Syria."

9. As Ocalan himself claimed in March 1993: "I control the organization. I can maintain that control." He even threatened to "kill" any PKK fighter who disobeyed his orders. "Ocalan Discusses Starting 'Political Process,'" *Nokta* (Istanbul), Mar. 2, 1993, pp. 18-19; as cited in *Foreign Broadcast Information Service—West Europe,* Mar. 26, 1993, p. 71; hereafter cited as *FBIS-WEU.* Ocalan also claimed: "I am the will of the Kurdish people." Sibylle Hammann, "I am the Will of My People," *Kurier* (Vienna), Oct. 3, 1993, p. 5; as cited in *FBIS-WEU,* Oct. 4, 1993, p. 55; and that he considered himself "the leader of the overwhelming majority" of the Kurdish people. "PKK Leader Ocalan Interviewed on Policy, Goals," Ankara Show Television in Turkish, 1840 GMT, May 18, 1992; as cited in *FBIS-WEU,* May 19, 1992, p. 40.

10. The following is largely based on "Profile of PKK Leader Ocalan," *Turkish Probe* (Ankara), Aug. 17, 1993, pp. 8-9; as cited in *FBIS-WEU,* Sept. 2, 1993, pp. 58-59. Also see Imset, *The PKK,* pp. 333-34.

11. Cited in "Report on Interview with PKK Leader Ocalan," Ankara TRT Television Network in Turkish, 2020 GMT, Jan. 21, 1993; as cited in *FBIS-WEU,* Jan. 25, 1993, p. 58.

12. This and the following citations were taken from "Meeting," *Berxwedan* (Bonn), May 16-20, 1993; as cited in *FBIS-WEU,* June 4, 1993, p. 44. This Armenian connection may help explain the ultranationalist Turkish leader Alpaslan Turkes's otherwise ludicrous claim that Ocalan is actually an Armenian conveniently called Hagop Hagopian, the same name carried by the notorious leader of the Armenian terrorist organization ASALA in the 1980s. By using this propagandistic technique of transfer, Turkes managed to give Turkish nationalists a double dosage of Kurd-bashing to chew on.

13. This and the following citations were taken from "Turkey: PKK's Ocalan Addresses Turkish People," London MED TV Television in Turkish, 1745 GMT, April 21, 1996; as cited in *FBIS-WEU,* April 25, 1996, p. 37.

14. Cited in Georgina Higueras, "We Are Not Terrorists, This Is a War," *El Pais* (Madrid), July 3, 1995, p. 6; as cited in *Foreign Broadcast Information Service—Near East & South Asia,* July 10, 1995, p. 55; hereafter cited as *FBIS-NES.*

15. Cited in *FBIS-WEU,* Sept. 2, 1993, p. 59. See note 10 for the full citation.
16. Cited in *FBIS-WEU,* Jan. 25, 1993, p. 59. See note 11 for the full citation.
17. Cited in *FBIS-NES,* July 10, 1995, p. 55. See note 14 above for the full citation. In an earlier interview, Ocalan told the famous Turkish journalist Mehmet Ali Birand that he "hated weapons," had never touched a gun, and loved birds and football games. "The Case of the 'Apo' Interview," *Briefing* (Ankara), June 20, 1988, pp. 17-18.
18. Cited in "Kurdish Leader Ocalan Announces Terrorism," *News* (Vienna), July 8, 1993, p. 41; as cited in *FBIS-WEU,* July 9, 1993, p. 58. In the same interview, Ocalan also added: "So much blood has been shed; so many people have been killed. I carry all these killings on my shoulders."
19. Cited in *ibid.*
20. Cited in *FBIS-WEU,* June 4, 1993, pp. 43, 44. See note 12 for the full citation. When sarcastically asked: "Are you contemplating an end similar to Jesus?" Ocalan replied: "No, but I highly resemble him when rendering of services and peace is concerned." Cited in Tayyar Safak, "Understanding Apo," *Tercuman* (Istanbul), Mar. 22, 1993, p. 2; as cited in *FBIS-WEU,* Mar. 31, 1993, p. 71.
21. Cited in *FBIS-WEU,* June 4, 1993, p. 43. See note 12 for the full citation. Ocalan continued: "I have always likened [the] PKK's emergence to the emergence of the prophets. We are carrying on the task of the prophets. . . . It would be a great mistake to regard the PKK as a nationalistic, or even a communist organization. It is a really tolerant movement that is closely attached to humanism." *Ibid.*
22. Cited in *FBIS-WEU,* May 19, 1992, p. 40. See note 9 for the full citation.
23. "Readers of Curukkaya's 'Verses of Apo' Attacked in Several European Towns," *TDN,* Oct. 14, 1994. Curukkaya's wife, Aysel (Medya) Curukkaya, had earlier been a leading PKK militant in the province of Amed (Diyarbakir).
24. PKK Central Committee, "Central Committee Statement of the PKK (Kurdistan Workers Party) Following the Fifth Congress of the PKK," Feb. 1995.
25. Cited in Imset, *The PKK,* p. 334.
26. Abdullah Ocalan, "The Guerrillas Handbook," [c. 1989]; as cited in *ibid.,* p. 151.
27. See, for example, Jake Border, "Orphan Guerrillas: Lonely Struggle of Kurdish Freedom Fighters," *Soldier of Fortune,* Oct. 1992, p. 42.
28. Oral Calislar, "Ocalan Interviewed on Socialism," *Cumhuriyet* (Istanbul), June 21, 1993, p. 10; as cited in *FBIS-WEU,* July 12, 1993, p. 53.
29. Cited in *FBIS-NES,* July 10, 1995, p. 56. See note 14 for the full citation. Kani Yilmaz, at the time possibly the third highest ranking member of the PKK, when questioned in August 1994 whether "the PKK was still a Marxist movement," described it as "a socialist one, with nationalist demands for freedom." Cited in Ismet G. Imset, "PKK to Escalate Attacks to Mark Anniversary," *TDN,* Aug. 15, 1994, pp. 1, 9; as cited in *FBIS-WEU,* Aug. 18, 1994, p. 42. A year later, a PKK publication put it this way: "The PKK is fighting for the national liberation of the Kurdish people and is striving towards a socialist society in which people live together in equality." Abdo Ziman, "Nationalism and the Kurdish National Liberation Movement," *Kurdistan Review* (London), Sept./Oct. 1995, p. 51.
30. The following data were taken from Hayri Birler, "PKK Revamps Top Political-Military Hierarchy," *TDN,* April 3, 1995; and interviews with knowledgeable Kurds.
31. "Profile of Kurdish Islamic Movement," Ankara Show Television in Turkish, 2045 GMT, Nov. 21, 1994; as cited in *FBIS-WEU,* Nov. 23, 1994, p. 57.

32. "PKK Leader Uses Islamic Theme in Conference Message," *TDN,* July 20, 1994, p. A2; as cited in *FBIS-WEU,* July 27, 1994. A recent PKK publication justified the party's new tolerance concerning religion by arguing that "it seems unrealistic to suppose that dreams, dogma and religion will one day all disappear. They are part of human nature." Ziman, "Nationalism and the Kurdish National Liberation Movement," p. 52.

33. For these figures, see Ismet G. Imset, "Interior Minister: PKK to be Wiped Out in 'Crackdown,'" *TDN,* July 3, 1993, pp. 1, 11. Six months later, Ismet gave the following figures: "ARGK: 8,000-10,000 full-time fighters, plus 35,000 active supporters [ERNK] and 370,000 sympathizers, mainly in the southeast." "Security is Better in the Cities, Little Improved in Rural Areas," *Turkish Times,* Feb. 1, 1994, p. 7. Also see Imset, "The PKK: Terrorists or Freedom Fighters," p. 46. Yet another estimate at about the same time declared that "the P.K.K. claims to have a hardcore force of 5,000 highly trained guerrillas [ARGK] operating inside Turkey, backed by as many as 150,000 militia men [ERNK] plus an estimated 2 million sympathizers." Frederick Painton, "From Banditry to Civil War," *Time,* Dec. 6, 1993, p. 44. These much larger figures for the ERNK and sympathizers would appear to be PKK exaggerations for propagandistic reasons.

34. Imset, *The PKK,* p. 133.

35. *Ibid.,* p. 143.

36. Cited in *FBIS-WEU,* Oct. 4, 1993, p. 54. See note 9 above for the full citation.

37. *FBIS-WEU,* Aug. 18, 1994, p. 42. See note 29 above for the full citation.

38. Cited in "PKK Reportedly Developing New Command Strategy," *TDN,* June 14, 1994, p. 2; as cited in *FBIS-WEU,* June 20, 1994, p. 48.

39. Durriyah Awni, "Interview with PKK Leader Ocalan on Terror, Foreign Ties," *Al-Musawwar* (Cairo), Sept. 13, 1996, pp. 24-25; as cited in *FBIS-WEU,* Sept. 20, 1996, p. 2. At the end of 1996, Ocalan narrowed this figure when he declared: "At the moment, we have more than 15,000 guerrillas . . . spread throughout Kurdistan." "London MED TV on Lebanese Paper's Interview with the PKK's Ocalan," London MED TV in Turkish, 1815 GMT, Dec. 26, 1996; as cited in *FBIS-WEU,* Dec. 26, 1996, p. 1. Whatever the precise number, it is clear that the PKK has had problems in enlarging the size of the ARGK.

40. Christopher Panico, "Turkey's Kurdish Problem," *Jane's Intelligence Review* 7 (April 1995), p. 172. Also see Tammy Arbuckle, "Winter Campaign in Kurdistan," *International Defense Review* 28 (Feb. 1995), p. 60, who puts the figure at 2500.

41. "Iran Says Turkish Raid Killed Nine," Reuter, Jan. 29, 1994; as cited in *The Kurds: Recent Wire Reports,* Jan. 30, 1994, p. 1.

42. Alan Makovsky, "Western Dreams and Eastern Problems," *Middle East Insight* 11 (May-June 1995), p. 26. In April 1993, Ocalan himself claimed that he had "a militant force of 10,000 people inside Turkey, 5,000 of them in the Botan area, 500 in Dersim, 500 in Amed, and a very high number in the Garzan district." See Ismet G. Imset, "PKK's Ocalan Interviewed on Issues, Developments," *TDN,* April 17, 1993, pp. 1, 11; as cited in *FBIS-WEU,* May 4, 1993, p. 57.

43. The following analysis is based, in part, on Ismet G. Imset, "PKK Commanders Discuss Cease-Fire Extension," *TDN,* April 20, 1993, pp. 1, 11; as cited in *FBIS-WEU,* May 6, 1993, pp. 59-61; and Ismet G. Imset, "PKK Leader Calls for Liberated Zones," *TDN,* Nov. 15, 1993.

44. The following data and citations were taken from a PKK document entitled "Central Committee of the PKK (Kurdistan Workers Party) Following the Fifth Congress of the PKK," Feb. 1995.
45. The following data and citations were taken from Border, "Orphan Guerrillas," p. 43.
46. The following data and citations were taken from Michael Ignatieff, *Blood & Belonging: Journeys into the New Nationalisms* (Toronto: Viking, 1993), pp. 153-55.
47. Ziman, "Nationalism and the Kurdish National Liberation Movement," p. 51. Ocalan himself recently declared: "We want to put an end to the stereotype of the old-fashioned kind of Kurdish woman; it is vile. I am trying to assist the women to become independent from men and to be self-reliant." Abdullah Ocalan, "Kurdish Women: A Great Surge Towards Freedom." *Kurdistan Report,* Nov./Dec. 1996, p. 56.
48. The following discussion is based on Border, "Orphan Guerrillas," pp. 41-42.
49. Hazhir Teimourian, "Turkey—The Challenge of the Kurdistan Workers' Party," *Jane's Intelligence Review* 5 (Jan. 1993), p. 32.
50. Border, "Orphan Guerrillas," p. 42.
51. Ayla Ganioglu, "Turkey: Gures 'Suspicious' of U.S. Support of Kurds," *TDN,* April 24, 1996, p. A4; as cited in *FBIS-WEU,* April 26, 1996, p. 26.
52. Kemal Yunteri, "PKK Acquires U.S. Missiles," *Cumhuriyet* (Istanbul), June 19, 1995, p. 4; as cited in *FBIS-WEU,* June 23, 1995, p. 56.
53. The following data and citations were taken from the parliament's publication entitled "Kurdistan Parliament in Exile," April 12-16, 1995.
54. Cited in Hussein Dakroub, "Marxist Ocalan Declares 'Jihad' against the West," *TDN,* April 15, 1995.
55. Ironically, the PKK contributed to this very "fratricidal war" in Iraqi Kurdistan by suddenly attacking Barzani's KDP in the Bahdinan area a few months later.
56. The following analysis is largely based on Imset, *The PKK,* pp. 15-17; and "Programme," *Serxwebun,* (PKK), Feb. 1983.
57. The following figures were taken from General Secretariat of the National Security Council (Turkey), *12 September in Turkey: Before and After* (Ankara: Ongun Kardesler Printing House, 1982), pp. 245-50.
58. *Ibid.,* p. 249.
59. The following citations were taken from Imset, *The PKK,* pp. 150 and 350.
60. This and the following citation were taken from "PKK Reportedly Developing New Command," *TDN,* June 14, 1994, p. 2; as cited in *FBIS-WEU,* June 20, 1994, p. 48.
61. This and the following citation were taken from "Kurdish Official Views Cudi Mountain Fighting," *Ozgur Ulke* (Istanbul), Aug. 6, 1994, p. 4; as cited in *FBIS-WEU,* Aug. 11, 1994, p. 42.
62. The following data and citations were taken from Imset, *The PKK,* pp. 75-77.
63. The following data and citations were taken from *ibid.,* pp. 228-29.
64. Cited in Ismet G. Imset, "PKK's Ocalan Interviewed on Issues, Developments," *TDN,* April 17, 1993, pp. 1, 11; as cited in *FBIS-WEU,* May 4, 1993, p. 56.
65. This and the following citation were taken from "Kurdish Official Calls for Dialogue, Federation," *La Libre Belgique* (Brussels), April 22, 1993, p. 4; as cited in *FBIS-WEU,* May 6, 1993, p. 58.

66. The following data and citations were taken from Sinan Yilmaz, "Current Year Critical for Kurdish Problem," *TDN*, May 7, 1994, pp. 1, 8; as cited in *FBIS-WEU*, May 11, 1994, p. 43.

67. International Conference on North West Kurdistan (South East Turkey), "Final Resolution," Brussels, Belgium, Mar. 12-13, 1994.

68. Cited in "PKK Leader Ocalan's Letter to West Detailed," *Ozgur Ulke*, Nov. 26, 1994, p. 4; as cited in *FBIS-WEU*, Nov. 30, 1994, pp. 55-57.

69. This and the following citations were taken from Ismet G. Imset, "A Historic Decision by the PKK Prior to the CSCE Summit," *Ozgur Ulke*, Dec. 5, 1994, p. 7; as cited in *FBIS-WEU*, Dec. 9, 1994, p. 55.

70. Hayri Birler, "PKK Congress Approves Exile Government, General Staff & Liberated Area," *TDN*, Dec. 27, 1994.

71. The following data and citations were largely taken from "Central Committee Statement of the PKK (Kurdistan Workers Party) Following the Fifth Congress of the PKK," Feb. 1995.

72. The following citation and data were taken from ERNK European Representation, Press Release #5, "Turkey Should Respect the Cease-Fire," Dec. 21, 1995. Largely ignored by both sides, the PKK formally called off this cease-fire in the summer of 1996.

73. This and the following citations were taken from "President Ocalan's Newroz Message," made available to this author by the American Kurdish Information Network [ERNK], Washington, D.C., April 4, 1996.

74. Imset, *The PKK*, p. 155.

75. "Paper Details PKK Activities in CIS States," *Turkish Probe* (Ankara), Nov. 4, 1994, p. 13; as cited in *FBIS-WEU*, Nov. 10, 1994, p. 66.

76. Painton, "From Banditry to Civil War," p. 26.

77 Patricia Tourancheau, "Turks Bled White by 'Revolutionary Tax,'" *Liberation* (Paris), May 5, 1992, pp. 28-29; as cited in *FBIS-WEU*, May 28, 1992, pp. 58-60.

78. Imset, *The PKK*, p. 156. Writing in the summer of 1995, Hayri Birler agreed with this figure of DM 500 annually from drug dealing. "PKK Involvement in Drug Trafficking Detailed," *TDN*, July 11, 1995, p. A8; as cited in *FBIS-WEU*, July 17, 1995, p. 27.

79. Ismet G. Imset, "Security is Better in the Cities, Little Improved in Rural Areas," *Turkish Times* (Washington, D.C.), Feb. 1, 1994, p. 7.

80. Cited in Higueras, "We Are not Terrorists," p. 6. See note 14 above for the full citation. Indeed, the Turkish parliament's commission to investigate killings by unknown persons reported that many people believed that JITEM, the intelligence service of the gendarmerie, was involved in such extralegal activities as arms and drug smuggling. See Martin van Bruinessen, "Turkey's Death Squads," *Middle East Report* no. 199 (April-June 1996), p. 22.

81. "Interview [by David Korn] with Abdullah Ocalan General Secretary of the Kurdistan Workers Party," distributed by the American Kurdish Information Network [ERNK], [June 1995]. Also see "PKK Leader on Party Ideology, U.S. Policy," *Serxwebun* (Cologne), April 1995, pp. 12-14, 23; as cited in *FBIS-WEU*, June 27, 1995, pp. 6-7.

82. Cited in "PKK Involvement in Drug Smuggling Detailed," *TDN*, Dec. 3, 1993, p. B1; as cited in *FBIS-WEU*, Dec. 7, 1993, p. 40.

83. The following discussion is based on "'Uniformed Gangs' and the Rule of Law," *Briefing*, Oct. 7, 1996, p. 10; "CHP Investigations in Southeast Uncover Drug Trafficking Activities," *Briefing*, Oct. 14, 1996, p. 2; and Kelly Couturier, "Security Forces Allegedly Involved in Turkish Criminal Gang," *Washington Post*, Nov. 27, 1996, p. A24. In January 1997, a German court declared that evidence indicated there were close ties between the Turkish government and heroin traffickers operating in Turkey and Europe. Kurdish clans employed by the government as village guards and Tansu Ciller were specifically named. The Turkish government indignantly denied the charges. Kelly Couturier, "Turkey Blasts German Court's Drug Claim," *Washington Post*, Jan. 23, 1997, p. A24.

84. *Hurriyet* (Istanbul), Nov. 1, 1995.

85. Robert Gelbard, "International Narcotics Strategy Report," United States Information Agency briefing, April 4, 1994; as cited in Human Rights Watch Arms Project, *Weapons Transfers and Violations of the Laws of War in Turkey* (Human Rights Watch: New York, 1995), p. 144.

86. Cited in Ugur Akinci, "United States: PKK Is Involved in Drug Traffic in Europe," *TDN*, May 1, 1995.

87. "German Parliamentarian: PKK a 'Political Problem,'" Ankara Turkiye Radyolari Network in Turkish, 1100 GMT, Oct. 22, 1992; as cited in *FBIS-WEU*, Oct. 27, 1992, p. 55.

88. Frank J. Gaffney, Jr., "Iraq's Kurdish Victims, Turkey's Kurdish Terrorists," *Wall Street Journal*, Mar. 26, 1992.

89. The following analysis and citations are taken from Alan Cowell, "Heroin Pouring Through Porous European Borders," *New York Times International*, Feb. 9, 1993, p. A3.

90. Ignatieef, *Blood & Belonging*, p. 152.

91. Cited in *FBIS-WEU*, July 17, 1995, p. 28. See note 78 above for the full citation.

92. "Armed Forces Discover Huge KWP Drugs Cache," *Sabah* (Istanbul), April 20, 1995. (Accessed over the internet.) Also see *ibid.*, which stated that "it was determined, during Turkey's six-week operation into northern Iraq . . . the PKK is also using this region for the production of drugs."

93. The following data and citations were taken from Scott Peterson, "Turkey—With Help From U.S.—Chokes Off Drug Trafficking," *Christian Science Monitor*, May 1, 1996. See also Richard Cole, "Terrorists Help Feed Heroin Need: DEA Taking Aim at Kurdish Pipeline," *Tennessean*, Dec. 16, 1996, p. 11A.

94. Nur Bilge Criss, "The Nature of PKK Terrorism in Turkey," *Studies in Conflict & Terrorism* 18 (January-March 1995), p. 29.

95. "Military View on Terror Expressed at Briefing," Ankara Anatolia in English, 1015 GMT, July 12, 1993; as cited in *FBIS-WEU*, July 12, 1993, p. 58.

96. "MED TV Interviews PKK Leader Ocalan," London MED TV Television in Turkish, 1945 GMT, Jan. 1, 1997; as cited *FBIS-WEU*, Jan. 1, 1997, p. 1.

97. Oliver Van Vaerenbergh, "Kurdish Leader Criticizes Belgium, Turkey for Police Raids," *Le Soir* (Brussels), Sept. 21-22, 1996, p. 33; as cited in *FBIS-WEU*, Sept. 26, 1996, p. 1.

98. "The Kurdish 'Temple' Has Been Ransacked!" American Kurdish Information Network, Press Release #14, Sept. 20, 1996.

## CHAPTER THREE

1. For an analysis of earlier events, see my *The Kurds in Turkey: A Political Dilemma* (Boulder: Westview Press, 1990). Parts of the ensuing analysis originally appeared in my *The Changing Kurdish Problem in Turkey*, no. 270 (London: Research Institute for the Study of Conflict and Terrorism, 1994), pp. 2-14, 17-23; and *The Kurds of Iraq: Tragedy and Hope* (New York: St. Martin's Press, 1992), pp. 98-106.

2. Martin van Bruinessen, *Agha, Shaikh and State: The Social and Political Structures of Kurdistan* (London: Zed Books, 1992), p. 32.

3. Hamit Bozarslan, "Political Aspects of the Kurdish Problem in Contemporary Turkey," in *The Kurds: A Contemporary Overview*, Philip G. Kreyenbroek and Stefan Sperl, eds. (London: Routledge, 1992), pp. 104-5.

4. This figure and the following citation were taken from Mehrdad R. Izady, *The Kurds: A Concise Handbook* (Washington: Crane Russak, 1992), p. 119. Corroborating Izady's figure, a report drawn up by the National Security Council (MGK) Secretariat in Turkey and released at the end of 1996, declared "the Kurdish people will make up 40 percent of the population in the year 2010. That they will increase to make up more than 50 percent of the population in the year 2025 is a possibility." Cited in "MIT Report on Antiterror Struggle Revealed," *Milliyet*, Dec. 18, 1996, p. 12; as cited in *Foreign Broadcast Information Service— West Europe*, Dec. 18, 1996, p. 2; hereafter cited as *FBIS-WEU*. On the other hand, another analysis of the size of the Kurdish population in Turkey disputes these figures by concluding that presently there are only slightly more than 7 million Kurds living in Turkey, which constitutes 12.60 percent of the country's total population, "far lower than the 12.5 million to 15 million claimed by some." Servet Mutlu, "Ethnic Kurds in Turkey: A Demographic Study," *International Journal of Middle East Studies* 28 (Nov. 1996), pp. 532, 533. Mutlu, however, did not try to explain why Turkey's late President Ozal himself had been one of those associated with the much higher figures.

5. Izady, *The Kurds*, p. 125.

6. Ankara TRT Television in Turkish, 1800 GMT, Oct. 14, 1992; as cited in *FBIS-WEU*, Oct. 15, 1992, p. 28. Mutlu, however, concluded that although the number of Kurds in the west had increased from one-fifth of their total population throughout Turkey in 1965 to one-third in 1990, "still, the number of Kurds in the west is far lower than often claimed" and certainly nowhere near the percentage asserted by Ozal. Mutlu, "Ethnic Kurds in Turkey," pp. 532-33.

7. The following discussion is based in part on "Pro-Turkish Terror and Ethnic Clashes Continue," *Briefing* (Ankara), Nov. 9, 1992, p. 6; and "Spread of Violence Beyond SE Brings New Dangers for Democracy," *Briefing*, Dec. 14, 1992, p. 12.

8. Helsinki Rights Watch, *Destroying Ethnic Identity: The Kurds of Turkey, An Update* (New York: Helsinki Rights Watch, 1990), pp. 13-18. Also see Martin van Bruinessen, "The Kurds in Turkey: Further Restrictions of Basic Rights," *International Commission of Jurists: The Review*, no. 45 (1990), pp. 46-52.

9. "Ozal Puts Up Brave Performance in Strasbourg—But Brussels Still Says 'No,'" *Briefing*, Oct. 2, 1989, p. 4.

10. Muserref Seckin and Ilter Sagirsoy, "Measures to Solve Kurdish Problem Proposed," *Nokta*, June 3, 1990, pp. 17-22; as cited in *FBIS-WEU*, Aug. 6, 1990, p. 38.

11. Sevket Okant and Murat Bardacki, "We Met with Abdullah Ocalan," *Hurriyet,* Apr. 1, 1990, p. 16; as cited in *FBIS-WEU,* Apr. 9, 1990, p. 26.

12. "The Southeast Report: What Does It Say?" *Briefing,* July 23, 1990, p. 5.

13. Sefik Kahramankaptan, "The Issue of Protecting the Kurds," *Tempo,* Feb. 2, 1991, pp. 16-17; as cited in *FBIS-WEU,* Feb. 22, 1991, p. 37.

14. Ilter Sagirsoy and Nedret Ersamel, "We Created 10 Million Kurds," *Nokta,* Feb. 10, 1991, pp. 20-27; as cited in *FBIS-WEU,* Mar. 6, 1991, p. 26.

15. "Reasons for Change Elaborated," Ankara Anatolia in English, 1510 GMT, Jan. 28, 1991; as cited in *FBIS-WEU,* Jan. 29, 1991, p. 56.

16. Cited in "Ozal Interviewed on Kurdish Issue, Violence," *Milliyet,* Aug. 23, 1992, p. 11; as cited in *FBIS-WEU,* Sept. 3, 1992, p. 39.

17. "Demirel Warns on Effects of Kurdish Issue," *Cumhuriyet* (Istanbul), Mar. 26, 1991, p. 4; as cited in *FBIS-WEU,* April 2, 1991, pp. 36-37.

18. "Unbanning of Kurdish Discussed, Examined," *Nokta,* Feb. 10, 1991, pp. 26-27; as cited in *FBIS-WEU,* Mar. 6, 1991, p. 29.

19. Ilter Sagirsoy, "No, Despite Ozal," *Nokta,* Feb. 24, 1991, pp. 28-29; as cited in *FBIS-WEU,* Mar. 26, 1991, pp. 41-42.

20. The following citations were taken from Institut Kurde de Paris, *Information and Liaison Bulletin,* no. 70, Jan. 1991, pp. 2-4; and "Language Freedom to Herald Democracy Drive?" *Briefing,* Feb. 11, 1991, pp. 6-9.

21. Sagirsoy and Ersanel, "We Created 10 Million Kurds," as cited in *FBIS-WEU,* Mar. 6, 1991, p. 27.

22. Mehmet Korkmaz, "Reactions from Kurdish Intellectuals," *Tempo,* Feb. 3-9, 1991, pp. 14-15; as cited in *FBIS-WEU,* Mar. 7, 1991, p. 37.

23. "Good-for-You to Ozal from Kurds," *Nokta,* Feb. 17, 1991, pp. 26-29; as cited in *FBIS-WEU,* Mar. 26, 1991, pp. 39-41.

24. Mehmet Ali Birand, "Interview with Abdullah Ocalan," *Milliyet,* Mar. 25, 1991, p. 19; as cited in *FBIS-WEU,* Apr. 2, 1991, p. 39.

25. "Kurdish Rebel Leader Proposes Talks with Ankara," Paris AFP in English, 0333 GMT, Mar. 23, 1991; as cited in *FBIS-WEU,* Mar. 25, 1991, pp. 44-45.

26. The following discussion and citations were taken from "Nationalist Uproar Spreads After Oath-Taking Incident," *Briefing,* Nov. 11, 1991, pp. 3-6.

27. Cited in "Demirel Warns on Effects of Kurdish Issue," *Cumhuriyet,* Mar. 26, 1991, p. 4; as cited in *FBIS-WEU,* Apr. 2, 1991, pp. 36-37. He repeated this figure a year after he had returned to power: "There are people of 26 different ethnic origins in Turkey." "Interview with Prime Minister Demirel," *Turkiye,* Oct. 10, 1992, p. 14; as cited in *FBIS-WEU,* Nov. 12, 1992, p. 54. In his ground-breaking, encyclopedic compilation of invaluable insights and statistics, Peter A. Andrews, ed., *Ethnic Groups in the Republic of Turkey* (Wiesbaden: Dr. Ludwig Reichert Verlag, 1989), p. 47, identified "forty-seven ethnic groups" in Turkey.

28. Ihsan Akdemir, "Restoration in Southeast," *Milliyet,* Dec. 2, 1991, p. 17; as cited in *FBIS-WEU,* Jan. 8, 1992, p. 58.

29. Cited in Meric Koyatasi, "Demirel on Domestic, Foreign Policy, Cyprus," *Hurriyet,* Nov. 26, 1991, p. 18; as cited in *FBIS-WEU,* Dec. 3, 1991, p. 46.

30. Kamran Qurrah Daghi, "Deputy Premier Inonu Explains Policy on Kurds," London *Al-Hayah,* Dec. 13, 1991, p. 4; as cited in *FBIS-WEU,* Dec. 17, 1991, p. 57.

31. Cited in "Coalition Outlines Plans for Southeast," *Milliyet,* Nov. 17, 1991, p. 16; as cited in *FBIS-WEU,* Dec. 18, 1991, pp. 55-56.

32. "Kurdish Reality Recognized," Ankara Anatolia in English, 1505 GMT, Dec. 8, 1991; as cited in *FBIS-WEU,* Dec. 9, 1991, p. 55.

33. This and the following citation were taken from "The Kurdish Question: From 1991 to 1992," *Briefing,* Jan. 6, 1992, pp. 9-10.

34. "Coalition Outlines Plans for Southeast," as cited in *FBIS-WEU,* Dec. 18, 1991, p. 55.

35. Ismet G. Imset, "Report on PKK, Dev Sol Camps in Lebanon," *Turkish Daily News,* Dec. 4, 1991, pp. 8, 11; as cited in *FBIS-WEU,* Dec. 18, 1991, p. 53.

36. "Part Two of Interview," *Turkish Daily News,* Nov. 26, 1991, p. 5; as cited in *FBIS-WEU,* Dec. 3, 1991, p. 56.

37. "Demirel Comments on PKK, German Ties," Ankara TRT Television Network in Turkish, 1700 GMT, Mar. 30, 1992; as cited in *FBIS-WEU,* Mar. 31, 1992, p. 25.

38. "SDPP Reports Set to Embarrass Leadership and Government," *Briefing,* Apr. 13, 1992, p. 6.

39. Helsinki Watch, "Kurds Massacred: Turkish Forces Kill Scores of Peaceful Demonstrators," June 1992, p. 14.

40. Caroline Moorehead, "'Secret War' Against Kurds in Turkey," *Independent,* Jan. 20, 1992.

41. Ismet G. Imset, "News Analysis: Who Really Controls the Kurdish Hezbollah?" *Turkish Daily News,* Sept. 7, 1993, p. 3; as cited in *FBIS-WEU,* Sept. 14, 1993, p. 67.

42. These figures were compiled by the Human Rights Foundation of Turkey as cited in Martin van Bruinessen, "Turkey's Death Squads," *Middle East Report,* no. 199 (April-June 1996), p. 23.

43. Ismet G. Imset, "Terrorist Acts in Southeast Detailed," *Turkish Daily News,* May 27, 1992, p. 3; as cited in *FBIS-WEU,* June 15, 1992, p. 43.

44. Cited in *ibid.*

45. The following discussion is based on Amnesty International, "Turkey: Walls of Glass," Nov. 1992, p. 14; and Helsinki Watch, "Turkey: Eight Journalists Killed Since February; A Ninth Critically Wounded," Aug. 1992. Subsequently, two more journalists and a newspaper distributor were killed, leading Helsinki Watch to conclude that "these murders suggest an on-going campaign to silence the dissident press in southeast Turkey." "Turkey: Censorship by Assassination," Dec. 1992, p. 2. Also see Helsinki Watch, "The Kurds of Turkey: Killings, Disappearances and Torture," Mar. 1993; and Helsinki Watch, "Turkey: Censorship by Assassination Continues," Feb. 1994.

46. This and the following citations were taken from "Interior Minister Views Terrorist Situation," *Turkish Daily News,* Aug. 14, 1992, p. 2; as cited in *FBIS-WEU,* Aug. 20, 1992, p. 57.

47. This and the following discussion are based on "Hizbullah: Both Friend and Enemy," *Briefing,* Feb. 22, 1993, pp. 7-9; "'Hizbullah Militant' Interviewed on Struggle," *Cumhuriyet,* Feb. 16, 1993, pp. 1, 9; as cited in *FBIS-WEU,* Feb. 22, 1993, pp. 45-46; and "'Anatolia People's Front' Said to be Force Fighting PKK," *Tercuman,* Mar. 8, 1993, pp. 2, 12; as cited in *FBIS-WEU,* Mar. 24, 1993, pp. 56-61.

48. Kemal Balci, "Report on Variant Hizbullah Structures, Links," *Turkish Daily News,* April 22, 1995, pp. 1, A8; as cited in *FBIS-WEU,* May 2, 1995, p. 42.

49. Aydin Engin, "'Hizbullah Militant' Interviewed on Struggle," *Cumhuriyet,* Feb. 16, 1993, pp. 1, 9; as cited in *FBIS-WEU,* Feb. 22, 1993, p. 45.

50. Aydin Engin, "Hizbullah Member on Affiliations, Fighting PKK," *Cumhuriyet,* Feb. 17, 1993, p. 17; as cited in *FBIS-WEU,* Feb. 24, 1993, p. 61.

51. Ali Oncu, "Part Five: AHC Leader Interviewed," *Tercuman,* Mar. 13, 1993, pp. 2, 11; as cited in *FBIS-WEU,* Mar. 24, 1993, p. 60.

52. The following discussion is based on Ismet G. Imset, "News Analysis: Who Really Controls the Kurdish Hezbollah?" *Turkish Daily News,* Sept. 7, 1993, p. 3; as cited in *FBIS-WEU,* Sept. 14, 1993, pp. 67-70; and Ismet G. Imset, "Is There a 'Nationalist' Connection to the Killings?" *Turkish Daily News,* Sept. 8, 1993, p. 8; as cited in *FBIS-WEU,* Sept. 13, 1993, pp. 69-73.

53. The following information was gathered from "The Crook, the Deputy, the Cop and the Lover," *Briefing,* Nov. 11, 1996, pp. 4-6; "Presidential Utterings Give Succor to Coalition," *Briefing,* Nov. 25, 1996, pp. 5-7; and Kelly Couturier, "Turkish Scandal Exposes Links Between Crime, State Officials," *Washington Post,* Jan. 1, 1997, pp. A21, A25.

54. Cited in Bruinessen, "Turkey's Death Squads," p. 22. Kurdish sources also blame Kanat, the late Turkish army intelligence officer Ahmet Cem Ersever, and Adem Yakin for the unsolved murder of DEP MP Mehmet Sincar in September 1993. Hatip Dicle, "To the Memory of Mehmet Sincar," *Ozgur Politika,* Sept. 4, 1996; as reprinted in American Kurdish Information Network, *Kurdish News,* Jan. 1997, p. 6. Some have also speculated about the role of the so-called gladio in Turkey's unsolved killings. The gladio was a secret guerrilla group created by the government during the cold war for use if Turkey were occupied by a foreign enemy.

55. "SDPP: Better in the Government or Out?" *Briefing,* Oct. 26, 1992, pp. 7-8.

56. This and the following citation were taken from "Appeals Court Judge Spokesman for Authoritarian Mood," *Briefing,* Sept. 14, 1992, p. 6.

57. "Demirel Denounces Attacks Against the State," Ankara TRT Television Network in Turkish, 1700 GMT, Sept. 22, 1992; as cited in *FBIS-WEU,* Sept. 23, 1992, p. 45.

58. "Chief of Staff Discusses PKK, Saratoga Incident," *Turkiye,* Oct. 8, 1992, p. 13; as cited in *FBIS-WEU,* Oct. 13, 1992, p. 37.

59. For analyses of the Turkish army's apparent destruction of much of this city on August 18, 1992, and the ensuing uprooting of its population, see "Military Aspect Emphasized at Meetings on Sirnak," *Briefing,* Aug. 31, 1992, pp. 3-5; and "A Parliamentary Report on the Events of Sirnak," in Institut Kurde de Paris, "The Situation in Turkish Kurdistan," pp. 15-18. The latter source of eight DYP and SDPP members of the Turkish parliament concluded that "it was the State who attacked the civilian population of Sirnak," *ibid.,* p. 18, a conclusion also reached by the former source. Also see Helsinki Watch, "Broken Promises: Torture and Killings Continue in Turkey," Dec. 1992, p. 53, where the analysis concludes that "the Sirnak episode was not the first time that troops had apparently decided to punish civilians for attacks against the military."

60. Ali Ozluer, "The PKK Has Declared War," *Hurriyet,* Mar. 24, 1992, p. 19; as cited in *FBIS-WEU,* Apr. 1, 1992, p. 39.

61. "Milliyet Interviews PKK Leader Ocalan, Part II," *Milliyet,* Mar. 24, 1992, p. 14; as cited in *FBIS-WEU,* Mar. 27, 1992, p. 42.

62. "Milliyet Interviews PKK Leader Ocalan, Part I," *Milliyet,* Mar. 23, 1992, p. 14; as cited in *FBIS-WEU,* Mar. 27, 1992, p. 42.

63. "Milliyet Interviews PKK Leader Ocalan, Part II," as cited in *FBIS-WEU,* Mar. 27, 1992, p. 43.

64. "Milliyet Interviews PKK Leader Ocalan, Part III," as cited in *FBIS-WEU,* Mar. 27, 1992, p. 44.
65. Donald L. Horowitz, *Ethnic Groups in Conflict* (Berkeley: University of California Press, 1985), p. 683.
66. *Ibid.,* p. 684.
67. Cited in "Ocalan Spokesman Denies Report," *Hurriyet,* Mar. 14, 1993, p. 22; as cited in *FBIS-WEU,* Mar. 15, 1993, p. 43.
68. The following citations were taken from Kamran Qurrah Daghi, "Ocalan Explains Peace Overtures," *Al-Hayah,* Mar. 17, 1993, pp. 1, 4; as cited in *FBIS-WEU,* Mar. 22, 1993, p. 42.
69. According to Robert Olson, "Sheikh Said had led the largest armed and most sustained Kurdish nationalist rebellion of the twentieth century." *The Emergence of Kurdish Nationalism and the Sheikh Said Rebellion, 1880-1925* (Austin: University of Texas, 1989), p. 127. After crushing his rebellion, the Turks hanged him on June 29, 1925. Bedr Khan Beg ruled the powerful Kurdish emirate of Botan—which at its height included much of present-day southeastern Turkey and even parts of Iraqi Kurdistan—from approximately 1821-1847. In 1847, the Turks forced him to surrender and sent him into exile where he died. See Bruinessen, *Agha, Shaikh and State,* pp. 177-82; and Thomas Bois and Vladimir Minorsky, "Kurds, Kurdistan," *The Encyclopedia of Islam* (new edition), V, 1981, p. 462. At a Kurdish conference in 1993, I met Sait T. Badrakhan from San Diego, California, a member of the family's current generation.
70. The following data and citations were taken from "PKK, PSK Leaders Issue Statement Following Meeting," (Clandestine) Voice of the People of Kurdistan in Arabic, 1630 GMT, Mar. 28, 1993; as cited in *FBIS-WEU,* Mar. 29, 1993, p. 60.
71. Cited in "Government Caught Out by Apo's Offer," *Briefing,* Mar. 22-29, 1993, p. 3.
72. "Can the Ceasefire Be Turned into a Peace?" *Briefing,* April 19, 1993, p. 9. General Dogan Gures, the chief of staff, declared that "the latest [October 1992] cross-border operations into northern Iraq broke PKK leader Abdullah Ocalan's strength." "Sabah Reports Chief of General Staff Interview," *Sabah,* Apr. 7, 1993, p. 16; as cited in *FBIS-WEU,* Apr. 13, 1993, p. 41. Interior Minister Ismet Sezgin claimed that the PKK had "received a strong blow in 1992" and "as a result of the loss of sympathy and prestige . . . decided to set aside their arms." "Sezgin Declares Nation, State United Against Terrorism," Ankara TRT Television Network in Turkish, 1700 GMT, Mar. 25, 1993; as cited in *FBIS-WEU,* Mar. 30, 1993, p. 52.
73. This and the following citation were taken from "PKK Puts Shocking End to a 'Peace' Which Ankara Never Gave a Chance," *Briefing,* May 31–June 7, 1993, p. 6.
74. Cited in Ali H. Yurtsever, "Abdullah Ocalan Defends PKK's Activities," *Milliyet,* May 27, 1993, p. 19; as cited in *FBIS-WEU,* June 2, 1993, p. 58.
75. Ismet G. Imset, "Kurdish Issue: Searching for Solutions," *Turkish Probe,* Apr. 6, 1993, pp. 2-5; as cited in *FBIS-WEU,* Apr. 21, pp. 59-60. Elsewhere Imset wrote: "There is no, repeat no state policy on Turkey's Kurds other than realizing the 'Kurdish identity,' whatever that means"; and "one of the problems in finding a solution to the problem is inevitably the Turkish mentality, which is still very much under the influence of the post-coup [i.e. military] regime." Ismet G. Imset, "Cease Fire on Razor's Edge as Ankara Ignores Kurdish Issue," *Turkish Probe,* May 4, 1993, pp. 6-8; as cited in *FBIS-WEU,* May 20, 1993, p. 41.

76. This and the following citation were taken from "Government Caught Out by Apo's Offer," p. 5. In fairness to Demirel, it should be pointed out that he encouraged the ending of the strife, arguing that "no one is pleased with bloodshed in the country and that it is not the state that causes the bloodshed." *Ibid.* Furthermore, of course, no government could simply agree suddenly to negotiate with those it for so long had denounced as "terrorists," a situation Ocalan himself recognized when he offered to step aside in favor of Kurdish parliamentarians in discussions with Ankara.

77  Cited in "Further on Demirel Comments on Terror," Ankara TRT Television Network in Turkish, 1800 GMT, Mar. 16, 1993; as cited in *FBIS-WEU*, Mar. 22, 1993, p. 41.

78. Cited in Fikret Bila, "Federation Cannot Be Established," *Milliyet*, Mar. 23, 1993, p. 12; as cited in *FBIS-WEU*, Mar. 30, 1993, p. 52. Ozal, on the other hand, was on record as being willing to discuss the concept of federation, even though he had added that he thought it wrong.

79. "Sabah Reports Chief of General Staff Interview," *Sabah*, Apr. 7, 1993, p. 16; as cited in *FBIS-WEU*, Apr. 13, 1993, p. 41.

80. This and the following citations were taken from Ismet G. Imset, "Wiping Out the PKK Again and Again . . . ," *Turkish Probe*, July 6, 1993, pp. 4-7; as cited in *FBIS-WEU*, July 29, 1993, p. 52.

81. Cited in "Talabani Interviewed on Ties with Turkey," *Ozgur Gundem*, Dec. 19, 1993, p. 11; as cited in *FBIS-WEU*, Dec. 27, 1993, p. 35. Talabani expressed similar sentiments concerning Ozal's intentions when I spoke with him at his home in Irbil, Iraqi Kurdistan, on Aug. 16, 1993.

82. This and the following citation were taken from Rafet Balli, "The Way Ocalan Views Turkish Leaders," *Milliyet*, Mar. 26, 1993, p. 20; as cited in *FBIS-WEU*, April 2, 1993, p. 65.

83. This and the following citation were taken from Ismet G. Imset, "PKK Leader Says Attacks Will Force 'Political Solution,'" *Turkish Daily News*, June 12, 1993, pp. 1, 11; as cited in *FBIS-WEU*, June 22, 1993, p. 75. Elsewhere Ocalan even went so far as to call Ozal's death from a heart attack "suspicious."

84. This and the following citations were taken from "Way Ocalan Views Turkish Leaders," as cited in *FBIS-WEU*, April 2, 1993, p. 65.

85. Shaikh Sait, as mentioned above, was hanged. Ocalan's reference was to Sezgin's recommendation that he surrender to "the compassionate arms of Turkish justice."

86. Cited in "PKK's Ocalan Announces End to Cease-Fire," London Kanal-6 Television in Turkish, 1630 GMT, June 8, 1993; as cited in *FBIS-WEU*, June 10, 1993, p. 70. Jalal Talabani specifically confirmed this information when I spoke at length with him in Irbil, Iraqi Kurdistan, on Aug. 16, 1993. Also see "PKK Puts Shocking End of a 'Peace' Which Ankara Never Gave a Chance," *Briefing*, May 31–June 7, 1993, p. 6, which declares: "it was common knowledge that the PKK massacre had been carried out without the knowledge of other PKK commanders. . . . Apo himself had not ordered the attack." Sakik's brother, Sirri Sakik, was a DEP member of the Turkish parliament from Mus.

87. Cited in "Government Adopts Military Thinking Despite Spattering of Appeals for Common Sense," *Briefing*, Nov. 15, 1993, p. 6.

88. Cited in "More of the Same in Store After Latest Crisis," *Briefing*, Nov. 1, 1993, p. 4.

89. Cited in Ismet G. Imset, "Southeast Crisis: Turning to Military Politics," *Turkish Probe,* July 20, 1993, pp. 2-5; as cited in *FBIS-WEU,* July 29, 1993, p. 56.

90. Imset, "Wiping Out the PKK Again," as cited in *FBIS-WEU,* July 29, 1993, p. 52.

91. This figure of 4,100 killed in 1993 was obtained from Alistar Lyon, "Turkey's Kurdish Crisis is Thorn in Ciller's Side," Reuters, Feb. 9, 1994. Some 2,650 had died in 1992, the highest previous annual total. Reuters, Dec. 12, 1993.

92. See "Tuzla Bombing a Symptom of Much More," *Briefing,* Feb. 21, 1994, p. 4.

93. "Kurds Holding U.S., New Zealand Citizens," Paris AFP in English, 2038 GMT, Oct. 15, 1993; as cited in *FBIS-WEU,* Oct. 18, 1993, p. 43.

94. Cited in "Kurds Sentence Tourism to Death," *The European,* June 15, 1995.

95. *Ibid.*

96. For these figures, see Aliza Marcus, "Turkish Writers from 'Closed University' Behind Bars," *Turkish Daily News,* Mar. 7, 1995; Rasit Gurdilek, "Turkey Counts Costs and Benefits of Iraq Incursion," *Turkish Probe,* April 21, 1995, p. 7; Alan Cowell, "War on Kurds Strains Turks' Ties to Allies," *International Herald Tribune,* Nov. 18, 1994; Human Rights Watch/Helsinki, "Turkey: Forced Displacement of Ethnic Kurds from Southeastern Turkey," Oct. 1994, p. 8; "Military Operations Don't Mean Prosperity," *Briefing,* May 20, 1996, p. 8; Umit Enginsoy, "Pro-Kurdish Party Figure Interviewed on Goals," Paris AFP in English, 0858 GMT, Dec. 22, 1995; as cited in *FBIS-WEU,* Dec. 22, 1995, p. 25; Eric Rouleau, "Turkey: Beyond Ataturk," *Foreign Policy,* no. 103 (Summer 1996), p. 81; and David McDowall, *A Modern History of the Kurds* (London: I.B. Taurus, 1996), p. 441. In addition, one should also factor in the so-called Apo compensation, the money the government pays to keep some 200,000 civil servants in the state of emergency region.

97. "PKK's Ocalan Threatens Pipeline, Vows Economic War," *Ozgur Gundem,* Oct. 18, 1993, p. 11; as cited in *FBIS-WEU,* Oct. 21, 1993, p. 58.

98. Servet Yildirim, "Turkish Current Deficit May Hit $6 Bln—Official," Reuters, Dec. 1, 1993.

99. "Military Operations Don't Mean Prosperity," *Briefing,* May 20, 1996, p. 8. Writing several years earlier, Morton I. Abramowitz, "Dateline Ankara: Turkey After Ozal," *Foreign Policy,* no. 91 (Summer 1993), p. 165, declared that the war was involving "perhaps as much as 30 percent of military forces."

100. The following discussion is based on "Government Discusses Regional Economy," *Briefing,* Oct. 5, 1992, pp. 6-7; and "Heightened Tensions Due to Embargo and Shootings," *Briefing,* Aug. 17, 1992, pp. 6-7.

101. This citation and the following discussion are based on "More of the Same in Store After Latest Crisis," *Briefing,* Nov. 1, 1993, p. 4; and "Demirel Hints Kurdish Situation Could Worsen," *Yeni Gunaydin* (Istanbul), Nov. 2, 1993, p. 11; as cited in *FBIS-WEU,* Nov. 4, 1993, p. 58.

102. "Demirel Hints Kurdish Situation Could Worsen," as cited in *FBIS-WEU,* Nov. 4, 1993, p. 58.

103. "Central Committee Statement of the PKK (Kurdistan Workers Party) Following the Fifth Congress of the PKK," Feb. 1995.

104. Cited in "Ocalan on PKK Strength," *Turkish Daily News,* Mar. 21, 1995, p. A4; as cited in *FBIS-WEU,* Mar. 24, 1995, p. 43.

105. This and the following citation were taken from Human Rights Watch Arms Project, *Weapons Transfers and Violations of the Laws of War in Turkey* (New York: Human Rights Watch, 1995), p. 54.

106. This and the following citation were taken from "PKK Leader Reportedly 'Incensed' Over Losses," *Turkish Daily News,* Oct. 17, 1994, pp. 1, A8; as cited in *FBIS-WEU,* Oct. 20, 1994, p. 55.

107. This and the following citation were taken from "Prosperity Party Leader Interviewed," Ankara Show Television in Turkish, 2030 GMT, Jan. 31, 1994; as cited in *FBIS-WEU,* Feb. 3, 1994, p. 41. In the rest of Turkey, of course, the government considered Erbakan's party a threat. For background, see Richard Tapper, ed., *Islam in Modern Turkey: Religion, Politics and Literature in a Secular State* (London: I. B. Tauris, 1994); and Serif Mardin, *Religion and Social Change in Modern Turkey: The Case of Bediuzzaman Said Nursi* (New York: State University of New York Press, 1989).

108. This and the following citations were taken from Kurt Seintz, "The Program of the Islamists," *Neue Kronen-Zeitung* (Vienna), June 29, 1996, pp. 4-5; as cited in *FBIS-WEU,* July 1, 1996, p. 41.

109. On this important point, see Paul B. Henze, *Turkey: Toward the Twenty-First Century* (Santa Monica: Rand Corporation, 1992), p. 24. Ironically, of course, the appeal to Islamic unity ran counter to the Turkish republican emphasis on nationalism and de-emphasis on religion originally set by Ataturk himself.

110. Cited in "Abdullah Ocalan Declares a Unilateral Ceasefire," *Kurdistan Report* (PKK), no. 23 (March–May 1996), p. 3.

111. The results of the national election on December 24, 1995, in percentage of the vote received and seats won in the parliament, were: Refah (Erbakan), 21.32 (158); ANAP (Yilmaz), 19.66 (132); DYP (Ciller), 19.20 (135); DSP (Ecevit), 14.65 (75); and CHP (Baykal), 10.71 (50). Turkes's NAP, 8.18 percent, and the pro-Kurdish HADEP, 4.17 percent, failed to reach the required threshold of 10 percent for seats in parliament.

112. Thomas L. Friedman, "Who Lost Turkey?" *New York Times,* Aug. 21, 1996, p. A17.

113. Cited in James Wyllie, "Turkey's New Posture: Change or Continuity?" *Jane's Intelligence Review,* Sept. 1, 1996. (Accessed via internet.)

114. "The First Nail in the New Policy's Coffin?" *Briefing,* Sept. 2, 1996, p. 7.

**CHAPTER FOUR**

1. See, for example, Ference A. Vali, *Bridge Across the Bosporus: The Foreign Policy of Turkey* (Baltimore: Johns Hopkins Press, 1971); Kemal H. Karpat, *Turkey's Foreign Policy in Transition, 1950-1974* (Leiden: E. J. Brill, 1975); Selim Deringil, *Turkish Foreign Policy During the Second World War: An 'Active' Neutrality* (Cambridge: Cambridge University Press, 1989); and C. H. Dodd, ed., *Turkish Foreign Policy: New Prospects* (Huntingdon: The Eothen Press, 1992).

More recently, however, see the following three articles by Robert Olson: "The Kurdish Question and Turkey's Foreign Policy, 1991-1995: From the Gulf War to the Incursion into Iraq," *Journal of South Asian and Middle Eastern Studies* 19 (Fall 1995), pp. 1-30; "The Kurdish Question and Geopolitic and Geostrategic Changes in the Middle East after the Gulf War," *Journal of South Asian and Middle Eastern Studies* 17 (Summer 1994), pp. 44-67; and "The Kurdish Question in the Aftermath of the Gulf War: Geopolitical and Geostrategic Changes in the Middle East," *Third World Quarterly* 13 (no. 3; 1992), pp. 475-99. Also see Henri J. Barkey, "Under the Gun: Turkish Foreign Policy and the Kurdish Question," in *The Kurdish Nationalist Movement in the 1990s: Its Impact on Turkey and the*

*Middle East,* Robert Olson, ed. (Lexington: University Press of Kentucky, 1996), pp. 65-83; and Graham E. Fuller and Ian O. Lesser, *Turkey's New Geopolitics: From the Balkans to Western China* (Boulder: Westview Press, 1993), pp. 25-27, 40-45. Portions of this chapter were originally published in my "The Kurdish Factor in Middle Eastern Politics," *International Journal of Kurdish Studies* 8 (nos. 1 & 2, 1995), pp. 94-109.

2. Robert Olson, *The Emergence of Kurdish Nationalism and the Sheikh Said Rebellion, 1880-1925* (Austin: University of Texas Press, 1989).

3. *Ibid.,* p. 151.

4. *Ibid.,* p. 161.

5. *Ibid.* Hatay, Syria (1938), Korea (1950-1953), and Cyprus (1974) are three exceptions.

6. *Ibid.*

7. *Ibid.* Given the increasing relevance for Turkey of the Kurdish problem regionally and even internationally, Olson's prediction would seem quite likely to be accurate.

8. "PKK Leader on War, Pipeline, Tourism, Drugs," *Ozgur Gundem* (Istanbul), Aug. 25, 1993, p. 8; as cited in *Foreign Broadcast Information Service—West Europe,* Sept. 9, 1993, p. 86; hereafter cited as *FBIS-WEU.*

9. Eleni Leontits, "We Cannot Be Defeated by the Turks," *Kiriakatiki Elevtherotipia* (Athens), July 18, 1993, pp. 28-29; as cited in *FBIS-WEU,* Aug. 17, 1993, p. 39.

10. "PKK Threatens to Target Caspian Pipeline," *Turkish Daily News,* Feb. 6, 1995, p. A4; as cited in *FBIS-WEU,* Feb. 9, 1995, p. 43.

11. The changes made in article 8 of the Anti-Terrorism Law are an example.

12. Kemal Kirisci, "Provide Comfort or Trouble: Kurdish Ethnicity and Turkish Foreign Policy," paper presented to the annual meeting of the Middle East Studies Association of North America, Research Triangle, North Carolina, Nov. 12, 1993, p. 2.

13. This and the following citation were taken from "Ciller Holds News Conference on Terrorism, PKK Fight," Ankara TRT Television Network in Turkish, 1100 GMT, Nov. 4, 1993; as cited in *FBIS-WEU,* Nov. 5, 1993, p. 56. In reply, Ocalan had admitted that "we might establish limited relations . . . with foreign powers if this would serve the interests of our people" but maintained that "in our view total dependence on foreign forces is a source of weakness." Cited in "PKK's Ocalan Views Turkish Military Operations," *Al-Nahar* (Beirut), April 10, 1995, p. 11; as cited in *FBIS-WEU,* April 17, 1995, p. 45.

14. M. S. Anderson, *The Eastern Question, 1774-1923: A Study in International Relations* (New York: St. Martin's Press, 1966); and Stanford J. Shaw and Ezel Kural Shaw, *History of the Ottoman Empire and Modern Turkey,* vol. II, *Reform, Revolution and Republic: The Rise of Modern Turkey, 1808-1975* (Cambridge: Cambridge University Press, 1977) will help give the reader a background and guide to further literature on this matter.

15. This and the following citation were taken from Olson, *Sheikh Said Rebellion,* p. 76.

16. Martin van Bruinessen, *Agha, Shaikh and State: The Social and Political Structure of Kurdistan* (London: Zed Books Ltd., 1992), p. 290.

17. See Kendal [Nezan], "Kurdistan in Turkey," in *People Without a Country: The Kurds and Kurdistan,* Gerard Chaliand, ed. (London: Zed Press, 1980), pp. 64-65.

18. Cited in "Turkey Prepares for the 'New Middle East,'" *Briefing* (Ankara), Nov. 22, 1993, p. 6.

19. Ismet Cheriff Vanly, "The Kurds in Syria and Lebanon," in *The Kurds: A Contemporary Overview,* Philip G. Kreyenbroek and Stefan Sperl, eds. (London: Routledge, 1992), p. 169. For further background, see Suha Bolukbasi, "Ankara, Damascus, Baghdad, and the Regionalization of Turkey's Kurdish Secessionism," *Journal of South Asian and Middle Eastern Studies* 14 (Summer 1991), pp. 15-36.

20. For useful analyses of GAP, see John Kolars, *The Euphrates River and the Southeast Anatolia Development Project* (Carbondale, IL: Southern Illinois University Press, 1991); Robert Olson, "The Impact of the Southeast Anatolian Project (GAP) on Kurdish Nationalism in Turkey," *International Journal of Kurdish Studies* 9 (nos. 1-2; 1996), pp. 95-102; Carl E. Nestor, "Dimensions of Turkey's Kurdish Question and the Potential Impact of the Southeast Anatolian Project (GAP): Part I," *International Journal of Kurdish Studies* 8 (nos. 1-2; 1995), pp. 33-78; and Suha Bolukbasi, "Turkey Challenges Iraq and Syria: The Euphrates Dispute," *Journal of South Asian and Middle Eastern Studies* 16 (Summer 1993), pp. 9-32.

21. The following discussion is based largely on "Sezgin to Give Syria Evidence of PKK Support," Ankara Anatolia in English, 1515 GMT, April 11, 1992; as cited in *FBIS-WEU,* April 13, 1992, p. 58.

22. "Sezgin Briefs Assembly on Syrian 'Promises,'" Ankara TRT Television Network in Turkish, 1700 GMT, April 21, 1992; as cited in *FBIS-WEU,* April 22, 1992, p. 40.

23. Cited in "Syria Not to be Asked to Extradite PKK Members," *Turkish Daily News,* April 23, 1992, pp. 1, 12; as cited in *FBIS-WEU,* May 4, 1992, p. 54.

24. Cited in "Turkey: Yilmaz Announces Reform Program," Ankara TRT Television Network, 0800 GMT, May 6, 1996; as cited in *FBIS-WEU,* May 8, 1996, p. 38.

25. Cited in Ayse Karabat, "Turkey: Syria Said Angered by Water Reduction," *Turkish Daily News,* April 24, 1996; as cited in *FBIS-WEU,* April 25, 1996, p. 34.

26. Cited in "Demirel on Terrorism, Ties with Syria," *Al-Musawwar* (Cairo), July 26, 1996, pp. 18-21, 82-83; as cited in *FBIS-WEU,* Aug. 5, 1996, p. 20.

27. For background analysis, see Suha Bolukbasi, "Turkey Copes with Revolutionary Iran," *Journal of South Asian and Middle Eastern Studies* 13 (Fall/Winter 1989), pp. 94-109.

28. The following data were taken from "Reviving Terrorism: Can It Be Contained?" *Briefing,* July 24, 1989, pp. 18-19.

29. The following data were taken from "The PKK: Botan Group at Verge of Destruction but Final Solution Still Far Away," *Briefing,* Aug. 14, 1989, p. 18.

30. This and the following citation were taken from Turan Yilmaz and Fahir Arikan, "PKK's New Camps Are in Iran," *Hurriyet* (Istanbul), July 16, 1993, p. 16; as cited in *FBIS-WEU,* July 20, 1993, p. 70.

31. Ugur Sefkat, "Iran's Mullahs Support the PKK," *Sabah* (Istanbul), Aug. 5, 1993, p. 16; as cited in *FBIS-WEU,* Aug. 10, 1993, p. 42.

32. The following analysis is partially based on Adnan Husayn, "Iraqi Kurds Accuse Kurdish Workers Party of Launching Military Operations Against 'Peshmerga,'" *Al-Sharq Al-Awsat* (London), Oct. 23, 1993, p. 6; as cited in *FBIS-WEU,* Oct. 27, 1993, p. 32.

33. Ugur Sefkat, "The 8 PKK Camps in Iran," *Sabah,* June 18, 1995, p. 19; as cited in *FBIS-WEU,* June 27, 1995, pp. 8-9.

34. Ertugrul Ozkok, "F-16 Aircraft Turned Back on 18 May," *Hurriyet,* June 10, 1995, p. 21; as cited in *FBIS-WEU,* June 14, 1995, p. 42.

35. Operation Provide Comfort, "Fact Sheet," May 6, 1993. For background, see Kemal Kirisci, "Turkey and the Kurdish Safe-Haven in Northern Iraq," *Journal of South Asian and Middle Eastern Studies* 19 (Spring 1996), pp. 21-39.

36. The stillborn Treaty of Sevres (1920), imposed by the victorious allies upon the defeated Ottoman Empire, was overturned by the Treaty of Lausanne (1923), which made no mention of a Kurdish state.

37. This and the following citation appeared in "Military and Assembly to Agree to Protection of Some Kurds," *Briefing,* June 22, 1992, p. 9.

38. "Learning to Live with 'Kurdistan,'" *Briefing,* June 1, 1992, p. 11.

39. "Ankara OKs Emergency Law But Crisis Only Deepens in SE," *Briefing,* June 29, 1992, p. 15.

40. For an analysis of these events, see my "A de Facto Kurdish State in Northern Iraq," *Third World Quarterly* 14 (No. 2; 1993), pp. 295-319; and Robert Olson, "The Creation of a Kurdish State in the 1990s?" *Journal of South Asian and Middle Eastern Studies* 15 (Summer 1992), pp. 1-25.

41. "A Common Interest in Ending the Embargo," *Briefing,* Aug. 30, 1993, p. 12.

42. Cited in "Iraqi Kurds Reportedly to Block Terrorist Attacks," Ankara TRT Television Network, 1600 GMT, April 8, 1992; as cited in *FBIS-WEU,* April 9, 1992, p. 43.

43. "Talabani Calls on PKK 'To End Armed Action,'" Ankara Anatolia in Turkish, 1415 GMT, Oct. 18, 1991; as cited in *FBIS-WEU,* Oct. 21, 1991, p. 58. Turkey was allocating some $12 million a year in economic aid to the Iraqi Kurds.

44. This and the following citation were taken from "Meets with Demirel," Ankara TRT Television Network in Turkish, 1600 GMT, June 9, 1992; as cited in *FBIS-WEU,* June 11, 1992, p. 42.

45. "Cetin on Iraq's Territorial Integrity," Ankara Anatolia in English, 1020 GMT, July 28, 1992; as cited in *FBIS-WEU,* July 28, 1992, p. 40.

46. For background analysis, see Philip Robins, "More Apparent Than Real? The Impact of the Kurdish Issue on Euro-Turkish Relations," in *The Kurdish Nationalist Movement in the 1990s: Its Impact on Turkey and the Middle East,* Robert Olson, ed. (Lexington: University Press of Kentucky, 1996), pp. 114-32.

47. These estimated figures were garnered from the following sources: Hazhir Teimourian, "The Making of Kurdish Militants," *European* (London), July 22-25, 1993, p. 10; as cited in *FBIS-WEU,* July 23, 1993, p. 54; Kevin Liffey, "Germany Clamps Down on Kurds After Attacks," Reuters, Nov. 5, 1993; and "Interior Minister Discusses Stance on PKK Terrorism," *West Europe Intelligence Report* (Brussels), Dec. 1, 1993.

48. Cited in "Reviving Terrorism: Can It Be Contained?" *Briefing,* July 24, 1989, p. 17.

49. Siyamend Othman, personal correspondence to the author, dated Mar. 13, 1987.

50. This and the following citations were taken from "Kurdish Separatists Strike Out at West Germany," *Armenian Reporter,* Jan. 7, 1988, p. 4.

51. In June 1987, the European Parliament declared Turkey's "denial of the existence of the Kurdish question . . . [*inter alia* presents] insurmountable obstacles to consideration of the possibility of Turkey's accession to the Community." The other reasons, of course, dealt with Turkey's non-Western heritage and Islamic culture.

52. Cited in "Agreement Reached in Bern Embassy Crisis," *Briefing,* July 5, 1993, p. 15.

53. Cited in "The Bern Crisis . . . On and Off and On," *Briefing,* July 12, 1993, p. 10.

54. Cited in "Agreement Reached in Bern Embassy Crisis."

55. Cited in Rolf Soderlind, "Germany Bans Kurdish Militants After Bombings," Reuters, Nov. 26, 1993.

56. Cited in John Follain, "France Bans Kurdish Groups for 'Terrorist' Links," Reuters, Nov. 30, 1993.

57. "Smiles in Ankara as Germany Bans PKK," *Briefing,* Nov. 29, 1993, p. 8.

58. Unal Cevikoz, personal correspondence to the author, dated Dec. 18, 1993.

59. Cited in Raf Casert, "Belgium-Kurds," Reuters, Jan. 3, 1994.

60. Cited in "Assorted Events in Europe Following Banning of Kurdish Organizations," *The Kurds: Recent Wire Reports,* Dec. 5, 1993, p. 2.

61. Cited in Soderlind, "Germany Bans Kurdish Militants After Bombings."

62. Cited in Follain, "France Bans Kurdish Groups for 'Terrorist' Links."

63. See Liffey, "Germany Clamps Down on Kurds After Attacks."

64. *Ibid.*

65. Cited in "Kurdish Disturbances Abroad Continue," *Turkish Daily News,* Mar. 21, 1995.

66. Cited in "Germany Vows End of Kurdish Terror," *Turkish Daily News,* Mar. 20, 1995.

67. Tony Paterson, "Bonn Feels Backlash of Kurdish Ban," *European,* Aug. 7-13, 1995.

68. Bill Powell, "Kurdistan's Second Front," *Newsweek,* April 10, 1995, p. 19. Disturbances also occurred in Austria, Belgium, Sweden, and Switzerland, among others.

69. "PKK Plans to Target German Police During Demonstrations," *Turkish Daily News,* Aug. 2, 1995. The ERNK accused Germany of pursuing a "fascist, chauvinist policy towards the Kurdish people's liberation struggle." *Ibid.*

70. These and the following figures and citation were taken from Paterson, "Bonn Feels Backlash of Kurdish Ban."

71. This and the following citations were taken from Christina Erck and Josef Hufelschulte, "You Should Be Glad," *Focus* (Munich), Dec. 22, 1995, pp. 18-21; as cited in *FBIS-WEU,* Dec. 28, 1995, pp. 24-26.

72. Cited in "Turkey: PKK's Ocalan Addresses Message to Arab Summit Leaders," London MED TV Television in Turkish, 1715 GMT, June 22, 1996; as cited in *FBIS-WEU,* June 24, 1996, pp. 39, 40.

73. Alain Lallemand and Olivier Van Vaerenbergh, "Police Raid PKK Offices, Arrest 20 Suspects," *Le Soir* (Brussels), Sept. 19, 1996, pp. 1, 17; as cited in *FBIS-WEU,* Oct. 11, 1996, pp. 3-4.

74. On this point, see Robins, "More Apparent Than Real?"

75. U.S. Department of Commerce, Bureau of Export Administration, Office of Strategic Industries and Economic Security, *European Diversification and Defense Market Assessment: A Comprehensive Guide for Entry into Overseas Markets* (Washington: U.S. Department of Commerce, 1995), p. 286; as cited in Human Rights Watch Arms Project, *Weapons Transfers and Violations of the Laws of War in Turkey* (New York: Human Rights Watch, 1995), p. 3. For background, see George S. Harris, *Troubled Alliance: Turkish-American Problems in Historical Perspective* (Washington: American Enterprise Institute, 1972); and Peter L. Thompson, "United States–Turkey Military Relations: Treaties and Implications," *International Journal of Kurdish Studies* 9 (nos. 1 & 2; 1996), pp. 103-113.

76. Ugur Akinci, "Gen. John M. Shalikashvili Defends Human Rights Progress in Turkey," *Turkish Daily News,* June 28, 1995.

77. Cited in "PKK Official Reacts to Ciller on Human Rights," *Ozgur Ulke,* July 9, 1994, p. 8; as cited in *FBIS-WEU,* July 22, 1994, p. 41.

78. This and the following citations were taken from "PKK Leader on Party Ideology, U.S. Policy," *Serxwebun* (PKK), April 1995, pp. 12-14; as cited in *FBIS-WEU,* June 27, 1995, p. 1.

79. Cited in "Turkey: PKK's Ocalan Addresses Message to Arab Summit Leaders," as cited in *FBIS-WEU,* June 24, 1996, p. 39.
80. "U.S. Said Aiding PKK Wounded," *Hurriyet,* Oct. 26, 1992, p. 22; as cited in *FBIS-WEU,* Oct. 29, 1992, p. 72.
81. Cited in "PKK Violence Shifts to Northeast," *Turkish Times,* Sept. 15, 1993, p. 11. For a background analysis on the Turkish-Armenian enmity, see my, *"Pursuing the Just Cause of their People": A Study of Contemporary Armenian Terrorism* (New York: Greenwood Press, 1986).
82. The following specifics were taken from "PKK Violence Shifts to Northeast."
83. "Armenian, PKK Military Moves Linked to Azerbaijani Oil Deal," *Turkish Daily News,* Aug. 25, 1993, pp. 1, 11; as cited in *FBIS-WEU,* Aug. 31, 1993, p. 56. Another report concluded, however, that "there was little evidence at the present time to corroborate the claim against Armenia that it is supporting the PKK." See "PKK Activity in Northeast Linked with Armenia," *Turkish Daily News,* Aug. 27, 1993, pp. 1, 11; as cited in *FBIS-WEU,* Sept. 1, 1993, p. 29.
84. The following data were taken from "The Armenian Connection," *Turkish Daily News,* Nov. 11, 1993. Muslim Turks and Kurds are circumcised, while Christian Armenians are not.
85. The following data were taken from Aydin Demir, "PKK Requests Camp Site from Armenia," *Sabah,* Sept. 22, 1992, p. 14; as cited in *FBIS-WEU,* Sept. 28, 1992, p. 43.
86. Tolga Sardan, "Armenia Supports PKK, Provides Camp Site," *Milliyet* (Istanbul), June 4, 1993, p. 10; as cited in *FBIS-WEU,* June 8, 1993, p. 59. Lachin was the capital of the so-called Red Kurdistan region set up by the Soviets for a brief period in the 1920s. See Ismet Cheriff Vanly, "The Kurds in the Soviet Union," in *The Kurds: A Contemporary Overview,* Philip G. Kreyenbroek and Stefan Sperl, eds. (London: Routledge, 1992), p. 201.
87. "Turkey Links PKK with Armenia," *Turkish Times,* Sept. 15, 1993, p. 1. As noted in Chapter 2, Ocalan recently illustrated that the Turks possessed no monopoly on the ludicrous, when he compared himself to Jesus Christ: "I feel myself closer to the type of person Jesus was. . . . I highly resemble him where rendering of services and peace is concerned." Cited in Tayyar Safak, "Understanding Apo," *Tercuman* (Istanbul), Mar. 22, 1993, p. 2; as cited in *FBIS-WEU,* Mar. 31, 1993, p. 71. Although Ocalan is clearly of Kurdish ancestry, he was born in Omerli, a village near Urfa formerly inhabited by Armenians.
88. "Profile of PKK Leader Ocalan," *Turkish Probe* (Ankara), Aug. 17, 1993, pp. 8-9; as cited in *FBIS-WEU,* Sept. 2, 1993, p. 58. As noted in Chapter 2, Turkes was apparently attempting to somehow identify Ocalan with Hagop Hagopian, the notorious leader of the Armenian Secret Army for the Liberation of Armenia (ASALA), a terrorist group that murdered a number of Turkish diplomats and citizens in the early 1980s. Hagopian himself was killed either by dissident Armenians or Turkish agents in Athens, Greece, in April 1988. See my *Transnational Armenian Activism,* Conflict Studies no. 229 (London: Research Institute for the Study of Conflict and Terrorism, 1990), p. 24.
89. This and the following citation were taken from "Chief of General Staff: Armenian Church Behind PKK," *Gunaydin* (Istanbul), Oct. 28, 1993, p. 8; as cited in *FBIS-WEU,* Nov. 1, 1993, p. 57.
90. The following data were taken from Ugur Sefkat, "Alliance Between the PKK and Armenians," *Sabah,* May 24, 1994, p. 13; as cited in *FBIS-WEU,* May 26, 1994, p. 45.

91. Sezai Sengun, "Joint Action by PKK and ASALA," *Hurriyet*, June 5, 1994, p. 18; as cited in *FBIS-WEU*, June 13, 1994, p. 54.

92. M. Can Yuce, "The Essence of the Current Enmity Toward Armenians," *Ozgur Gundem* (Istanbul), Dec. 20, 1993, p. 2; as cited in *FBIS-WEU*, Dec. 27, 1993, p. 39.

93. Cited in *ibid.*, p. 40.

94. "Turkey Moves to Sever Armenia-PKK Bridge," *Turkish Daily News*, April 29, 1995.

95. For an excellent analysis of recent relations, see Tozun Bahcheli, *Greek-Turkish Relations Since 1955* (Boulder: Westview Press, 1990).

96. Cited in Eleni Leontits, "We Cannot Be Defeated by the Turks," *Kiriakatiki Elevtherotipia* (Athens) July 18, 1993, pp. 28-29; as cited in *FBIS-WEU*, Aug. 17, 1993, p. 38.

97. This and the following data were taken from *Nokta* (Ankara), April 5, 1992; as cited in *Turkish Times*, May 1, 1992, p. 13.

98. This and the following citations and data were taken from Mumtaz Soysal, "Foreign Support and Internal Obstacles," *Hurriyet*, July 28, 1993, p. 9; as cited in *FBIS-WEU*, July 30, 1993, p. 40.

99. The following data were taken from Ugur Sevkat, "Athens Supplies Antitank Missiles to PKK Leader Ocalan," *Sabah*, Dec. 7, 1993, p. 18; as cited in *FBIS-WEU*, Dec. 17, 1993, p. 55.

100. "Greece Supports Kurdish Fight for Independence," Reuters, Dec. 4, 1993.

101. "Greece's EU Presidency: No Blank Cheque," *Briefing*, Dec. 13, 1993, p. 13. Given the fact that only Germany and France had actually banned the PKK as of January 1994, the accuracy of this source may be questioned.

102. Stelios Vervirakis, "Athens Presents a Shield to Ocalan," *Sabah*, June 22, 1995, p. 14; as cited in *FBIS-WEU*, June 27, 1995, p. 29.

103. Emin Demirel, "PKK's Bomb Expert Arrested," *Hurriyet*, May 13, 1994, p. 22; as cited in *FBIS-WEU*, May 17, 1994, p. 58; and "NSC Discusses Tension with Greece, Cyprus, PKK," *Aydinlik* (Istanbul), April 11, 1994, p. 11; as cited in *FBIS-WEU*, April 18, 1994, p. 58. See also "Greek Spy Agency Tied to Terror Group: Athens Backed Anti-Turkish Kurds," *Washington Times*, Sept. 10, 1996 (accessed via internet).

104. See, for example, Paul Henze, "Turkish Government Tackles Problem of Kurdish Insurgency," *Christian Science Monitor*, Oct. 30, 1985, p. 8.

105. The following discussion is based on "PKK Expands Activities in CIS," *Turkish Probe*, Nov. 4, 1994, p. 13; and "PKK Opens 'Kurdish House' in Moscow," *Turkish Daily News*, Dec. 27, 1994.

106. The following discussion is largely based on Robert Olson, "The Kurdish Question and Chechnya: Turkish and Russian Foreign Policies Since the Gulf War," *Middle East Policy* 4 (March 1996), pp. 106-118.

## CHAPTER FIVE

1. On divisions in Kurdish society, see Martin van Bruinessen, *Agha, Shaikh and State: The Social and Political Structures of Kurdistan* (London: Zed Books Ltd., 1992); Amir Hassanpour, *Nationalism and Language in Kurdistan, 1918-1985* (San Francisco: Mellen Research University Press, 1992); and David McDowall, *A Modern History of the Kurds* (London: I. B. Tauris & Co. Ltd., 1996). Portions of the following analysis originally appeared in my "Kurdish Infighting: The PKK-

KDP Conflict," in *The Kurdish Nationalist Movement in the 1990s: Its Impact on Turkey and the Middle East,* Robert Olson, ed. (Lexington: University Press of Kentucky, 1996), pp. 50-62.

2. The KDP was established on August 16, 1946, by the legendary Iraqi Kurdish leader Mulla Mustafa Barzani (1903-1979). Currently led by his son Massoud Barzani (1946–), it has been described as rightist, conservative, feudal, tribal, and nationalist. It also is associated with the Kurmanji-speaking, Bahdinani area of northwestern Iraqi Kurdistan. For further analyses, see my *The Kurds of Iraq: Tragedy and Hope* (New York: St. Martin's Press, 1992), pp. 21-24; Edmund Ghareeb, *The Kurdish Question in Iraq* (Syracuse: Syracuse University Press, 1981), pp. 35-41; Sa'ad Jawad, *Iraq and the Kurdish Question, 1958-1970* (London: Ithaca Press, 1981), pp. 17-24; and McDowall, *Modern History of the Kurds,* pp. 296-300, 315-20, 343-47.

3. The PUK was established by Jalal Talabani (1933–) in Damascus on June 1, 1975, following the collapse of Mulla Mustafa Barzani's revolt against Baghdad the previous March. It has been described as leftist, socialist, and progressive, and it is associated with the Sorani-speaking area of southeastern Iraqi Kurdistan. For further analyses, see Nader Entessar, *Kurdish Ethnonationalism* (Boulder, CO: Lynne Rienner Publishers, 1992), pp. 78-80, 130-33; and McDowall, *Modern History of the Kurds,* pp. 343-47. For a recent analysis of the KDP-PUK struggle in northern Iraq, see my "The KDP-PUK Conflict in Northern Iraq," *Middle East Journal* 50 (Spring 1996), pp. 225-41.

4. This and the following data were taken from Ismet G. Imset, "PKK: The Deception of Terror (Countering Stability in Turkey), Part II," *Briefing* (Ankara), June 6, 1988, p. 20.

5. "On Elections, PKK, Independence," *Milliyet* (Istanbul), Feb. 23, 1992, p. 7; as cited in *Foreign Broadcast Information Service—West Europe,* Feb. 26, 1992, p. 26. Hereafter cited as *FBIS-WEU.*

6. This and the following citation appeared in Imset, "PKK: Deception of Terror."

7. "A Good-Will Gesture: But at What Cost?" *Briefing,* Sept. 12, 1988, p. 6.

8. "Will the PKK Be a Regional Issue?" *Briefing,* Mar. 14, 1988, p. 11.

9. "Talabani's Meeting with PKK Leader Reported," *Hurriyet* (Istanbul), Dec. 22, 1991, p. 16; as cited in *FBIS-WEU,* Dec. 27, 1991, p. 12.

10. "Formation of PKK-Affiliated Party Reported," *Cumhuriyet* (Istanbul), Nov. 1, 1991, p. 10; as cited in *FBIS-WEU,* Dec. 18, 1991, p. 55.

11. Cited in "Iraqi Kurds Reportedly to Block Terrorist Attacks," Ankara TRT Television Network in Turkish, 1600 GMT, April 8, 1992; as cited in *FBIS-WEU,* April 9, 1992, p. 43.

12. "Talabani Calls on PKK To End Armed Action," Ankara Anatolia in Turkish, 1415 GMT, Oct. 18, 1991; as cited in *FBIS-WEU,* Oct. 21, 1991, p. 58.

13. Cited in "Talabani Calls on PKK To End Armed Action."

14. "PKK Said To Suspend Armed Activity Until March," *Gunaydin* (Istanbul), Nov. 28, 1991, p. 8; as cited in *FBIS-WEU,* Dec. 3, 1991, p. 50.

15. Ismet G. Imset, "PKK Promises No More Military Attacks," *Turkish Daily News,* Dec. 10, 1991, pp. 1, 11; as cited in *FBIS-WEU,* Dec. 16, 1991, p. 42.

16. This and the following citations were taken from "PKK's Ocalan on Turkish, U.S., Syrian Policies," *2000 Ikibin'e Dogru* (Istanbul), March 22, 1992, pp. 18-29; as cited in *FBIS-WEU,* April 23, 1992, p. 28.

17. This and the following citation were taken from *ibid.*, p. 29.
18. Cited in "Talabani Comments on Ankara, Talks, PKK," *Turkish Daily News,* June 16, 1992, p. 2; as cited in *FBIS-WEU,* June 29, 1992, p. 54.
19. "Talabani: Iraq Preparing for War Against Turkey," Ankara TRT Television Network in Turkish, 1600 GMT, June 14, 1992; as cited in *FBIS-WEU,* June 15, 1992, p. 39.
20. "DPK Political Bureau Criticizes PKK, Ankara," (Clandestine) Voice of the Iraqi People in Arabic, 1700 GMT, March 25, 1992; as cited in *Foreign Broadcast Information Service—Near East & South Asia,* March 26, 1992, p. 15. Hereafter cited as *FBIS-NES.*
21. "Barzani Arrives, Criticizes PKK Savagery," Ankara Radyolari Network in Turkish, 2000 GMT, March 30, 1992; as cited in *FBIS-WEU,* March 31, 1992, p. 27.
22. "PKK Denounces Barzani as Collaborator," *Hurriyet,* Feb. 24, 1992, p. 14; as cited in *FBIS-WEU,* Feb. 28, 1992, p. 44.
23. This and the following citation were taken from "Ocalan Said To Order Deaths of Barzani, Talabani," *Tercuman* (Istanbul), Jan. 24, 1992, p. 11; as cited in *FBIS-WEU,* Jan. 27, 1992, p. 43.
24. This and the following citations were taken from "Ocalan Interviewed on Foreign Support for PKK," *Milliyet,* March 26, 1992, p. 14; as cited in *FBIS-WEU,* March 30, 1992, p. 36.
25. Abdullah Ocalan, "The Outlook for Political Struggle and the Autonomy Talks in Southern Kurdistan," *Serxwebun* (Germany), July 1991, pp. 1, 7-11; as cited in *FBIS-WEU,* Aug. 29, 1991, p. 42.
26. "Ocalan on Foreign Support," as cited in *FBIS-WEU,* Mar. 30, 1992, p. 36.
27. The following analysis is largely based on Ismet G. Imset, "Analysis," *Turkish Daily News,* Aug. 10, 1992, pp. 1, 12; as cited in *FBIS-WEU,* Aug. 18, 1992, pp. 40-42; and Ismet G. Imset, "Ankara Still Silent on PKK Blockade," *Turkish Daily News,* Aug. 12, 1992, pp. 1, 12; as cited in *FBIS-WEU,* Aug. 19, 1992, pp. 27-28.
28. Cited in "KDP's Barzani Interviewed on Federation, Plans," *Al-Akhbar,* Nov. 22, 1992, p. 4; as cited in *FBIS-NES,* Dec. 1, 1992, p. 26.
29. "Talabani Interviewed on Agreement with PKK," *Nokta* (Istanbul), Nov. 29, 1992, pp. 10-21; as cited in *FBIS-NES,* Dec. 14, 1992, p. 21.
30. This and the following citation were taken from "Kurdistan Government Statement Criticizes PKK," (Clandestine) Voice of the People of Kurdistan in Arabic, 1700 GMT, Aug. 5, 1992; as cited in *FBIS-NES,* Aug. 7, 1992, p. 20.
31. Cited in "Iraqi Kurdistan Prime Minister Interviewed," *Avanti* (Rome), Oct. 31, 1992, p. 16; as cited in *FBIS-NES,* Nov. 4, 1992, p. 21. Barzani similarly argued that the PKK was "supported by Iran, Iraq, and Syria, which are all against Kurdish independence." Cited in Jim Muir, "Iraqi Kurds Question Aims of Turkish Incursion into Iraq," *Christian Science Monitor,* Nov. 9, 1992, p. 4.
32. Cited in "Operation Kills 2,000 Guerrillas," Paris AFP in English, 1126 GMT, Nov. 4, 1992; as cited in *FBIS-WEU,* Nov. 4, 1992, p. 30. Also see Chris Hedges, "An Odd Alliance Subdues Turkey's Kurdish Rebels," *New York Times,* Nov. 24, 1992, pp. A1, A8.
33. Cited in "Sabah Reports Chief of General Staff Interview," *Sabah* (Istanbul), April 7, 1993, p. 16; as cited in *FBIS-WEU,* April 13, 1993, p. 41.
34. This scaled-down figure was given to me by Hoshyar Zebari, a member of the KDP politburo with responsibility for foreign relations, when I spoke at length with him

in Irbil, Iraqi Kurdistan on August 17, 1993. Nevertheless, Zebari still emphasized that there had been serious fighting the previous October.

35. Ismet Imset, "Talabani Scenarios: How Much Are They Worth?" *Turkish Daily News*, Nov. 12, 1993; and Rasit Gurdilek, "Turkey, Iraqi Kurds Discuss Post-Incursion Security," *Turkish Probe*, May 9, 1995, p. 9.

36. Kani Xulam, representative of the American Kurdish Information Network (PKK affiliate), interview with the author, Washington, D.C., Dec. 8, 1995.

37. "Kurds Accuse Iran, Syria of Backing PKK To Ruin Truce," Paris AFP in English, 2307 GMT, Sept. 2, 1995; as cited in *FBIS-NES*, Sept. 7, 1995, p. 46.

38. "Ocalan on Reasons Behind Weekend Attacks," Paris AFP in English, 0807 GMT, Aug. 29, 1995; as cited in *FBIS-NES*, Aug. 30, 1995, p. 51.

39. This and the following citations were taken from "A Political and Military Challenge: PKK Operation Against the KDP in South Kurdistan," *Kurdistan Report* (London/PKK affiliate), no. 22 (September/October 1995), pp. 25-27.

40. This and the following citations and data were taken from "MED TV Interviews PKK's Abdullah Ocalan," London MED TV Television in Turkish, 1630 GMT, Sept. 18, 1995; as cited in *FBIS-WEU*, Sept. 22, 1995, P. 37.

41. Bucak was a Turkish Kurdish lawyer from Urfa in Turkey who headed the Kurdish Democratic Party of Turkey. Following his murder, the party split into two hostile groups; both fled to Iraqi Kurdistan. There, under circumstances that remain obscure, both of the new leaders (Dr. Shivan [Sait Kirmizitoprak] and Sait Elci) were killed and their organizations largely eliminated. Some say that Mulla Mustafa Barzani executed Shivan for killing Elci, while others say that it was the result of provocation by the Turkish intelligence service, the MIT.

42. Ugur Sefkat, "PKK's Plan on Northern Iraq," *Sabah*, May 15, 1994, p. 25; as cited in *FBIS-WEU*, June 1, 1994, p. 67.

43. "KDP Appeals To PKK Fighters To Surrender," (Clandestine) Voice of Iraqi Kurdistan in Arabic, 1815 GMT, Sept. 3, 1995; as cited in *FBIS-NES*, Sept. 7, 1995, p. 43.

44. Cited in Bayram Baran *et al.*, "We Met Mas'ud Barzani at the Battle Front," *Zaman* (Istanbul), Sept. 1, 1995, p. 11; as cited in *FBIS-WEU*, Sept. 5, 1995, p. 30.

45. "KDP Radio Reports PKK Surprise Attack," (Clandestine) Voice of Iraqi Kurdistan in Arabic, 1810 GMT, Aug. 26, 1995; as cited in *FBIS-NES*, Aug. 29, 1995, p. 44.

46. This and the following citations were taken from "Kurdish Leader on Victories Over PKK," (Clandestine) Voice of Iraqi Kurdistan in Arabic, 1820 GMT, Oct. 22, 1995; as cited in *FBIS-NES*, Oct. 26, 1995, p. 44.

47. Hoshyar Zebari (KDP spokesman), "Press Release," Salahuddin, Iraqi Kurdistan, Oct. 23, 1995.

48. The following data and citations were taken from "Turkey: PKK's Ocalan Addresses Message to Arab Summit Leaders," London MED TV Television in Turkish, 1715 GMT, June 22, 1996; as cited in *FBIS-WEU*, June 24, 1996, p. 37.

49. "Ocalan Statement Marks 17th Anniversary of PKK," London MED TV Television in Turkish, 1730 GMT, Nov. 26, 1995; as cited in *FBIS-WEU*, Nov. 30, 1995, p. 30.

50. This and the following citation were taken from "Ocalan Discusses Ties with U.S., Middle East," London MED TV Television in Turkish, 1730 GMT, April 26, 1996; as cited in *FBIS-WEU*, April 30, 1996, p. 27.

51. "PKK's Ocalan Offers to Form 'Peace Force' Between Kurds," London MED TV Television in Turkish, 1715 GMT, Aug. 31, 1996; as cited in *FBIS-WEU*, Oct. 17, 1996, p. 1.

52. "PKK Leader Calls for 'National Mobilization,' 'War,'" London MED TV Television in Turkish, 1715 GMT, Sept. 5, 1996; as cited in *FBIS-WEU,* Oct. 17, 1996, p. 1.

53. "MED TV Urges Kurds to Get Rid Of Barzani, Talabani," London MED TV Television in Turkish, 1715 GMT, Oct. 27, 1996; as cited in *FBIS-WEU,* Oct. 29, 1996, p. 2.

## CHAPTER SIX

1. The following figures and citations were taken from Sinan Yilmaz, "Report: Kurds Oppose Separate State," *Turkish Daily News* (Ankara), Aug. 4, 1995, p. A2; as cited in *Foreign Broadcast Information Service—West Europe,* Aug. 8, 1995, p. 27-30. Hereafter cited as *FBIS-WEU.*

2. Zaza—a popular, but somewhat derogatory, term for those who speak Dimili—is a Kurdish dialect that some would call a separate Kurdish language. Although the Turkish government treats the Zaza as a separate ethnic group, most authorities on the subject regard them as Kurdish. On the Kurdish language, see Amir Hassanpour, *Nationalism and Language in Kurdistan, 1918-1985* (San Francisco: Mellen Research University Press, 1992); Mehrdad R. Izady, *The Kurds: A Concise Handbook* (Washington: Crane Russak, 1992), pp. 167-82; and Philip G. Kreyenbroek, "On the Kurdish Language," in *The Kurds: A Contemporary Overview,* Philip G. Kreyenbroek and Stefan Sperl, eds. (London: Routledge, 1992), pp. 68-83.

3. Other evidence indicates that Kurdish men are much more likely than Kurdish women to know Turkish as a second language because they are much more likely to work outside of the home. Therefore, since 90 percent of the respondents were male, this final figure of only 3.7 percent who did not know a second language is probably much too small.

    In the past, to try to minimize the size of its Kurdish population, the Turkish government counted as Kurdish only those who spoke no other language. Since many Kurds did speak some Turkish as a second language, they were not counted as Kurds. Moreover, after 1965 the government stopped counting Kurds at all. In addition, of course, many ethnic Kurds have been partially or fully assimilated. As a result, only estimates—at times widely differing—exist of the Kurdish population.

4. Ergil's classifications here are rather incongruous. Sufi simply refers to various Islamic orders practicing different forms of mysticism. Although Ataturk banned them, they continued underground. In general, see Martin van Bruinessen, *Agha, Shaikh and State: The Social and Political Structures of Kurdistan* (London: Zed Books, 1992), pp. 210-16. Hanefi refers to one of the four recognized schools of law in Sunni Islam. Traditionally, most Sunni Muslim Turks were of the Hanefite school, while Turkish Kurds who were Sunni Muslim were of the Shafii jurisprudence. Alevi refers to a heterodox form of Islam in Turkey that some would consider beyond the Islamic pale. At least 10 percent of the population in Turkey is Alevi, with claims as high as 30-40 percent. See Peter A. Andrews, ed., *Ethnic Groups in the Republic of Turkey* (Wiesbaden: Dr. Ludwig Reichert Verlag, 1989), p. 57. Maybe 30 percent of the Kurds in Turkey are Alevi. See *ibid.,* p. 116.

5. This low figure also probably illustrates a higher proportion of urban respondents than exists in the actual population. Nevertheless, in the past few years meat and agricultural prices dependent on production in the southeast have skyrocketed in Turkey due to the destruction caused to the countryside by the war.

6. "Conservatives Lambast Ergil, TOBB Report," *Turkish Probe* (Ankara), Aug. 11,

1995; and "Political Leaders Criticize TOBB Report," *Turkish Daily News,* Aug. 8, 1995, pp. 1, A8; as cited in *FBIS-WEU,* Aug. 11, 1995, pp. 39-40.

7. Cited in "Dogu Ergil: The Report Was My Duty As a Citizen," *Turkish Daily News,* Aug. 19, 1995.

8. The following data and citation were taken from an article written by Firat Kayakiran and carried by the Reuters news agency on Nov. 7, 1995, from where it was accessed over the Internet.

9. "No Politics in Sabanci's Southeast Report," *Briefing* (Ankara), Nov. 27, 1995, p. 8.

10. Cited in Tilman Mueller, "Our Press Is Full of Propaganda," *Stern* (Hamburg), April 20, 1995, p. 214; as cited in *FBIS-WEU,* April 21, 1995, p. 44. Boyner's party, however, received barely one-third of one percent of the vote in the national elections of December 1995.

11. The following citations were taken from Hans Rauscher, "Turkish Prime Minister Criticizes SPOe's Kurdish Policy," *Kurier* (Vienna), June 27, 1996, p. 6; as cited in *FBIS-WEU,* June 28, 1996, p. 27.

12. This and the following citations were taken from Nese Duzel, "We Would Hold Them Accountable," *Hurriyet* (Istanbul), April 2, 1995, pp. 1, 7; as cited in *FBIS-WEU,* May 2, 1995, p. 38.

13. Cited in "PKK Leader Calls for Federal Arrangement," *Ozgur Gundem* (Istanbul), April 14, 1994, p. 8; as cited in *FBIS-WEU,* May 5, 1994, p. 57.

14. Cited in Dieter Bednary and Romain Leick, "The Chancellor Is My Role Model," *Der Spiegel* (Hamburg), May 13, 1996, pp. 166-71; as cited in *FBIS-WEU,* May 14, 1996, p. 30.

15. Cited in "PKK Leader on Party Ideology, U.S. Policy," *Serxwebun* (Cologne), April 1995, pp. 12-14, 23; as cited in *FBIS-WEU,* June 27, 1995, p. 2.

16. The following data and citations were taken from Alparslan Esmer, "DKP: 'The Party of the Oppressed,'" *Turkish Daily News,* Jan. 17, 1997. Given the fate of previous pro-Kurdish parties, Elci's new party had, at best, a difficult road to travel.

17. Cited in "The General Takes Command, Discretely but Indisputably," *Briefing,* Dec. 30, 1996, p. 1.

18. Meaningful economic measures—as distinct from the mere rhetoric of the past—are also a *sine qua non,* of course, for helping to solve the Kurdish problem. Hopefully, projects such as GAP will prove for Turkey's southeast what the TVA proved for the United States's southeast. Ocalan recently declared, "an economic plan for the Kurdish provinces is necessary. . . . Our militants . . . must be drawn into productive fields." "Ihlas Agency Interviews PKK's Ocalan," London MED TV Television in Turkish, 1945 GMT, Jan. 5, 1997; as cited in *FBIS-WEU,* Jan. 5, 1997, p. 9.

# SELECTED BIBLIOGRAPHY

Since this book is a sequel to my earlier study, *The Kurds in Turkey: A Political Dilemma,* 1990, most of the entries in this bibliography come after that date. For works before that date, see the bibliography in my earlier study. Also for numerous additional references to specific articles in newspapers, weeklies, or that appeared in translation or news clippings services, see the notes at the end of each chapter.

## INTERVIEWS AND CORRESPONDENCE

Barzani, Massoud. Chairman of the Kurdistan Democratic Party (Iraq). Salahuddin, Iraqi Kurdistan, Aug. 16, 1993.

Barzani, Nechirvan. Member of the Politburo of the Kurdistan Democratic Party (Iraq). Salahuddin, Iraqi Kurdistan, Aug. 19, 1993.

Cevikoz, Unal. Turkish diplomat in Belgium. Correspondence, Dec. 18, 1993.

"Dilan." PKK official. Millpitas, CA, Aug. 7, 1993.

Fuller, Graham. Senior political scientist at Rand. Washington, D.C., June 15, 1994.

Izady, Mehrdad. Kurdish academician. New York, July 20, 1995.

Kandemir, Nuzhet. Turkish Ambassador to the United States. Washington, D.C., April 10, 1990.

Karadaghi, Kamran. Senior correspondent *Al-Hayah* (London). Tel Aviv, Israel, April 25, 1994.

Karim, Najmaldin. President, Kurdish National Congress of North America. Washington, D.C., Dec. 8, 1995.

Karpat, Kemal. Professor of History, University of Wisconsin. Correspondence, Dec. 9, 1994.

Kaya, Yasar. President, Kurdistan Parliament-in-Exile. Irvine, CA, July 22, 1995.

Lowry, Heath. Ataturk Professor of Ottoman and Modern Turkish Studies, Princeton University. Washington, D.C., April 1, 1994.

Makovsky, Alan. Senior Fellow, The Washington Institute for Near East Policy. Washington, D.C., June 15, 1994.

Nezan, Kendal. Director, Institut Kurde de Paris. Irvine, CA, July 22, 1995.

Olson, Robert. Professor of History, University of Kentucky. Washington, D.C., Dec. 8, 1995.

Othman, Siyamend. Member, Institut Kurde de Paris. Correspondence, Mar. 13, 1987.

Rahman, Sami Abdal. Member of the Politburo of the Kurdistan Democratic Party (Iraq). Irbil, Iraqi Kurdistan, Aug. 14, 1993.

Salih, Barham. Member of the Politburo of the Patriotic Union of Kurdistan (Iraq). Washington, D.C., May 16, 1996.

Talabani, Jalal. Chairman of the Patriotic Union of Kurdistan (Iraq). Irbil, Iraqi Kurdistan, Aug. 17, 1993.

Uthman, Mahmud. Former member of the Politburo of the Kurdistan Democratic Party (Iraq). Milpitas, CA, Aug. 7, 1993.

Vanly, Ismet Cheriff. Kurdish academician. Salahuddin, Iraqi Kurdistan, Aug. 16, 1993.
Xulam, Kani. Representative of the American Kurdish Information Network (ERNK affiliate). Washington, D.C., Dec. 8, 1995.
Zana, Mehdi. Former mayor of Diyarbakir, Turkey. Milpitas, CA, Aug. 7, 1993.
Zebari, Hoshyar. Member of the Politburo of the Kurdistan Democratic Party (Iraq). Irbil, Iraqi Kurdistan, Aug. 17, 1993.

## TRANSLATIONS AND NEWS CLIPPINGS SERVICES

*Foreign Broadcast Information Service—Near East & South Asia.* Referred to as *FBIS-NES.*
*Foreign Broadcast Information Service—West Europe.* Referred to as *FBIS-WEU.*
Institut Kurde de Paris, *Information and Liaison Bulletin.*
Kurdish Institute of Brussels, *Quarterly Newsletter.*
*The Kurds: Recent Wire Reports.* (Reuters).
TRKNWS-L/Turkish Radio Hour (Received over the Internet via trh@netcom.com), Haywood, CA.

## NEWSPAPERS, WEEKLIES, ETC.

*Briefing* (Ankara)
*Christian Science Monitor*
*Economist*
*European* (London)
*International Herald Tribune*
*Kurdistan Report* (London/PKK)
*New York Times*
*Newsweek*
*Time*
*Turkey Today* (Turkish Embassy/Washington)
*Turkish Daily News* (Ankara)
*Turkish Probe* (Ankara)
*Turkish Times* (Washington)
*Washington Post*
*Wall Street Journal*

## ARTICLES, REPORTS, MONOGRAPHS, AND BOOKS

Abramowitz, Morton L. "Dateline Ankara: Turkey After Ozal." *Foreign Policy* no. 91 (Summer 1993), pp. 164-85.
Ahmad, Feroz. *The Making of Modern Turkey.* London: Routledge, 1993.
———. *The Turkish Experiment in Democracy, 1950-1975.* London: C. Hurst & Company, 1977.
Amnesty International. *Human Rights and U.S. Security.* New York: Amnesty International, 1995.
———. "Turkey: A Policy of Denial." Feb. 1995.
———. "Turkey: Dissident Voices Jailed Again." June 1994.
———. "Turkey: Human Rights Defenders at Risk." Sept. 1994.
———. "Turkey: Unfulfilled Promise of Reform." Sept. 1995.
———. "Turkey: Walls of Glass." Nov. 1992.
Anderson, M. S. *The Eastern Question, 1774-1923: A Study in International Relations.* New York: St. Martin's Press, 1966.
Andrews, Peter A., ed. *Ethnic Groups in the Republic of Turkey.* Wiesbaden: Dr. Ludwig Reichert Verlag, 1989.
Anter, Musa. *Hatiralarim* [My Memoirs]. Istanbul: Yon Yayincilik, 1991.

Arbuckle, Tammy. "Winter Campaign in Kurdistan." *International Defense Review* 28 (Feb. 1995), pp. 59-61.
Avebury, Eric. "Turkey's Kurdish Policy in the Nineties." *International Journal of Kurdish Studies* 9 (nos. 1 & 2; 1996), pp. 3-34.
Bahcheli, Tozun. *Greek-Turkish Relations Since 1955.* Boulder: Westview Press, 1990.
Barkey, Henri. "Turkey, Islamic Politics, and the Kurdish Question." *World Policy Journal* 13 (no. 1; 1996), pp. 43-52.
———. "Turkey's Kurdish Dilemma." *Survival* 35 (Winter 1993), pp. 51-70.
———. "Under the Gun: Turkish Foreign Policy and the Kurdish Question," in Robert Olson, ed., *The Kurdish Nationalist Movement in the 1990s: Its Impact on Turkey and the Middle East.* Lexington: University Press of Kentucky, 1996, pp. 65-83.
Barkey, Henri and Graham E. Fuller. "Turkey's Kurdish Question: Critical Turning Points and Missed Opportunities." *Middle East Journal* 51 (Winter 1997), pp. 59-79.
Bayrak, Mehmet. *Kurtler ve Ulusal-Demokratik Mucadeleleri* [The Kurds and Their National-Democratic Struggles]. Ankara: Oz-Ge Yayinlari, 1993.
Besikci, Ismail. *Kurdistan & Turkish Colonialism: Selected Writings.* London: Kurdistan Solidarity Committee and Kurdistan Information Centre, 1991.
Bois, Thomas and Vladimir Minorsky. "Kurds, Kurdistan." *The Encyclopedia of Islam* (new edition), vol. 5, 1981, pp. 438-86.
Bolugiray, Nevzat. *Separatist Terror During the Ozal Era (1983-1991).* Ankara: Tekin Yayinevi, 1992.
Bolukbasi, Suha. "Ankara, Damascus, Baghdad, and the Regionalization of Turkey's Kurdish Secessionism." *Journal of South Asian and Middle Eastern Studies* 14 (Summer 1991), pp. 15-36.
———. "Turkey Challenges Iraq and Syria: The Euphrates Dispute." *Journal of South Asian and Middle Eastern Studies* 16 (Summer 1993), pp. 9-32.
———. "Turkey Copes with Revolutionary Iran." *Journal of South Asian and Middle Eastern Studies* 13 (Fall/Winter 1989), pp. 94-109.
Border, Jake. "Orphan Guerrillas: Lonely Struggle of Kurdish Freedom Fighters." *Soldier of Fortune* (Oct. 1992), pp. 38-43, 80.
Bozarslan, Hamit. "Political Aspects of the Kurdish Problem in Contemporary Turkey," in Philip G. Kreyenbroek and Stefan Sperl, eds., *The Kurds: A Contemporary Overview.* London: Routledge, 1992, pp. 95-114.
———. "Political Crisis and the Kurdish Issue in Turkey," in Robert Olson, ed., *The Kurdish Nationalist Movement in the 1990s: Its Impact on Turkey and the Middle East.* Lexington: University Press of Kentucky, 1996, pp. 135-53.
———. "Turkey's Elections and the Kurds." *Middle East Report* no. 199 (April-June 1996), pp. 16-19.
Bozeman, Adda. *The Future of Law in a Multicultural World.* Princeton: Princeton University Press, 1970.
———. *Politics and Culture in International History.* Princeton: Princeton University Press, 1960.
Brown, James. "The Turkish Imbroglio: Its Kurds." *The Annals of the American Academy of Political and Social Science* no. 541 (Sept. 1995), pp. 116-29.
Bruinessen, Martin van. *Agha, Sheikh and State: The Social and Political Structures of Kurdistan.* London: Zed Books Ltd., 1992.
———. "Between Guerrilla War and Political Murder: The Workers' Party of Kurdistan." *Middle East Report* no. 153 (July-August 1988), pp. 40-42, 44-46, 50.

————. "Kurdish Society, Ethnicity, Nationalism and Refugee Problems," in Philip G. Kreyenbroek and Stefan Sperl, eds., *The Kurds: A Contemporary Overview.* London: Routledge, 1992.

————. "The Kurds in Turkey." *MERIP Reports* no. 121 (Feb. 1984), pp. 6-12.

————. "The Kurds in Turkey: Further Restrictions of Basic Rights." *International Commission of Jurists: The Review* no. 45 (1990), pp. 46-52.

————. "Turkey's Death Squads." *Middle East Report* no. 199 (April-June 1996), pp. 20-23.

Bulloch, John and Harvey Morris. *No Friends But the Mountains: The Tragic History of the Kurds.* New York: Oxford University Press, 1992.

Burkay, Kemal. *Gecmisten Bugune Kurtler ve Kurdistan* [The Kurds and Kurdistan from the Past until Today]. Istanbul: Deng Yayinlari, 1992.

Button, Stephen E. "Turkey Struggles with Kurdish Separatism." *Military Review* (Dec. 1994 - Jan./Feb. 1995), pp. 70-83.

Chaliand, Gerard, ed. *A People without a Country: The Kurds and Kurdistan.* New York: Olive Branch Press, 1993.

————. *The Kurdish Tragedy.* London: Zed Books Ltd, 1994.

Criss, Nur Bilge. "The Nature of PKK Terrorism in Turkey." *Studies in Conflict & Terrorism* 18 (January-March 1995), pp. 17-37.

Dunn, Michael Collins. "The Kurdish 'Question': Is There an Answer?" *Middle East Policy* 4 (Sept. 1995), pp. 72-86.

Entessar, Nader. *Kurdish Ethnonationalism.* Boulder: Lynne Rienner Publishers, 1992.

Ersever, Ahmet Cem. *Kurds, PKK and A. Ocalan.* [1992]. Accessed from the Internet.

Etzioni, Amitai. "The Evils of Self-Determination." *Foreign Policy* no. 89 (Winter 1992-93), pp. 21-35.

Frelick, Bill. "Operation Provide Comfort: False Promises to the Kurds." in Gerard Chaliand, ed., *A People Without a Country: The Kurds and Kurdistan.* New York: Olive Branch Press, 1993, pp. 231-37.

Fuller, Graham E. "The Fate of the Kurds." *Foreign Affairs* 72 (Spring 1993), pp. 108-21.

Fuller, Graham E. and Ian O. Lesser. *Turkey's New Geopolitics: From the Balkans to Western China.* Boulder: Westview Press, 1993.

General Secretariat of the National Security Council (Turkey). *12 September in Turkey: Before and After.* Ankara: Ongun Kardesler Printing House, 1982.

Ghareeb, Edmund. *The Kurdish Question in Iraq.* Syracuse: Syracuse University Press, 1981.

Gunter, Michael M. *The Changing Kurdish Problem in Turkey.* no. 270. London: Research Institute for the Study of Conflict & Terrorism, 1994.

————. *The Kurds in Turkey: A Political Dilemma.* Boulder: Westview Press, 1990.

————. *The Kurds of Iraq: Tragedy and Hope.* New York: St. Martin's Press, 1992.

————. "A De Facto Kurdish State in Northern Iraq." *Third World Quarterly* 14 (no. 2; 1993), pp. 295-319.

————. "The KDP-PUK Conflict in Northern Iraq." *Middle East Journal* 50 (Spring 1996), pp. 225-41.

————. "The Kurdish Factor in Middle Eastern Politics." *International Journal of Kurdish Studies* 8 (nos. 1 & 2; 1995), 94-109.

————. "The Kurdish Insurgency in Turkey." *Journal of South Asian and Middle Eastern Studies* 13 (Summer 1990), pp. 57-81.

————. "The Kurdish Problem in Turkey." *Middle East Journal* 42 (Summer 1988), pp. 389-406.

——. "Turkey and the Kurds: New Developments in 1991." *Journal of South Asian and Middle Eastern Studies* 15 (Winter 1991), pp. 32-45.

Hale, William. *Turkish Politics and the Military.* London: Routledge, 1994.

Harris, George S. *Troubled Alliance: Turkish-American Problems in Historical Perspective.* Washington, D.C.: American Enterprise Institute, 1972.

——. "Ethnic Conflict and the Kurds." *Annals of the American Academy of Political and Social Science* no. 433 (Sept. 1977), pp. 112-24.

Hassanpour, Amir. *Nationalism and Language in Kurdistan, 1918-1985.* San Francisco: Mellen Research University Press, 1992.

Helsinki Rights Watch. *Destroying Ethnic Identity: The Kurds of Turkey, An Update.* New York: Helsinki Rights Watch, 1990.

Helsinki Watch. "Broken Promises: Torture and Killings Continue in Turkey." Dec. 1992.

——. "Free Expression in Turkey, 1993: Killings, Convictions, Confiscations." Aug. 1993.

——. "Kurds Massacred: Turkish Forces Kill Scores of Peaceful Demonstrators." June 1992.

——. "The Kurds of Turkey: Killings, Disappearances and Torture." Mar. 1993.

——. "Turkey: Censorship by Assassination." Dec. 1992.

——. "Turkey: Censorship by Assassination Continues." Feb. 1994.

——. "Turkey: Eight Journalists Killed Since February; A Ninth Critically Wounded." Aug. 1992.

Henze, Paul. *Turkey: Toward the Twenty-First Century.* Santa Monica, CA: Rand, 1992.

Herschlag, Zvi Yehuda. *The Contemporary Turkish Economy.* London: Routledge, 1988.

Hitchens, Christopher. "Struggle of the Kurds." *National Geographic.* 182 (August 1992), pp. 32-61.

Horowitz, Donald L. *Ethnic Groups in Conflict.* Berkeley: University of California Press, 1985.

Human Rights Watch Arms Project. *Weapons Transfers and Violations of the Laws of War in Turkey.* New York: Human Rights Watch, 1995.

Ignatieff, Michael. *Blood & Belonging: Journeys into the New Nationalism.* Toronto: Viking, 1993.

Imset, Ismet G. *The PKK: A Report on Separatist Violence in Turkey (1973-1992).* Istanbul: Turkish Daily News Publications, 1992.

——. "The PKK: Terrorists or Freedom Fighters?" *International Journal of Kurdish Studies* 10 (nos. 1 & 2; 1996), pp. 45-100.

International Conference on North West Kurdistan (South East Turkey). "Final Resolution." Brussels, Belgium, Mar. 12-13, 1994.

Izady, Mehrdad. *The Kurds: A Concise Handbook.* Washington: Crane Russak, 1992.

Kalpakian, Jack. "Waning Crescent: Turkey in Kurdistan." unpublished paper, Old Dominion University, Norfolk, VA, 1995.

Karpat, Kemal. *Turkey's Politics: The Transition to a Multi-Party System.* Princeton: Princeton University Press, 1959.

——. *The Turkish Experiment in Democracy, 1950-1975.* London: C. Hurst & Company, 1977.

——. ed. *Turkey's Foreign Policy in Transition: 1950-1974.* Leiden: E. J. Brill, 1975.

——. ed. *Turkish Foreign Policy: Recent Developments.* Madison, WI: University of Wisconsin Press, 1996.

Kazancigil, Ali and Ergun Ozbudun, eds., *Ataturk: Founder of a Modern State.* London: C. Hurst & Company, 1981.

Kinnane, Derk. *The Kurds and Kurdistan.* London: Oxford University, 1964.

Kinross, Lord. *Ataturk: A Biography of Mustafa Kemal, Father of Modern Turkey.* New York: William Morrow and Company, 1965.

Kirisci, Kemal. "Provide Comfort or Trouble: Kurdish Ethnicity and Turkish Foreign Policy." Paper presented at the 27th annual meeting of the Middle East Studies Association of North America, Research Triangle, NC, Nov. 12, 1993.

———. "Turkey and the Kurdish Safe-Haven in Northern Iraq." *Journal of South Asian and Middle Eastern Studies* 19 (Spring 1996), pp. 21-39.

Kolars, John. *The Euphrates River and the Southeast Anatolia Development Project.* Carbondale, IL: Southern Illinois University Press, 1991.

Kreyenbroek, Philip G. and Stefan Sperl, eds. *The Kurds: A Contemporary Overview.* London: Routledge, 1992.

Kuniholm, Bruce R. "Turkey and the West." *Foreign Affairs* 70 (Spring 1991), pp. 34-48.

"Kurdistan Parliament in Exile." The Hague, The Netherlands, April 12/16, 1995.

Kurkcu, Ertugrul. "The Crisis of the Turkish State." *Middle East Report* no. 199 (April-June 1996), pp. 2-9.

Kutschera, Chris. "Mad Dreams of Independence: The Kurds of Turkey and the PKK." *Middle East Report* no. 189 (July-August 1994), pp. 12-15.

Laizer, Sheri. *Martyrs, Traitors and Patriots: Kurdistan after the Gulf War.* London: Zed Books, 1996.

Lewis, Bernard. *The Emergence of Modern Turkey.* 2 ed. London: Oxford University Press, 1968.

McDowall, David. *The Kurds.* no. 96/4. London: Minority Rights Group, 1996.

———. *The Kurds: A Nation Denied.* London: Minority Rights Publications, 1992.

———. *A Modern History of the Kurds.* London: I. B. Tauris, 1996.

Macfie, A.L. *Ataturk.* Harlow: Longman, 1994.

Magnarella, Paul J. "The Legal, Political and Cultural Structures of Human Rights Protections and Abuses in Turkey." *Journal of International Law and Practice* 3 (1994), pp. 439-67.

Makovsky, Alan. "Western Dreams and Eastern Problems." *Middle East Insight* 11 (May-June 1995), pp. 23-28.

Mango, Andrew. *Turkey: The Challenge of a New Role.* Westport, CT: Praeger, 1994.

———. "Turks and Kurds." *Middle Eastern Studies* 30 (October 1994), pp. 975-97.

Marcus, Aliza. "City in the War Zone." *Middle East Report* no. 189 (July-August 1994), pp. 16-19.

———. "Turkey's Kurds After the Gulf War: A Report from the Southeast," in Gerard Chaliand, ed., *A People without a Country: The Kurds and Kurdistan.* New York: Olive Branch Press, 1993, pp. 238-47.

Mardin, Serif. *Religion and Social Change in Modern Turkey: The Case of Bediuzzaman Said Nursi.* New York: State University of New York Press, 1989.

Muller, Mark. "Nationalism and the Rule of Law in Turkey: The Elimination of Kurdish Representation During the 1990s." *International Journal of Kurdish Studies* 10 (nos. 1 & 2; 1996), pp. 9-44.

Mutlu, Servet. "Ethnic Kurds in Turkey: A Demographic Study." *International Journal Of Middle East Studies* 28 (Nov. 1996), pp. 517-41.

National Foreign Assessment Center (U.S. Central Intelligence Agency). *The Kurdish Problem in Perspective.* Aug. 1979.

Nestor, Carl E. "Dimensions of Turkey's Kurdish Question and the Potential Impact of the Southeast Anatolian Project (GAP): Part I." *International Journal of Kurdish Studies* 8 (nos. 1-2; 1995), pp. 33-78.

———. "The Southeast Anatolian Project (GAP) and Turkey's Kurdish Question: Part II." *International Journal of Kurdish Studies* 9 (nos. 1-2; 1996), pp. 35-78.

Nezan, Kendal. "Kurdistan in Turkey," in Gerard Chaliand, ed., *People without a Country: The Kurds and Kurdistan.* London: Zed Press, 1980, pp. 47-106.

Nigogosian, Aram. "Turkey's Kurdish Problem: Recent Trends," in Robert Olson, ed., *The Kurdish Nationalist Movement in the 1990s: Its Impact on Turkey and the Middle East.* Lexington: University Press of Kentucky, 1996, pp. 38-49.

O'Ballance, Edgar. *The Kurdish Struggle 1920-94.* New York: St. Martin's Press, 1996.

Olson, Robert. *The Emergence of Kurdish Nationalism and the Sheikh Said Rebellion, 1880-1925.* Austin: University of Texas Press, 1989.

———. ed. *The Kurdish Nationalist Movement in the 1990s: Its Impact on Turkey and the Middle East.* Lexington: University Press of Kentucky, 1996.

———. "The Creation of a Kurdish State in the 1990s?" *Journal of South Asian and Middle Eastern Studies* 15 (Summer 1992), pp. 1-25.

———. "The Impact of the Southeast Anatolian Project (GAP) on Kurdish Nationalism in Turkey." *International Journal of Kurdish Studies* 9 (nos. 1-2; 1996), pp. 95-102.

———. "The Kurdish Question and Chechnya: Turkish and Russian Foreign Policies Since the Gulf War." *Middle East Policy* 4 (March 1996), pp. 106-118.

———. "The Kurdish Question and Geopolitic and Geostrategic Changes in the Middle East after the Gulf War." *Journal of South Asian and Middle Eastern Studies* 17 (Summer 1994), pp. 44-67.

———. "The Kurdish Question and Turkey's Foreign Policy, 1991-95." *Journal of South Asian and Middle Eastern Studies* 19 (Fall 1995), pp. 1-30.

———. "The Kurdish Question in the Aftermath of the Gulf War: Geopolitical and Geostrategic Changes in the Middle East." *Third World Quarterly* 13 (No. 3; 1992), pp. 475-99.

———. "Kurds and Turks: Two Documents Concerning Kurdish Autonomy in 1922 and 1923." *Journal of South Asian and Middle Eastern Studies* 15 (Winter 1991), pp. 20-31.

Operation Provide Comfort. "Fact Sheet." May 6, 1993.

Panico, Christopher. "Turkey's Kurdish Problem." *Jane's Intelligence Review* 7 (April 1995), pp. 170-74.

PKK Central Committee. "Central Committee Statement of the PKK (Kurdistan Workers Party) Following the Fifth Congress of the PKK." Feb. 1995.

Robbins, Philip. *Turkey and the Middle East.* New York: Council on Foreign Relations Press, 1991.

———. "Between Sentiment and Self-Interest: Turkey's Policy toward Azerbaijan and the Central Asian States." *Middle East Journal* 47 (Autumn 1993), pp. 593-609.

———. "More Apparent Than Real? The Impact of the Kurdish Issue on Euro-Turkish Relations," in Robert Olson, ed., *The Kurdish Nationalist Movement in the 1990s: Its Impact on Turkey and the Middle East.* Lexington: University Press of Kentucky, 1996, pp. 114-32.

———. "The Overlord State: Turkish Policy and the Kurdish Issue." *International Affairs* 69 (October 1993), pp. 657-76.

Robinson, Richard D. *The First Turkish Republic: A Case Study in National Development.* Cambridge: Harvard University Press, 1963.

Rothschild, Joseph. *Ethnopolitics: A Conceptual Framework.* New York: Columbia University Press, 1981.

Rouleau, Eric. "Turkey: Beyond Ataturk." *Foreign Policy* no. 103 (Summer 1996), pp. 70-87.

Rugman, Jonathan and Roger Hutchings. *Ataturk's Children: Turkey and the Kurds.* London and New York: Cassell, 1996.

Sezer, Duygu Bazoglu. *State and Society in Turkey: Continuity and Change.* Santa Monica, CA: Rand, 1993.

Shaw, Stanford and Ezel Shaw. *History of the Ottoman Empire and Modern Turkey.* Vol. II: *Reform, Revolution, and Republic: The Rise of Modern Turkey, 1805-1917.* Cambridge: Cambridge University Press, 1977.

Soguk, Nevzat. "A Study of the Historico Cultural Reasons for Turkey's 'Inconclusive' Democracy." *New Political Science* no. 26 (Fall 1993), pp. 89-116.

Tachau, Frank. *Turkey: Authority, Democracy and Development.* New York: Praeger, 1984.

Tapper, Richard, ed., *Islam in Modern Turkey: Religion, Politics and Literature in a Secular State.* London: I. B. Tauris and Co. Ltd., 1991.

Teimourian, Hazhir. "Turkey—The Challenge of the Kurdistan Workers' Party." *Jane's Intelligence Review* 5 (Jan. 1993), pp. 29-32.

Thompson, Peter L. "United States–Turkey Military Relations: Treaties and Implications." *International Journal of Kurdish Studies* 9 (nos. 1 & 2; 1996), pp. 103-113.

U.S. Department of State. "Turkey Human Rights Practices, 1995." Mar. 1996, received via the Internet.

Vanly, Ismet Cheriff. "The Kurds in Syria and Lebanon," in Philip G. Kreyenbroek and Stefan Sperl, eds., *The Kurds: A Contemporary Overview.* London: Routledge, 1992, pp. 143-70.

———. "The Kurds in the Soviet Union," in Philip G. Kreyenbroek and Stefan Sperl, eds., *The Kurds: A Contemporary Overview.* London: Routledge, 1992, pp. 193-218.

Weiker, Walter F. *Political Tutelage and Democracy in Turkey: The Free Party and Its Aftermath.* Leiden: E. J. Brill, 1973.

Yalcin-Heckmann, Lale. *Tribe and Kinship among the Kurds.* Frankfurt am Main: Peter Lang, 1991.

———. "Ethnic Islam and Nationalism among the Kurds," in Richard Tapper, ed., *Islam in Modern Turkey: Religion, Politics and Literature in a Secular State.* London: I. B. Tauris and Co. Ltd., 1991, pp. 102-20.

Yegan, Mesut. "The Turkish Discourse and the Exclusion of Kurdish Identity." *Middle Eastern Studies* 32 (April 1996), pp. 216-29.

Zubaida, Sami. "Turkish Islam and National Identity." *Middle East Report* no. 199 (April-June 1996), pp. 10-15.

Zurcher, Erik. *Opposition in the Early Turkish Republic: The Progressive Republican Party, 1924-1925.* Leiden: E. J. Brill, 1991.

———. *Turkey: A Modern History.* London: I. B. Tauris, 1993.

# INDEX